Praise for Harvey's
Times Bestselling Books:

Lou Holtz—"Harvey Mackay may be the most talented man I have met."

Billy Graham—"Harvey's business acumen shows through on every page . . . There's so much warmth, wisdom, and wittiness in this book that it would be well for everyone to read every page."

Ted Koppel—"Harvey Mackay takes you on an easy reader ride to success in the business world. He got his; now, in a burst of compassion, he's drafted the guidelines so that you can get yours."

Rabbi Harold Kushner—"Harvey Mackay has no equal when it comes to understanding what makes people tick."

Gloria Steinem—"He is fast, smart, funny—and frighteningly right."

Tom Peters—"Harvey Mackay joins Bob Townsend (*Up the Organization*) as master of brief, biting, and brilliant business wit and wisdom."

Ken Blanchard—"I love this book! Mackay strips away the veneer and hits us between the eyes with the naked truth about succeeding in the real world. Impossibly, he delivers more in his second book than in his record-shattering first."

Donald Trump—"Harvey's uncanny ability to get people to talk and reveal their darkest and brightest hours is unsurpassed."

Stephen Covey—"A mother lode of timely, hard-earned, bite-size, street-smart golden nuggets . . . invaluable for job seekers, employed or unemployed."

Mark Victor Hansen and Jack Canfield—"Enjoy Harvey's cookbook for success—it gives the reader the best of his wisdom—truly, the best kind of chicken soup for anyone and everyone in business and in life."

Larry King—"Harvey Mackay is the only person I'll listen to while standing in shark-infested waters . . . real stories from the real world with real solutions."

Norman Vincent Peale—"Harvey Mackay is one of the greatest writers of our time."

**USE YOUR HEAD
TO GET YOUR
FOOT IN THE DOOR**

OTHER BOOKS BY HARVEY MACKAY:

Swim with the Sharks Without Being Eaten Alive

Beware the Naked Man Who Offers You His Shirt

Dig Your Well Before You're Thirsty

Pushing the Envelope All the Way to the Top

We Got Fired! . . . And It's the Best Thing That Ever Happened to Us

The Harvey Mackay Rolodex Network Builder

USE YOUR HEAD TO GET YOUR FOOT IN THE DOOR

Job Search Secrets No One Else Will Tell You

HARVEY MACKAY

piatkus

PIATKUS

First published in the US in 2010 by Portfolio, a member of Penguin Group (USA) Inc.
First published in Great Britain in 2010 by Piatkus

A CIP catalogue record for this book
is available from the British Library.

ISBN 978-0-7499-5430-7

Designed by Joy O'Meara
Typeset in Janson
Printed in the UK by CPI Mackays, Chatham ME5 8TD

Papers used by Piatkus are natural, renewable and
recyclable products sourced from well-managed forests and certified
in accordance with the rules of the Forest Stewardship Council.

Mixed Sources
Product group from well-managed
forests and other controlled sources
www.fsc.org Cert no. SGS-COC-004081
© 1996 Forest Stewardship Council
FSC

Piatkus
An imprint of
Little, Brown Book Group
100 Victoria Embankment
London EC4Y 0DY

An Hachette UK Company
www.hachette.co.uk

www.piatkus.co.uk

Dedication

This book is dedicated to the dedicated . . . those millions of people who are resolved to make a career comeback, no matter how trying and challenging that triumph may be.

- Dedicated to maintaining a positive attitude, knowing full well that every day's frustrations—big and small—can easily drain the enthusiasm and energy to make a breakthrough.
- Dedicated to learning, accepting, and then acting on the hard facts of how they really rank in the job market, and committed to improve their lot through focused hard work.
- Dedicated to taking stock of their entire skill set and determined that they will be as techno-smart as their next competitor.
- Dedicated to keeping their network of personal contacts alive, fresh, and relevant to their career plan.
- Dedicated to the realization that getting a job is far harder than having a job, and willing to work the hours and to discipline their time far beyond how they might when they collected a regular paycheck.
- Dedicated to exhaustive preparation in advance of any job-search step—be it polishing a résumé, approaching a recruiter, or appearing for an interview.

- Dedicated to the inescapable truth that modern life is no
  one-stop search, but a perpetual journey through multiple
  job and career changes.

*This book is dedicated to those who want to climb back into the ring . . . because I want
nothing more than to share these pointers that will land you the knockout win you so
deeply desire.*

Ten Reasons to Buy This Book

These pages will teach you the surefire techniques to secure a job in the worst economy in decades. It also gives you the tools to conduct the *lifetime* search you can expect with the three to five career shifts and the twelve to fifteen job changes of the typical person's working life:

1. Master the winning attitude and positive psychology necessary to re-enter the workforce successfully after having been fired, reorganized, downsized, or reengineered out of a job.

2. Build, expand, and energize the network of contacts and power figures that will open the doors to your ultimate career opportunities.

3. Learn the secret preparation tools that will enable you to design a foolproof résumé in the Internet age.

4. Bolster your confidence to overcome disabling rejection and maneuver decisively in making new contacts.

5. Develop the personal awareness and planning disciplines needed to execute a flawless job interview.

6. Explain the most difficult, disappointing, and embarrassing lapses in your career and personal development.

7. Absorb the negotiation skills to exit your last job with maximum advantage and to enter your newest responsibility with optimum opportunity.

8. Understand the demanding world of recruiters, employment directors, and industrial psychologists and learn the messages they long to hear.

9. Grasp use of the latest communications technology and databases to give you #1 positioning in the candidate pool for the best jobs.

10. Build the "staging strategy" you will need to identify and secure your next job targets while you use your present position for your and your employer's best benefit.

Acknowledgments

In *Use Your Head to Get Your Foot in the Door*, only a stellar team could have gotten the job done:

Ron Beyma can take a diamond in the rough and turn it into a sparkling gem. His masterful editorial judgment, trend-spotting abilities, and superior organizational skills combine to keep me on track. He delivers, rain or shine, at the speed of light. Ron has been a valued member of my editorial team because he truly knows how to use his head!

The term *chief of staff* understates the pivotal contributions Greg Bailey has made to this book in every way. Greg continues to be my right hand—and so much more—in the entire spectrum of my professional life. An inexhaustible source of topic leads; an unparalleled administrator in marshaling all of this book's supporting resources; an incredible eye for detail as well as proportion in sizing up a manuscript and helping me set direction. And this always is done with an effortless ease with people that is awesomely low-key.

Margie Resnick Blickman—an editor whose eye for excellence is unsurpassed—is foremost a loving sister and friend. Hey, not even Stradivarius could imagine a better sounding board.

To call Mary Anne Bailey a proofreader doesn't begin to do justice to her discerning judgment in weighing a phrase or her mastery of detail in polishing prose. She's a consummate professional with an uncanny sense of rightness in the written word.

My agent, Jan Miller, is the prototype of a new generation of dynamo in the publishing world: people friendly, resourceful, and unbelievably efficient. Jan and her staff of energetic young professionals have sent a fresh wind rustling through the publishing industry. Her A-team roster of authors are the All Stars of the business and motivational world.

When I wrote *Swim with the Sharks*, I praised the professionalism, poise, and friendship of my then editor Adrian Zackheim. That respect has only grown in luster over the years. Adrian is more than tops in the industry, he's a publishing legend who is building the Portfolio imprint of Penguin Books into a powerhouse.

You'll doubtless note the deft touch of David Moldawer, an exacting editorial talent and a gifted ear for what matters to today's audiences. I thank David for helping to polish the structure and to road test the messages.

Allison Sweet McLean, the third member of the Portfolio team, is the outfit's publicity whiz. She knows the magic steps in building buzz in the book market and has the boundless energy to play all the cards with verve.

Scott Mitchell, CEO of MackayMitchell Envelope Company, has a sixth sense for modern management priorities. That includes what execs look for when hiring others.

As to Neil Naftalin, the reason why things run so well in our world of books, columns, and speeches is we live by the adage "Run it by Neil"—the closest person I know to the gold standard of judgment and a trusted friend and adviser for more than fifty years.

Jan Beyma is both a resourceful researcher who knows the ways of the Web and a dedicated document manager who understands how to present text and track changes with easy-to-cipher precision.

Kathy Hanlin, my administrative assistant, is the unrivaled utility player on our team. Effortlessly, she shifts her skills and attention to the varied needs of an often hectic office and closes loop after open loop.

If you want to dress up a book, Rachel Roddy is your lady. What Paris and Milan can do to make design on the catwalk sizzle, Rachel delivers for a book jacket time and again—ironing out every last wrinkle till it lies just right.

Judy Olausen is the world's #1 serial photographer—and the best, too. Not only has she photographed me for the cover of every one of my books, she managed to photograph me for this one more times than all the others combined!

Planned Television Arts has proven itself as much the master of publicity in the age of twitters and tweets as it has been in the rapidly evolving world of print. That's because it has such agile knowledge workers as David Hahn at the helm of its campaigns.

Teresa Mazzitelli—whom we affectionately term "the Bulldog" at MackayMitchell Envelope Company—gave me an eagle-eyed view of the executive recruiting business. She also unearthed inspiring stories of folks who became stellar successes in a sour economy. Her relentless determination to find talent has helped us time and again.

If you enjoy the wry chuckles from the *New Yorker* that dot these pages, part of the thanks goes to Merrideth Miller, the Cartoon Bank administrator who helped arrange their appearance.

I thank Sam Richter, the guru of *warm call* sales strategy, for sharing the ingenious ways you can apply door-opening sales gambits to getting your foot in the door of even the most tightly shut employment offices.

The pros at United Feature Syndicate, who zip my weekly column to publications throughout the country, deserve a big thank you as always. My columns helped secure valuable reader input about job experiences and successes in these trying times.

I want to extend appreciation to everyone at MackayMitchell Envelope Company, especially our human resources manager, Elaine Sampson. Our employees have taught me a lot about people priorities in business, and you have my respect and admiration every day.

Two family members helped with the book's jacket, my film-director son, David, and my ever-loving wife, Carol Ann. Her encouragement and patience have enabled each of my books to come to fruition. She pushed me over the cliff when she said, "You have to write this book!"

Contents

Acknowledgments   xi

Preface   xix

Dark Days

1 Against All Odds . . . How Preparation Prevailed   3

2 7 Danger Signals You May Soon Be out of a Job   8

3 Play for Keeps—Hold On to Your Job, A Survivor's Handbook   10

  Quickie—How Bad Can Things Get?   12

4 Things Change . . . and It Pays to Know How   14

5 12 Herculean Labors to Keep You on the Payroll   16

6 The Last to Learn   21

  Quickie—Fine-Tune Your Job Description Without Being Asked   24

7 Yours to Lose   25

  Quickie—Misery Is Contagious, Too   27

8 Beat Rejection Before It Beats You   28

9 Parting Words: Canned Remarks upon Getting Canned   32

  Quickie—The Stretch Marks of Experience   34

10 A Checklist for Checking Out   36

  Quickie—Crying Societies or Support Groups?   38

11 Gone to Potter   39

Reconstruct Your Attitude

12 Anger Is Only One Letter from Danger   43

13 You're Never a Failure Until You Think You Are   46

14 Being Your Best with Things at Their Worst   49

15 Pitchmanship: Applying Marketing Nichemanship to Job Hunting 52

Quickie—Should You Go Under the Knife After You Get the Ax?   55
16 The Continuity of Contrarians   56
17 Is This the Time to Get That MBA?   58
Quickie—The Lecture Room in Your Laptop   61
18 When It's OK Not to Act Your Age!   63
Quickie—Moonlighting: The Wisdom of Having a Second Skill   66
19 Electronic Résumé Screening: Use Language That Computes   67
Quickie—The Acid Test for Hiring   69
20 Headhunters: Making Yourself Delectable   70

Re-employment: Your Extreme Preparation Guide

21 The Mackay Daily Planner for the Unemployed   79
Quickie—Million Dollar Baby!   82
22 Getting a Job Is a Job   83
23 Want to Become an Entrepreneur? Better Be One First!   92
24 The One-Stop Job Shop   99
Quickie—Rebirth Certificate   101
25 Use Your Head, but Follow Your Heart!   102
26 Adjust to What You <u>Aren't</u>: Résumé Fine Tuning After Setbacks   108
Quickie—How Not to Waste Your Time on the Internet   110
27 Expose Yourself in the Privacy of Your Own Home   112
Quickie—Encore! Encore!   116
28 The Age of the Agile Exec   117

Mobilize Your Network

29 Job Hunting Is a Contact Sport   127
Quickie—Don't Lose Your Face in Facebook   130
30 Mackay's Deadwood Network Pruner   131
Quickie—Network to New Work   134
31 Bass Are Still Where You Find 'Em   135
Quickie—Ageless Alumni   138
32 The Octopus Exercise   139
33 Matchmaker, Matchmaker, Find Me a Job!   141
Quickie—One Sweet Tweet   144
34 Don't Be Blackballed by Your BlackBerry   146
Quickie—Twitter: Risk and Risqué   149

Fill In the Blanks

35 Plugging Holes in Your Résumé   153
36 Imagination: There's Just No Substitute   156
37 Psychological Evaluations: Shrink to Grow   159
38 Shrinks: A Skull Session   162
   Quickie—Take Pride in Stride   168
39 Mackay 44 Interview Prep Checklist   169
40 Footlights and Footwork   172
   Quickie—The Mother of All Questions   176
41 In a Job Hunt, Make Sure Your Ducks Are in a Row   177
   Quickie—Rehearsing Job Interview Questions   180
42 9 Motivators to Make Them Want to Return Your Call   181
   Quickie—Lubricate Gatekeepers to Oil the Gate   183
43 No Isn't an Answer . . . It's a Question   184

D-Day: Plan the Attack

44 Bytes: Researching the Hands That Will Feed You   189
45 Early Birds Get the Worm, Late Birds Get the Job   198
   Quickie—Pickiness Pays   201
46 A Winning Suit Trumps   202
47 Speed-Reading Reception Areas   205
48 A Business Lunch Is No Picnic   208
49 Art of the Ask: It's Not Just Your Answers   215
   Quickie—One in a Hundred   218.
50 Post-Interview Homework   219
51 The Mackay 22   222
52 The Second-Round Interview: How to Get to the Finals   225

Get Hired

53 Job Search of a Twenty-Something   231
54 Shriveling Your Way into a Job   240
   Quickie—What Personnel Types Prize   242
55 Fly Under Fetching Colors   243
   Quickie—Timing Is Everything   246
56 Winning the Circuit: The *Why* Behind Multiple Interviews   247
   Quickie—The Ninety-Day Guarantee   249

57 Landing the Ideal Job   250
58 Your Designer Job   252
   Quickie—No One Is Immune   255
59 Negotiating Terms in Your Next Position   257
60 Before You Take the Job They *Offer*, Take the Job You *Want*   260

Stay Afloat

61 The Multi-Task Master   267
   Quickie—Setting Clear Job Measurement Standards   270
62 Knowing When to Upsize: Asking for a Raise   271
   Quickie—Peers and Partners   275
63 This Time Around: Swearing Off Career Obsolescence   276

Afterthoughts

   Kurt Einstein's and Harvey Mackay's 20 Most Revealing
      Interview Questions   281
   The Mackay Lucky 13: A List of Life-Changing Books   291
   University of Southern California (USC)—MBA
      Commencement Speech, May 15, 2009   303
   Appendix: An Open Book   317
   Index   319
   Money-back Guarantee   330

Preface

A recent *New York Times* article pointed out that public libraries across the country have become combat zones as millions of people line up outside of cubicles to attempt online job searches, and tempers flare. Some have never sent e-mails, and many more don't have a clue about assembling and submitting a résumé in the electronic age.

The unemployment rate was 10.2 percent in November 2009, the highest in more than a quarter century. The personal bankruptcies, divorces, broken families, and shattered plans for a college education are the more common and widespread aftermaths.

Statistics paint a powerful portrait of the changing world of work, and this book pinpoints some of the most dramatic ones like these. A 2007 Gallup poll in *Time* magazine reported 77 percent of all Americans hated their jobs . . . and, according to current labor statistics, the average person will have at least three to five career changes and ten to fourteen different jobs by age thirty-eight.

Many people think they have embarked on the most important job search of their life. The truth that's now sinking in is this: We are all engaged in a lifetime job search. The illusion of a lifetime job is a myth that died along with a gold retirement watch twenty years ago. What people need today is a lifetime job strategy and the tools to make it continuously successful.

That's what this book is about. I've mentored hundreds of new grads and seasoned veterans, and I can help you, too.

Harvey Mackay, February 1, 2010

USE YOUR HEAD
TO GET YOUR
FOOT IN THE DOOR

*"It's the whole kindergarten thing, Mom. I'm alone
in there, swimming with the sharks."*

DARK DAYS

Chapter 1

Against All Odds . . .
How Preparation Prevailed

Early in 2008, we had a get-together at our home in Phoenix. Two hundred visitors bustled around the grounds on a pleasantly cool evening. As the clock neared midnight, I noticed one guest was lingering. It was Vinny Del Negro, assistant general manager of the Phoenix Suns. He finally marched up and asked if he could see me alone. I knew this had to be big time. We adjourned to my office, and Vinny's wife, Lynn, strolled off to poolside with my spouse, Carol Ann.

Vinny Del Negro's dad played basketball at the University of Kentucky under one of the all-time great coaches, Adolph Rupp. Like father, like son. Vinny was elected to the All-Atlantic Coast Conference (All-ACC) team after leading the North Carolina State Wolfpack to the laurels in the 1987 ACC Tournament, and Vinny was singled out as Most Valuable Player (MVP) for setting the pace.

During his National Basketball Association (NBA) career, Vinny started for six years for the San Antonio Spurs before stints with the Milwaukee Bucks and the Golden State Warriors. A trade brought him to the Phoenix Suns in 2000. In 2003, after retiring as a player, he did television and radio commentary for the Suns and was soon promoted, first to director of player personnel and then to assistant general manager.

What's on Vinny's mind on this starry Arizona evening?

"I enjoy working in the front office, Harvey, but I want to be an NBA head coach," he says.

That takes my breath away. "Well," I said, "that's one stretchy objective. Let's start by taking a look at your track record. I know you've never coached in the NBA, but you surely did some college coaching along the way."

"No."

"I s-e-e . . ." I comment hesitantly before I probe a little deeper. "Well, even though it was a long time ago, you surely helped your high school coach as an assistant?"

"No, never did."

"Grade school . . . Maybe you did some coaching in grade school?"

"No sir, can't say that I had the chance, Harvey."

"You really want to do this, Vinny?"

"More than anything."

"You've never coached a day in your life, and the job you're aiming at is that of head coach?" Since that coaching position had opened up for the Phoenix Suns, what better opportunity could present itself?

He nodded.

"I will guarantee you one thing in blood." I sighed. "I know Suns' owner Robert Sarver very well. This guy is the youngest person in American history to establish a national bank. He got where he is by surrounding himself with experienced people. He is only going to go with a known coach."

Vinny didn't flinch, and I could see the determination burning in his eyes.

"Vinny, if you want to come over tomorrow for four hours with your legal pad in hand, I'll teach you how to do the interview. You're not going to get this job, but I can't imagine a better trial run because you are already so deep into the Phoenix organization. If you handle this opportunity right, despite your total void in coaching experience, I guarantee you'll be a finalist in coaching searches in the future. That will stick, as long as there's the NBA."

The next day Vinny drops by. Over bagels and apple juice, we do our chalk talk. Off he goes, and in the coming weeks, he handles, I should say aces, his interview with the Suns.

"Harvey, I think I'm going to be considered very seriously."

"That's great, Vinny," I say. "Remember everything you say and do, because this is the most important job you'll never get."

Days pass. Vinny calls. "Harvey, guess what? I didn't get the job. They hired Terry Porter, who, as you know, had been head coach with the Bucks and then an assistant in Detroit."

"We're batting a thousand," I say. "What do you have in mind next?" I ask.

"I'm heading to Orlando for the predraft camp, and when I get back I will reevaluate everything and move forward."

While in Orlando, Vinny has a chance to sit down with John Paxson, the general manager of the Chicago Bulls. At the time, Jim Boylan's role as interim coach in Chicago had ended. Another opportunity presented itself for Vinny.

"Go get 'em," I say.

The first interview is promising. Vinny says, "I really do believe I have a chance to be a finalist." Second interview, and Vinny reaches me at the office, saying, "I am a finalist."

"Vinny," I remind him, "I told you you'd be a finalist, but the Bulls are probably the bluest-chip franchise in the entire NBA. The third interview is with the owner, Jerry Reinsdorf. I know this guy. You'll do well, but go back and study the apple juice–stained notes of yours from our powwow."

On June 10, 2008, Vinny calls and catches me with clients at a baseball game.

I was wrong. His preparation, perseverance, and passion prevailed.

He got the top job!

Vinny Del Negro was named the new head coach of the Chicago Bulls.

In April–May 2009, the Bulls faced the Boston Celtics in the NBA playoffs.

Vinny asked my assistant, Greg, to send him a stack of my thirty-five best columns on motivation to share with his players. Did they help? Who knows? But this I do know. Due in large measure to the unscalable determination of Vinny Del Negro, the Bulls battled the Celtics to seven games, two in overtime, one in double overtime, and one in triple overtime. Hardwood devotees consider it to have been the best first round of NBA postseason play ever.

There are lessons here, to be sure. The most important?

- **Networking and relevant experience are the investment that builds a great career.** The only place where opportunity springs up out of the blue is in the movies . . . and any actor will tell you: You won't even get a chance to play those zany, surreal parts without grueling, methodical experience and knowing the right people.

- **There are few substitutes for determination and self-confidence in getting a shot at the job you want.** With those two mighty engines, you will level the thickest steel-reinforced doors with a few swift kicks. But knocking down the door, as crucial as that is, is not locking up the job.

- **And there is absolutely, positively no substitute for preparation in aiming the shots you get so that they land squarely in the bull's-eye.** You can have the finest moves in the talent contest, you can boast a trophy speed-dial list on your iPhone, you can possess the single-mindedness of Paul Revere and be as self-assured as Muhammad Ali . . . and you still won't nail the job, unless you know how to mold and merchandise your personal pitch.

If this is true when times are booming—and it is—you can only imagine how true it is in times like these.

This book is about bundling that crushing zigzag lightning you have recently absorbed and hurling it back in one focused thunderbolt to land you on the payroll and to keep you there.

"At this point, I'm just happy to still have a job."

Chapter 2

7 Danger Signals
You May Soon Be out of a Job

- **It's not your bad breath keeping you on the outskirts:** Suddenly your boss invites your second-in-command to meetings you usually attend . . . but forgets to ask you. Or your office is abruptly relocated two floors away from the C-suite or your department's power alley. Or you are transferred to Novosibirsk or Chişinău, Moldova, with a glorious opportunity to build a brand-new market . . . and report back in five years.

- **Your organization chart is rerouted**. You now report to somebody with much less clout or stature than your last chief. Perhaps your new boss is the outfit's Attila the Hun, who specializes in dirty work like axing longtimers. Your prize subordinate (and backup) is reassigned. An overqualified new hire is parked in your department until "the right spot" opens up.

- **The meat is trimmed off meetings with your boss.** Those weekly half-hour status sessions become monthly fifteen-minute rush jobs, if they happen at all. However, when he or she does see you, the talk is all about hard-fisted goals, especially the ones that you are having the toughest time achieving.

- **Communication "chat content" drops to zero.** The e-mails and phone calls you get are strictly about measurement against the numbers or measurable benchmarks. And watch for this dead giveaway: Bad news or criticism is repeated to you twice, spoken slowly and clearly . . . or sent to you in writing when it would normally have been an offhand comment.

- **You are put decidedly out of the loop.** Your department is up for restructuring, but no one's asking your opinions. Suddenly your boss makes your decision for you, the one you've been weighing for the last two months. You're no longer asked to train new staff members. You vanish off the mail trail, especially for insider plans on competition and strategy. You are now seen as fully qualified for your job: Why waste time sending you to training programs?

- **You are the object of a neatness campaign**. Control freaks from the personnel department descend on you and your staff. Your boss wants the box score on all your timing-and-action calendars, and, by the way, how about a copy of your CMS—contact management system—with all those phone numbers and e-mail addresses? You call up your personnel records, and, overnight, every typo and sloppy entry has been airbrushed away.

- **You feel like you have been cordoned off in quarantine.** Nobody asks for your photo to tack on to the house blog. Buddies in other departments "forget" to invite you for an after-hours watering hole stop. When the company is quoted in the press, other voices say the things you were once asked to utter. And, after not hearing from him for sixteen days, your boss has just texted you this message on your BlackBerry: He wants to have a talk with you . . . next week . . . away from the office. Now I wonder what the topic might be?

Chapter 3

Play for Keeps—
Hold On to Your Job,
A Survivor's Handbook

In the last half century, there has been a torrent of new laws and prin-ciples in medicine, economics, business, the sciences, and, of course, the legal system. None astonishes me more than Moore's Law formulated by Gordon E. Moore in 1965. A cofounder of Intel, Moore contended that the number of transistors that could be economically loaded on an integrated circuit would double about every two years. The Caltech PhD was right as rain, and so appreciative of the good schooling he got that he and his wife have since enriched Caltech by a crisp $600 million, the biggest donation in history to a college or university.

What's so peachy about Moore's Law? Moore is describing the enormous increase in memory within computers, cars, phones, and nearly every other gadget we use. The most incredible thing of all: Moore's Law is expected to continue to prevail until the year 2015.

In case somebody hasn't formulated it yet—and somebody may well have done so—let me throw a new one at you. I'll call it Mackay's Law, and it works this way: Take the number of people in your department. Let's say it's twenty-five. My projection is, in five years, that number is likely to be fifteen. That means an average attrition rate of two bodies a year.

Moore's Law is part of the reason. As computer memory skyrockets, not only does the volume of machine-made calculations increase, the complexity of things computers can do will also multiply . . . and in amazing ways. If a Toyota robotic trumpeter can already belt out a flawless version of "Somewhere over the Rainbow," you can be sure unimaginable labor- and management-savings technology is headed our way. The innovations will be over the moon! They will slay us . . . literally . . . at the rate of two per year in the workplace.

Keeping your job will be a lot like navigating a *Survivor* obstacle course in reality TV. In Greek mythology, mighty Hercules had to perform twelve labors of repentance. One of the labors of Hercules was death defying, like bringing back Cerberus, the vicious multiheaded guard dog of Hades. And he had to do it bare-handed. A second labor was to wash out the biggest, rankest cattle stalls found in glorious old Greece. Suicide mission . . . and sloughing through deep doo-doo. Sounds like "all in a day's work" for the modern manager.

Mackay's Moral: In the future world of jobs,
Moore means less.

Quickie—
How Bad Can Things Get?

One day, as I sat musing . . . sad and lonely and without a friend,
I heard a voice out of nowhere say:
   "Cheer up. Things could be worse."
   So I cheered up. And, sure enough, things got worse!

"Oh them—they're just the ghosts of all the people we've terminated."

Chapter 4

Things Change . . .
and It Pays to Know How

When I was growing up as a kid, the U.S. GDP was in the hundreds of millions . . . then it went to billions. According to CNBC that number in the second quarter of 2009 was $13.7 trillion. The media is constantly confusing billions with trillions and vice versa. We have been so desensitized with these numbers, it's hard to comprehend them.

A quick little drill: I'm going to ask you to count from one to a trillion right now, and please stay awake until you finish this little assignment. How long will this take? 31,658 YEARS!

When I graduated from the University of Minnesota in 1954:

- A gallon of milk cost ninety-two cents.
- A loaf of bread: seventeen cents.
- The high for the Dow Jones was 338.
- And I drove a fire-engine red Pontiac Star Chief with a sticker price of $2,500.

In 1981–82:

- Milk had risen to $2.23 a gallon.
- Bread had climbed to fifty-three cents a loaf.
- The Dow was at about 900.
- And a Pontiac Firebird went for around $8,000.

Fall 2009:

- A gallon of milk is $2.69.
- A loaf of bread is $2.80.
- The Dow has bounced back above 9,000.
- And the Pontiac? That make won't even be around by next year.

Recently I saw a video on YouTube that Sony played at an executive conference this year. It points out how dramatically the world has changed and is changing:

- China will soon become the #1 English-speaking country in the world.
- Incidentally, when I was at the Olympic Games in China last summer, I learned that three hundred million people play basketball in China—the same number of people who live in the United States.
- The 25 percent of India's population with the highest IQs . . . is greater than the total population of the United States. Translation: India has more honors kids than America has kids.
- We are living in times of exponential growth—there are thirty-one billion searches on Google every month. In 2006, this number was less than a billion.
- For students starting a four-year technical degree, half of what they learn in their first year of study will be outdated by their third year of study.

Changes such as these can have a direct impact on you because they have a dramatic effect on the global employment market.

Mackay's Moral: What you don't know can hurt you, and it usually draws first blood from your pocketbook.

---

Chapter 5

12 Herculean Labors
to Keep You on the Payroll

1.   **Make yourself indispensable.** There are as many ways to make yourself indispensable as there are reasons for your boss to cut you loose. It pays to whip up the glue that will help you stick around.

Does your sales manager beef that no one is a team player? Hand off the ball every chance you get and then dive in blocking to help the other guy score a touchdown.

No one wants to touch the export trade opportunities to Upper Catatonia because their tariff laws are so complex, even though the CEO thinks this is the Mother of All Untapped Markets. Spend your weekends tracking down every detail you can on the Web. Maybe even hire an international trade law student to help you dig through the downloads.

The otherwise bright human resources director's administrative assistant thinks a .jpg file is something you stick on a message board. In an instant, you see your opening to become the most gifted and patient IT skills tutor on the company team.

2.   **Rev up your horsepower and flash it.** Holiday Inn founder Kemmons Wilson always believed you could get by working half days, and it didn't matter much if you worked the first twelve hours of the day or the second. If the hours for your job are 8 a.m. to 5 p.m., clock in at 7 a.m. and out at 6 p.m. And really spend that extra time *working*. There will be few others there for you to waste your precious minutes jawing. The clock doesn't care how you spend your time—6 p.m. will still come at 6 p.m.

If the guy or gal in the next cubicle is working a straight forty and making pretty much the same dough, it won't take long before the boss figures out that you're a bargain by a factor of 1.5.

Let's say your boss likes to work late; there can be a schmooze percentage if you do, too. Or, your boss may like to work late and values having someone reliable cover the bases while he sleeps in. There's no magic formula, but it's up to you to figure out the hours that will yield the biggest personal payoff for you.

3. **Volunteer.** In the army, never volunteering is the eleventh commandment. In business, volunteering may well be the First Opportunity. What does your boss hate to do? Is it sitting at his notebook and entering the weekly status report? How can you do it for him? There will always be a place in this world for the person who says, "I'll take care of it." And then does it.

4. **Stick out and shine.** "The invisible guy is first to go," warns executive recruiter Stephen Viscusi in a recent *Fortune* article. It doesn't matter how you shine, as long as it's positive for the company. Play third base on the softball team. If your boss's favorite charity is a soup kitchen for the down-and-out, learn how to ladle. Shoot the marketing VP that hot-off-the-press competitor's brochure a customer left in your office. Sprinkle your profile all over the company landscape. It's a lot harder to terminate a face than a social security number.

5. **Don't hang out with gloom and doom.** You know the types: They constantly gripe about the pay scale, the benefits, and the career opportunities. Management always makes the wrong calls, as they see it. The people who are dismissed never deserve to be. And the company's market strategy? It's headed to hell in a handbasket. Even if you never utter a negative word, tag along with this bunch and odds are high you'll be written off as a silent sympathizer.

6. **Be a builder . . . and a rebuilder.** When staff cutbacks happen, be the first to help the new streamlined organization to work, even when it costs extra hours and sweat. If the sales department loses a big account because of quality problems and you're in manufacturing, be the first to step up and say the client was right . . . and here's what we can do to help win that account back.

7. **Always position yourself as number two to your next career opportunity.** If you report directly to the head of your department or division, your first waking thought in the morning is what you will do that day to improve your chances of being the chief's backup. That includes the great idea you have been dreaming up to get that honcho promoted. The Law of Large Numbers guarantees that some #2 somewhere will be #1 someday. With surprising frequency, that #2 is an inside dark horse.

8. **Persevere.** In a rotten economy, it's so easy to throw in the towel. Hey, why not the whole linen closet? Top managers always have an eye out for people who do the opposite and engage themselves in tough problems, the ones who stick with finding a solution even after many reversals. And especially the ones who can keep up departmental morale among subordinates and peers in the darkest hours.

9. **Educate yourself one notch up.** Skilled marketers practice nichemanship in defining a tightly focused market and then bombarding it with custom-designed products. Savvy career survivors practice notchmanship. They study the résumés of managers on the next level and do their best to match and even surpass their career credentials. That isn't just restricted to formal degrees. It means loading up on those books, business journals, trade industry reports, Web sites, and bloggers that your firm's leading lights favor.

10. **Pay attention to your duds.** The clothes you wear—as I explain in the chapter "A Winning Suit Trumps"—assert your authority to subordinates, peers, the media, and most of all, to customers. Companies spend fortunes on their image. Your career is much likelier to blossom if you look like an extension of the company's public face rather than an eyesore who escaped from the deep-storage vault.

11. **Think big picture.** Your annual performance review is next week and the departmental budget is stretched—recalling retired CBS anchorman Dan Rather—"as tight as a too-small bathing suit on a too-hot car ride back from the beach." Back off. Maybe you come out and say the review can wait, there are more important priorities. Chances are you won't need to say anything at all. Cynics may brand you as a chump. In the tug-of-war to stay employed, you're likelier to come across as the champ who still has a desk.

12. And lastly, practice modesty. Indeed, you should do your best to make yourself indispensable. Indeed, you should not boast about it. Wisdom worthy to be reflected on each day: "If you think you're indispensable, put your finger in a bowl of water and check out the hole it leaves when you pull it out." The trick is to *be* indispensable . . . not to strut around the office as though you were.

"As usual, the employees are the last to know."

Chapter 6

The Last to Learn

It's a sad truth that employees are often the last to learn that their companies are in serious trouble and about to embark on a major downsizing program. The internal rumor mill is usually the *least* reliable source to counteract this. First, notorious gossipers crave sensational news. For them, dramatic counts far more than factual. Second, many companies know how to manage the rumor mill by feeding it just the kind of unreliable news that keeps employees and everyone else off balance.

Is there anything you can do to improve your chances of getting dependable first-alert warnings on your employer? Every employee in today's world needs to assemble his or her own personal intelligence system. That's not done overnight:

- Executive recruiters can be an excellent information source. Consider regularly contacting the recruiter who placed you in your job and building a trust factor so that he or she might share information about industry trends and issues.
- Financial analysts always monitor quarterly financial reports to see if a large number of executive stock options are exercised. It's public information for public companies, and you can access it over the Internet.
- Watch your boss. Often in impending crises, managers are given strict orders not to say anything. That causes more

21

than a few people to button up about everything. When you notice a sudden outbreak of tight-lippedness, an alarm bell should start clanging in your mind.

- Stay on the lookout for unusual corporate behaviors. Analysts in the Middle East always keep a watchful eye when a government stocks up on hospital beds in a potential hot spot or when the spouses and children of top leaders in a particular district are all abroad at the same time. Similarly, is the personnel department working unusually late hours? Are corporate meeting rooms blocked out for some unexplained period? One corporate insider I knew always sensed something was afoot when the number of bags coming out of the corporate shredder room suddenly spiked.

- Vendors and suppliers can be rich sources, especially ones who have been around long enough to read the tea leaves. A major reduction in raw materials orders is a nearly certain signal that production is going to be cut back.

- Let's say your boss, unbeknownst to you, has picked up a tip that the ax will soon be swinging. He or she is out on the market aggressively shopping the next job opportunity with competitors. That may cause a competitor to call you or a colleague, aware that a feeding frenzy for available candidates may be in the making. Be aware of any sudden change in the level of competitor interest in recruiting people from your firm.

- If a competitor's headquarters has a nearby watering hole, there is often much to be learned just by dropping by on a Friday evening and listening to the chatter. Competitors make it their business to learn about the ups and downs of rivals and may talk about the other guys far more freely than they would their own business.

The truth is that change happens like wildfire these days. Even if you do all the above, lightning may still strike you. There will, however, be a big difference. Rather than living a complacent life, you will expect that a jolt is on the horizon and you will likely be undertaking measures to dodge it.

Mackay's Moral: A reliable handle on tomorrow's news is one way to get a grip on an ax poised to swing.

Quickie—
Fine-Tune Your Job Description
Without Being Asked

"Living in fear of loss of job and income," management guru Peter Drucker once wrote, "is incompatible with taking responsibility for job and work group, for output and performance."

When Drucker wrote this he was chiefly talking about the safety nets of unemployment compensation and severance pay, but he also added: "Wherever a business has provided real job and income security, resistance to change or to innovation has disappeared."

There is also a powerful hidden lesson in this outlook when you apply it to today's job world: *The reason why so many people are casualties of massive company cutbacks is often that they did not take the initiative themselves to redefine their own jobs and make them more relevant.* Every several months, you should take a look at your job description and make some notes on it:

- What things are you spending time doing that your boss thinks are less/more important today than they may have been several months ago?
- What things are being done by your boss that he or she sees as significant drains on his or her time and which you could perhaps help with and share his or her burden?
- What are customers complaining about that is reversing their buying decisions or undercutting their loyalty to your firm . . . and which of these fall into your scope or responsibility?

Constantly initiate change to your own job to keep pace with company innovations and new market conditions. The best road to job security is to keep your job relevant.

Chapter 7

Yours to Lose

Widgitronics Global Resources is about to staff its marketing director position. You are the leading contender for the job. In fact, you are the proverbial shoo-in. You have eight years' experience with Widgitronics in consumer affairs. To broaden your exposure to the overall workings of the firm, you have just spent eight successful additional years on assignment in new product development and sales.

Everyone is convinced the marketing directorship is yours to lose. A loosely organized token search is conducted just to verify that no outside contender could be anywhere near as qualified as you are. Your colleagues have drafted their congratulatory messages and are just waiting to plug in the dates. Soon the victory balloons will be heaving in a net over your office desk waiting to cascade down when the announcement is made.

After a few weeks of deliberation, management announces its decision.

The verdict: You lose.

Stunned, you are determined to analyze the loss:

- Because there was such certainty you would win, your supporters never organized a cohesive campaign to back you.
- Your biggest advocate was the retiring marketing director, who—larger than life—chimed in with impromptu endorsements and gratuitously diminished the competition.
- You failed to brush up on the details of your own achieve-

ments in consumer affairs several years ago and slipped up
in responses to questions in your own interviews.

- A whole new group of entry-level marketing staff members
  had staged a relentless campaign with management saying
  that a grassroots change was needed in marketing management, one that was highly responsive to the Internet age.

Unlikely scenario? Consider how Hillary Clinton lost the Demo-
cratic presidential nomination in 2008.

- Her campaign was never properly organized and managed.
- Her husband, the popular former president Bill Clinton,
  was viewed at times as a meddlesome surrogate.
- Muddled recollections about a Bosnia visit in 1996 tarnished
  the credibility of her first lady experience.
- She cultivated the old guard of the party, at the expense of a
  powerfully organized and digitally able younger generation.

Mackay's Moral: In the staffing game, overconfidence and a
flawed plan can pull defeat from the jaws of victory.

Quickie—
Misery Is Contagious, Too

A wimpy guy walks into a bar and is hovering over his drink.

All of a sudden a six-foot-six monster guy—wearing boots, chains, and tattoos—elbows him off the bar stool.

Godzilla grabs the wimp's drink, inhales it, and hollers at him, "How do you like that, sonny?"

"Hey, mister, I'm having a bad day," the wimpy guy replies. "I got up early this morning and went to work, only to find out I got downsized out of my job. I went home at noon to tell my wife the bad news, and she left me. They stole my car this afternoon. And now I come in here to commit suicide . . . and you drink my poison."

Chapter 8

Beat Rejection
Before It Beats You

"How are you getting along?" asked the old timer of the new sales rep.

"Not so good," came the sales rep's disgusted reply. "I've been insulted in every place I made a call."

"That's funny," said the old timer. "I've been on the road forty years. I've had my samples flung in the street, been tossed downstairs, manhandled by janitors, and rolled in the gutter. But insulted—never!"

If you're reeling from just being fired or re-engineered out of a job, then you've just swallowed one heaping serving of rejection. Be mindful of what Sylvester Stallone said: "I take rejection as someone blowing a bugle in my ear to wake me up and get going, rather than retreat."

We all deal with rejection differently. But if you're in the sales game, you better get used to it because rejection is—and always will be—part of business. Too many people just give up. Ascending the career ladder of life is a matter of getting nods of approval from the powers that be. In order to get the yeses, you must hear the nos.

Here is my advice in dealing with rejection, because Lord knows, I've had plenty over my career:

- **Don't take it personally**. Don't consider yourself a failure if you get rejected. You're a much bigger person than the way your last job packaged you. Take stock of your personal inventory. The sooner you think in terms of your breadth of skills and talents, the quicker you will find constructive ways to move on.

- **Leave the last door open**. While you may be retooling your new identity, don't waste time with venom for the past. So what if the job wasn't tailor-made for you? Blaming your last boss and your former company gets you nowhere. Consider that experience to have been invaluable to get you to the next run. Embrace the philosophy I underscore in the title of my book *We Got Fired! . . . And It's the Best Thing That Ever Happened to Us*. Visualize the day when you can visit your last employer and actually *thank him or her* for the opportunity that was opened up for you. Remember as well that, on a practical level, you will need these people for references and goodwill within your industry.

- **Never say no for the other person**. Don't anticipate rejection based on your immediate past experience. Indeed, you may have to polish up your attitude and credentials. On the other hand, you may also find employers who like you very much as you are. Be flexible, and test the market. Find out what feels natural for you, but also listen to others—recruiters, interviewers, and trusted friends and advisers. You'll have to present yourself in a way that's both digestible for the marketplace and acceptable to you.

- **Analyze every failure, but never wallow in one**. I always want to know *why* people say no, and I'm not afraid to ask. Was it me? Was it the condition of the economy? How about the particular needs of the firm or the department of that point in time? Be wide open to changing yourself, but be careful about trying to remake yourself to answer circumstances beyond your control.

- **Remember past achievements**. Reflect on your past career and business successes. How did you feel? When did you shine your best? And be honest and up to date. Don't spotlight the kinds of career successes that are no longer possible in an industry or market that has changed forever.

- **Take a break**. If you're feeling down, do something you like—exercise, read a motivational book, listen to a favorite song. Just don't stay away too long. And never take a break when you're on a hot streak, only when you're in a slump. If a sudden streak of contacts and job prospects springs up, you may have already made the necessary adjustments in how you're presenting yourself.

As a young actor and comedian, Jerry Seinfeld had a small, recurring role as a mail carrier on the TV sitcom *Benson*. One day, Jerry showed up for a script read-through only to find that he hadn't been issued a script. When he asked why, he was told that he'd been fired. No one had remembered to inform him.

Embarrassed, Jerry left the studio determined to stay out of sitcoms until he had more control over the process. A few years later he succeeded, in more ways than one, when he cocreated the hit series *Seinfeld*, which ran for nine seasons on NBC and topped the Nielsen ratings for two years.

Getting fired, downsized, laid off, let go, or whatever term you want to use, once left a stigma. Now it is standard procedure. More and more people find themselves looking for work. And things are not going to change soon.

Rejection is the order of the day. It's acceptance that's the exception.

Two men wrote a book containing a collection of inspirational stories. The two authors figured it would take about three months to find a publisher. What happened next is as uplifting as any of the stories in their book.

The first publisher they approached said, "No."

The second publisher said, "No."

The third publisher said, "No."

The next thirty publishers said, "No."

Altogether, they received thirty-three rejections over a period of three years. So what did they do? They submitted their book to still another publisher.

The thirty-fourth publisher said, "Yes."

After thirty-three rejections, that one "yes" launched the spectacular publishing success of *Chicken Soup for the Soul*, written and compiled by my good friends Jack Canfield and Mark Victor Hansen. The Chicken Soup for the Soul series has so far sold more than thirty million copies—all because Canfield and Hansen had the willingness to fail over and over, and to keep going until they succeeded.

Mackay's Moral: Don't get dejected if you've been rejected— just get your new you perfected!

Chapter 9

Parting Words:
Canned Remarks upon Getting Canned

When people are fired, many look at their last words as a chance to ventilate all the venom and frustration that may be within them. It's their final chance to retaliate before clearing out their desk—the career equivalent of a trip to the firing squad.

Be very careful about that attitude. It can be costly and dangerously terminal for your career.

The best way to part company with your present employer is almost always on as good a set of terms as reality allows. The situation is strikingly similar to losing a customer when you are in sales. In sales, you have to understand that how you exit an account is just as critical as how you enter into a relationship.

Regaining the goodwill of former employers can be as important as pursuing a new one. It may seem refreshing to dive into a new pool of contacts today. But first, don't forget this: From an efficiency standpoint, you already have an established relationship on which to build. It's simply one that has, for some reason, gone awry. That means how you end an association is fundamental to the possibility of beginning a new one. Second, the person to whom you choose to rage may well be answering a recruiter's call in a reference check, or even working for an entirely new employer months from now.

When you lose a job, consider the first thing we say to a lost customer at MackayMitchell Envelope Company: "Thank you for giving us your business all these years." And we say it with sincerity and mean it. The next is: "What can we do to make it an easy transition for you?"

And finally: "If things don't work out, we're ready, willing, and able to consider stepping right back in. We sure would love to keep in touch with you from time to time." And we do.

Let's say the job you are losing is one you dearly wanted to keep or an affiliation with an organization you deeply loved. Surely, look at all your options. But from the moment you lose that spot, start to visualize the day you will win them back. Imagine the lunch or the golf game you will enjoy together to celebrate your return. Then plan out each painstaking, detailed, and hard-to-swallow step you would need to take to reinstate yourself. Don't make it an obsession, but do make it an option.

Mackay's Moral: He or she who burns bridges better be a damn good swimmer.

Quickie—
The Stretch Marks of Experience

"Man's mind, once stretched by a new idea, never regains its original dimensions," said Justice Oliver Wendell Holmes, Jr.— one of history's most distinguished members of the Supreme Court.

Reflect for a moment on Holmes' wisdom: "*A mind stretched by a new experience can never go back to its old dimensions.*"

Every time you search out a new job, and the trail proves to be a dead end . . . frustration takes the wind out of your sails.

Every interview that goes badly and leads to rejection . . . sparks a feeling of failure.

Every last-round candidacy where you *almost* land a job . . . sinks you into depression.

Those negative, self-destructive reactions earmark defeatist thinking.

Debrief yourself after each reversal, and you will usually find a wealth of learning about how to improve:

- your résumé,
- your pitch,
- your positioning,
- your explanation of why you lost your last job,
- and your plan for making your next job a success.

When does a setback become a real loss? If you *didn't* learn something new and important about yourself and your capabilities.

"Jim, say hi to Tom, our severance consultant."

Chapter 10

A Checklist
for Checking Out

It's as important to negotiate your termination from your present employer as well as you negotiate your next position with a new organization. Below are just some of the considerations. While you want to receive everything that you are entitled to get, it's always in your best interest to maintain positive relationships and not to burn bridges to future opportunities.

- Have a clear, written understanding of what your former company will say about your termination.
- If you're not terminated for cause, poor performance, or violation of company policy, try to secure letters of recommendation from former supervisors.
- Know if you can ask prospective employers to contact the company as references. If former bosses will say unflattering things about you, do your best to find this out in advance.
- If there is a possibility your company will rehire you in a better economy, see if the termination can be repositioned as a leave of absence. You may forgo some severance pay, but your résumé may look better as a result.
- If you are considering a return to school, the leave of absence may also be a natural explanation.
- If you are asked to take early retirement, make sure your benefits are carefully calculated.

- If you don't have another employer lined up, examine what you need to do to extend health care coverage.
- How will perquisites, such as club memberships or company cars, be addressed?
- If you have unused vacation or sick day credits, how can this time be converted into hard cash?
- If you are eligible for a partial-year bonus or stock options, establish how and when payments will be made.
- Confirm what items of information you are entitled to retain, such as client and prospect lists.
- Review any employment agreements to determine if you are bound by any "non-compete" clauses.

Quickie—
Crying Societies or Support Groups?

Losing a job is traumatic, especially if it's your first time through the meat slicer . . . and if your financial situation is already a tightrope walk. Because the job-loss experience sabotages confidence, a support group can be made to order to rebuild self-confidence. Internet support groups have both convenience advantages and privacy risks, which I'll describe in a moment.

- A support group is positive when it helps restore confidence and negative when it degenerates into a crying society. Remember that Job #1 when you lose a job is getting a job. Spending a lot of time with similarly out-of-work people may strengthen your feeling of moral outrage that you were unjustly fired. It may also do nothing about your getting a job and might in fact amplify the unhealthy feelings that you are an unwanted, flawed human being.
- Dr. Marc D. Feldman of the University of Alabama has "warned about sympathy-seekers who invade Internet support groups . . . People can invent or induce fictitious illnesses in themselves or others in order to gain sympathy." What holds true for illness-based alliances can afflict any sort of support group. Often people who are either unafflicted or mildy affected will exhaust the group's time and subvert its positive purposes.
- As with any Internet-based communication, be conscious that anyone can be listening in—and that includes former employers and executive recruiters.

Chapter 11

Gone to Potter

If you go out of your way to get yourself fired, do it to build a bridge to your next career. According to Inc.com, J. K. Rowling was a "former secretary who was once fired for writing short stories at her computer and used her severance pay to help finance the first Harry Potter" book. Rowling knows how to take risks that leave an impression. Once asked about a project she was considering, she said, "There is no point in doing it unless it is amazing." Today, Rowling's net worth is estimated at almost $800 million.

Enlightened firing can take many forms:

- Some highly qualified people are culled from companies in re-engineering-style mass firings. Confident in their own skills and their ability to land on their feet, wise individuals use their severance to finance a sabbatical. They invest in strengthening their present skills or learning a new special-ized second or third skill.

- Let's say you've been fired because your company forced you to engage in unethical practices, and your ex-employer has developed a reputation for doing business on dimly lit streets. You could appeal to firms priding themselves as ethical beacons.

- Perhaps you know you're due for a one-way ticket to the headsman's block. If you're a manager whose performance relies on the contributions of others, who will you need in your new job to be a success? I recall one executive who often hopped from one turnaround assignment to another. The executives who made up his new dirty dozen as he ricocheted from one new gig to another were rarely the same. And, even more important, were often not people he liked. In fact, he considered picking team members on the basis of liking them to be a big mistake. He picked people he respected and could play a meaningful role in solving the problems of the new business he was taking on.

Mackay's Moral: As Harry Potter put it, "You sort of start thinking anything's possible if you've got enough nerve."

RECONSTRUCT
YOUR ATTITUDE

Chapter 12

Anger Is Only One Letter
from Danger

The more you grow up, the less you blow up.

There was a father who had a son with a bad temper. The father knew the danger of anger, so he gave his son a bag of nails and told him that every time he lost his temper, he must hammer a nail into the back of the fence. The first day the boy had driven twenty-seven nails into the fence. Over the next few weeks, as the son learned to control his anger, the number of nails he hammered daily gradually dwindled.

The son discovered it was easier to hold his temper than to drive those nails into the fence. Finally, the day came when the boy didn't lose his temper at all. He told his father about it, and the father suggested that the boy now pull out one nail for each day that he was able to hold his temper.

The days passed and the young boy was finally able to tell his father that all the nails were gone. The father took his son by the hand and led him to the fence. He said, "You have done well, my son, but look at the holes in the fence. The fence will never be the same. When you say things in anger, they leave a scar just like this one."

Anger is a natural human emotion. The problem is not anger; the problem is the mismanagement of anger. Mismanaged anger and rage is the major cause of conflict in our personal and professional relationships.

One out of five Americans has an anger-management problem. Some of the problems that we hear about daily in the media are domestic abuse, road rage, workplace violence, divorce, and addiction.

People get angry or upset an average of ten to fourteen times a day. And anger is especially prevalent in the workplace. The most common triggers of anger at work are favoritism, unfair performance appraisals, and perceived sexual harassment. How do you keep hold of your temper before it flares into a heated storm or, worse, violence? Here are some tips:

- **Acknowledge your anger.** Don't pretend it's not there or ignore it in the hope that it will go away.
- **Don't be hyper about slights.** If a coworker doesn't acknowledge you as you pass in the hallway, it may simply mean he or she is racing to get to the bathroom.
- **Know what's ticking you off.** If you've had a fight with your spouse, leave your baggage at home. Or if you're under the gun on a project, don't take it out on a coworker.
- **Don't get angry just because someone else is.** If your coworker is mad at something or someone, it doesn't mean you have to be angry, too.
- **Track your anger signals.** Anger reveals itself physically through a racing pulse, shortness of breath, or pacing. Read the signs before your anger gets out of hand.
- **Chill out.** Find ways to temper your temper before it flares. Do breathing exercises, take a walk, or even do busy work.
- **Log it.** If someone's pushed your anger button, write down the reason. Be brutally honest for your purposes, but don't send it to the person. Just the act of logging it in your notebook will help you feel better.
- **Deal in a friend.** If it's unwise to direct your anger at the source, confide in a friend.

A young job candidate was in the reception area of a major company on a hot, humid day after an interview. He stopped to make a call on his iPhone, and apparently got some bad news. Not quite under his breath, he rattled off a string of unrepeatable words.

The receptionist could sense all the other visitors in the waiting area were embarrassed by the outburst of profanity. Realizing his gaffe, the angry job seeker tiptoed to the exit. As he pushed the elegant brass-paneled door open, the receptionist calmly said, "Sir, I believe you are leaving something behind."

He quickly turned and asked innocently, "Oh, what's that?"

"A very bad impression," the receptionist responded.

Mackay's Moral: When a person strikes in anger, he or she usually misses the mark.

Chapter 13

You're Never a Failure
Until You Think You Are

The devil offered all the tools of his trade, the old fable goes, to anyone who would pay the price. They were spread out on the table, each one labeled—hatred, malice, envy, despair, sickness—all the weapons that everyone knows so well. But off on one side, apart from the rest, lay a harmless-looking, wedge-shaped instrument marked "discouragement." It was old and worn, but it was priced far above all the rest.

When asked the reason why, the devil explained, "Because I can use this one so much more easily than the others. No one knows that it belongs to me, so with it I can open doors that are tightly bolted against the others. Once I get inside, I can use any tool that suits me best."

A very real problem within all of us that can cause an attitude crash is discouragement. In fact, I've always gone out of my way to stay away from negative people. I like to surround myself with positive, upbeat people who constantly encourage me.

The word *encouragement* means "to put courage into." Conversely, discouragement takes courage out. How can you reach for the stars, go bravely where no man has gone before, or climb the highest mountain if you lack courage?

Author Glenn Van Ekeren outlines the four pitfalls of discouragement:

1. Discouragement hurts our self-image.
2. Discouragement causes us to see ourselves as less than we really are.

3. Discouragement causes us to blame others for our predicament.
4. Discouragement causes us to blur the facts.

One of the greatest novels in American literature was the result of a very discouraging day for the author. Nathaniel Hawthorne had lost his job at a customhouse, and went home to break the news to his wife, Sophia. Rather than the reaction he expected, she was joyous. "Now you can write your book," she told him.

Unconvinced, Hawthorne asked her, "And what shall we live on while I am writing it?"

Sophia opened a drawer that contained a substantial amount of money and told him, "I have always known that you were a man of genius. I knew that someday you would write a masterpiece." She went on to explain that she had saved some of the household money each week, and had accumulated enough to last for a year. And with that, Hawthorne set to work on *The Scarlet Letter*, required reading for many of us in our high school English classes. And all because Sophia Hawthorne refused to let her husband be discouraged.

In her book *The Right Words at the Right Time*, Marlo Thomas tells the story of Shaquille O'Neal, the NBA superstar center. When he was fourteen, he attended a basketball camp expecting to astound the coaches with his brilliance. He was in for a rude shock. He had been a star in his San Antonio high school, but at the camp he was just one of many star athletes. Not getting the attention he was accustomed to from the coaches, he began to worry that perhaps he wasn't good enough to make the grade. His self-confidence took a nosedive.

Discouraged, he turned to his parents for advice. I've had some conversations with Shaq's mother, Lucille, about that advice. She told him, "You must fulfill your dreams while there's still room for you to do so. Attack them with a full head of steam. There's no opportunity like now. This is the time you can show people."

His confidence almost gone, Shaq told his mother, "I can't do that right now. Maybe later." Then, says Shaq, his mother said the words that he remembers changed his life: "Later doesn't always come to everybody."

Mackay's Moral: You aren't finished when you are defeated; you are finished when you quit.

"By god, you're not a man who's afraid to fail."

Chapter 14

Being Your Best with
Things at Their Worst

If at first you don't succeed . . . you're doing about average.

Rebounding from rejection is an essential skill to acquire, especially in job hunting. Here are five tips for beating rejection:

- **Ten setbacks are the going price for any worthwhile win.** If you look at the major league baseball standings at the end of any season, you'll find that, out of thirty teams, only eight make the playoffs, and only one of those winds up winning the World Series. Are those annual standings the end of the world for the twenty-nine losers? Hardly.

- **Analyze every failure, but never wallow in one.** President Harry Truman once said, "As soon as I realize I've made one damned fool mistake, I rush out and make another one." Failure is a condition all of us experience. It's our reaction to our failures that distinguishes winners from losers.
  What makes a great racehorse as compared to a cheap claimer is not just speed, it's heart. A claimer usually makes just one run. Once the horse is passed, that's it, the animal quits and the race is over. But stakes horses, the best of the breed, are different. Even if they fall behind, they'll come back and try to regain the lead. There's no quit in them. Like National Football League (NFL) coaching legend Vince Lombardi's teams, they never lose, they just run out of time. Defeats are temporary. Heart and class are permanent.

- **Don't rationalize away the hurt.** You didn't get the job? Turned down for a raise? Denied admission to the college of your choice? Don't kid yourself and try to cover up the hurt with "Gee, I didn't really want it anyway." Of course you wanted it. "I suppose I didn't deserve it." Of course you did. Self-delusion and self-hatred aren't the answer. Don't let your worth be defined by others. Point your head in the right direction and get back in the game.

  It's not a permanent condition; it's a short-term setback. You have a goal. The particular job or raise or school may have been a stepping-stone to that goal, but that's all it was. There's more than one way to cross a river. Now you're going to have to rethink the path, but that doesn't mean you have to abandon the goal.

- **Don't walk around as if you're wearing a scarlet letter.** For heaven's sake, who knows you were turned down for a job or for admission to Harvard? It's not going to be the lead story on the evening news. Rejection is only as big as you make it. Take an inventory of human emotional responses, like love, hate, greed, fear, jealousy, grief, envy, gratitude, compassion. Now compare them to self-pity. Of all the emotions on the list—some constructive, some not so constructive—I'd venture that self-pity probably has fewer positive applications, and can do less for you than just about any of them. Whatever you do, don't take rejection personally. It may have nothing at all to do with you.

- **Start worrying when they stop considering you as a contender.** Cary Grant, Marilyn Monroe, Alfred Hitchcock, and Richard Burton never won an Oscar. Babe Ruth was never named MVP. Thomas Jefferson, John Quincy Adams, and Andrew Jackson all lost elections for the presidency before they won one. Losers? No. Legends.

Mackay's Moral: Failure is not falling down, but staying down.

Victoria Roberts

*"If you want a positive outlook, you're going to
have to turn your chair around, Walter."*

Chapter 15

Pitchmanship: Applying
Marketing Nichemanship to Job Hunting

Niche marketing is a bona fide and well-tested approach to strategic selling. Some firms have had stellar success building their business around their pursuit of specialized niches. They say it pays to know your niche as well as your name.

Pitchmanship is a term I use to describe how to apply niche marketing principles to pitching yourself in a job search. There are some perilous myths surrounding niche marketing. Similarly, there are dangerous assumptions you steer clear of when you pitch yourself and your credentials for a job.

Myth one: **A pitch has to be chic.** Don't assume that organizations are always on the prowl for cutting-edge talent. Some companies posture themselves so low-key that they expect their people to have state-of-the-art skills, but the culture demands they present themselves with "Aw, shucks!" understatement. Study the organization and the style of the CEO in speeches and articles. It may be impractical to tailor your résumé for each and every company you pursue, but your cover letter should reflect some understanding of what the organization is about.

I call this the Turtle Wax Lesson because of how this old car-care staple is marketed. Turtle Wax has held a dependable—and sizable—share of the car-wax market for decades. This task is synonymous with something people hate to do. They do it with a product that has a reputation for being harder to apply than others, by exploiting a niche out there of people who literally "love" their cars. What better way to show dedication to your set of wheels than by lavishing care and devotion on the object of one's affections? Working hard to get a shine that shines through. Romantic stuff, huh?

Turtle Wax–style employers don't like people with instant, easy solutions. They cherish people who love to apply elbow grease in liberal quantities. And they tend to be skeptical of people who are finished products—people whom they can't change or polish in their own style.

Myth two: A pitch has to be flashy. There are a lot of companies that are going back to basics. That mantra has become one of the hottest marketing mantras in the present downturn. This doesn't mean accountants are now being recruited for their skills with an abacus or their ability to chisel Roman numerals onto slate. In a back-to-basics organization, hard-nosed skeptics are generally rewarded. They find a way to make do with what the organization has. The back-to-basics types often overlap with the Turtle Wax sorts, but not always. Some back-to-basics advocates have no interest at all in working harder. They just don't want things to cost more.

Myth three: A pitch shouldn't be too narrow in its demands. Don't assume that because your niche is larger, it's better. In marketing, wouldn't you rather be fighting for half of a 28 percent segment than one-seventh of a 44 percent one?

You may have lost your job as IT director for a mature $200-million company. An offer comes along for a position with the same title at a $100-million company with high growth prospects at half the salary. Many companies, as I point out elsewhere, are skeptical about people willing to take large salary cuts. However, if you really want the job, you can make a convincing case that you're committed to signing up with a shooting star. After all, doesn't the fact you're on the pavement say it all about the risks of being attached to a butchered cash cow?

Myth four: A pitch has to be neat. Although *most* searches are much more sharply defined these days, not all of them have the sharpness of a surgeon's scalpel. On the retail sales front, there are liquor stores in the toniest sections of Manhattan, Chicago's Gold Coast, and Beverly Hills that do as much volume in Château Ripple, vintage Wednesday, as Château Lafite-Rothschild, vintage 1895.

Again, research is king. Some companies are wildly inconsistent in the way they are willing to spend money. The corporate offices could be lavish, but everyone may be expected to travel coach and lunchtime dining could mean a trip to the fast-food court. Learn the profile and do your best to squeeze yourself into the company suit.

Mackay's Moral: You'll never please everyone, but you only have to please a few people to get an offer.

Quickie—
Should You Go Under the Knife
After You Get the Ax?

- A 2009 article in the *Chicago Tribune* says, "People who lost stable jobs in 1982 suffered an immediate 30 percent drop in their earnings, according to Social Security and other government records. As a group, they never recovered . . . A decade later, their earnings were down 20 percent compared with workers with similar profiles who avoided a layoff. After 15 years, they made 10 percent less. Even 20 years down the road, they hadn't caught up."
- This is tough news to take, especially if you're over fifty. This trend will not change for people losing jobs today. In fact, it may get worse.
- A personal makeover is the solution. Retrain the mind and keep one's skill sets up to date. Stay abreast of the latest in trend information and current events. Physical wellness and fitness are an absolute top priority.
- Some people think more drastic measures—like a tummy tuck, whittling away those love handles, or breast reduction—can make you look younger and more employable.
- A 2009 ABC News report noted, "The American Academy of Facial Plastic and Reconstructive Surgery reported that 75 percent of its members have patients asking for cosmetic surgery to stay competitive in the workplace."
- I've judged beauty pageants, including Miss America, but in my mind the jury is still out: Can you face-lift yourself into a new career? Fitness, continuous learning, and social awareness are—I believe—the core skills that will make you desirable to an employer. If you don't have these, no surgeon in the world can compensate for them.

Chapter 16

The Continuity of Contrarians

You're smart, or they wouldn't have hired you. You've read the tea leaves about job and career changes, and you know how frequently they happen. The head-office people figure you're probably good for five years. Then you'll either bolt . . . or could be they'll stretch you out on the chopping block during the next downsizing "harvest."

Almost all of your other entering "classmates" in this year's crop of new hires will be playing exactly the same hop-to-happiness game.

The truth is somewhat different. Organizations have to be agile enough to change, but they also crave continuity. While they expect a huge portion of the organization to turn over rapidly, headquarters also yearns for those stable human pillars who anchor cultural values.

So, imagine that you think "company career" is for you rather than dancing from job to job. What if you become an "I'm-sticking-around" contrarian? You may need to "announce" your intentions with an unusual accent:

- "If you need someone to babysit new recruits and help orient them to the company, I'm available."
- "You say you can't do my annual review on time? I can wait. I know I can count on you to be fair."
- "What can I do to make your job easier? Boss, what parts of your job description would be easy for you to delegate to me?"

- "Are there confrontational aspects of your job that you would just as soon someone else handle for you?"
- "I know you have a do-or-die presentation tomorrow. I'm great at speech bubbles and custom animations. How can I PowerPoint you to—in Star Trek terms—'go where no one has gone before'?"

Some might write off this overly helpful attitude as being too subservient at best. But hold the phone:

- Will you likely be wrenching your family through a transfer every five years?
- Do you have a passion for the stable life or prefer that of today's career nomad?
- If you stick around, are your odds better for *making* the decisions about who sticks around in the inevitable next personnel cut . . . or for being one of the decisions?

Mackay's Moral: Most people are willing to meet each other halfway; trouble is, most people are pretty poor judges of distance.

Chapter 17

Is This the Time
to Get That MBA?

When business is booming, managers complain they can't free up good people to train them. When business is bust, the cupboard is bare to finance training. Ideally, the best time to train is the off-season. And a downturn can be a perfect window to either get your MBA or at least start work on one.

Debate is hot about the value of an MBA. Up until 2008, an MBA was viewed—wrongly, to be sure—as an overnight meal ticket to gourmet dining in a hotshot Wall Street firm. It may be years before that play gets a revival, if it ever does.

You're much smarter to regard the MBA as advanced survival training in a very competitive employment world. Take time to do hard research:

- Identify managers and professionals in positions you aspire to be in within the next ten years. Do they have an MBA in addition to their other college degrees?
- What parts of the MBA degree are most vital to their success? Is it the finance, the marketing, the strategic planning? Knowing the focus of your MBA needs may help you pick where you should study. (All MBA programs are not alike.) You also might decide you don't really need an MBA as much as some selected business courses.
- During wartime, armies have long used officer candidate schools for two- or three-month crash courses. Similarly, many business schools offer advanced management pro-

grams to give managers a mini-MBA. Will this meet your needs? At age thirty-five, I attended Stanford's Advanced Management program. It lasted ten weeks with one hundred attendees representing twenty countries. To this day, it was the best business decision I ever made in my career.

- Can you negotiate funding for an advanced management program or even all or part of an MBA as part of your severance package from your current employer? For you, this option can be pennies from heaven in more ways than one: First, it can cover up a crater in your résumé. Second, when the economy swings around, your present employer may decide he needs you more than he thought he did, especially with your additional credentials. Third, that fresh sheepskin makes you more marketable, of course.

In January 2009, the *Times* of London published an article titled "Downturn Is Right Time to Take an MBA" by Steve Coomber. It included some noteworthy factors:

- "In a downturn, the opportunity costs of putting a career into neutral for a year or two are more attractive than during a boom, when people worry about missing out on quick promotions and big bonuses. In a recession, an MBA allows you to boost skills, ready for when the green shoots of recovery appear."
- "In coming years, there will be far less money to be made in finance than over the last decade," Arnoud De Meyer, the director of Judge Business School at Cambridge University, said. "The nature of the jobs will change and there will not be the same huge bonuses and salaries." Still, who can knock a business degree out of schools like Michigan, Northwestern, Stanford, Wharton, USC, or Harvard?

For those MBA students determined to work in the finance and banking sector, the best business schools have powerful networks, so be sure to use them.

If you have not stashed away enough grain in your silo for getting an MBA to be an option, then you should do a little reading before the *next* recession—and there will be another one, too. You can learn a lot from that old Greek named Aesop and his tale called *The Ant and the Grasshopper.*

Mackay's Moral: MBA can mean master of business administration or it can spell my best alternative when the economy nose-dives.

Quickie—
The Lecture Room in Your Laptop

Before you go out and spend megabucks on higher education, make sure that you get a load of the highest education . . . for nothing. Nothing!

- **TED (Technology, Entertainment, Design)** is an annual conference committed to "ideas worth spreading." These lectures, known as TED Talks, include business and technology. Among TED lecturers are Bill Gates and Google founders Sergey Brin and Larry Page. There are more than four hundred TED Talks that can be seen free online. According to April 2009 data, these speeches have been seen over one hundred million times.
- MIT has a free lecture program online called "Open-CourseWare."
- According to the *New York Times*, "Yale put some of its most popular undergraduate courses and professors online free. The list includes Controversies in Astrophysics with Charles Bailyn, Modern Poetry with Langdon Hammer and Introduction to the Old Testament with Christine Hayes."
- There are heaps of free programs on the Internet on accounting skills and information technology. Just be sure to read the fine print for those services that are without charge and those that intend to extract a price.

How you spend your viewing time is your business, but there's a noticeable difference on the gray matter scales between "I Dream of Jeannie" and "I Dream of Genius."

"*Would you take the guy at Table 4? I used to be his broker.*"

Chapter 18

When It's OK
Not to Act Your Age!

A few years ago, the MacArthur Foundation underwrote a landmark study that included the importance of "lifestyle choices" to maintaining productivity as one ages. The findings were summarized in a book titled *Successful Aging* by Dr. John W. Rowe, president of Mount Sinai Hospital, and Robert L. Kahn, PhD, from the University of Michigan.

Three groups of factors have an influence on productivity as one's age advances: mental and physical function, friendship and social relations, and enduring personal characteristics.

Among the book's remarkable findings:

- "Most age-related reductions in physical performance are avoidable and many are reversible."
- "Exercise dramatically increases physical fitness, muscle size, and strength in older individuals."
- "When it comes to sexual activity . . . chronological age itself is not the critical factor."
- "The more frequent the [physical] exercise, the greater the benefit, but you don't have to overdo it. Moderate exercise . . . [as measured in a major study] proved to be nearly as protective as vigorous exercise."
- "While most people assume that genes play the dominant role, new research suggests that environment and lifestyle may in fact be more important in terms of the risk factors associated with aging."

The authors also cite the famous African American baseball pitcher Satchel Paige who was still hurling from the mound after the age most big leaguers retire to read their press clippings and dust their trophies. When asked how old he was, Paige's answer was, "'How old would *you* be if you didn't know how old you was?'"

The more concessions to age that people make, the older they will act and the older they will seem. Among these I would include The Decisive Seven:

1. Awareness of the importance of nutrition and exercise.
2. Pride in personal appearance.
3. Breadth and diversity of personal network.
4. Scope of friends and engagement in socializing.
5. Participation in learning opportunities and continuing education.
6. Attention to current events and important trends in human behavior.
7. Resilience in facing and overcoming setbacks.

It's hard to make a meaningful effort on any of these fronts without faith in yourself. "Faith in oneself is the best and safest course," Michelangelo maintained. He left his design for the dome of St. Peter's unfinished when he died at the age of 88 in 1564. He remained unafraid of failure throughout his life, and this was decisive.

"The greater danger for most of us lies not in setting our aim too high and falling short," Michelangelo believed, "but in setting our aim too low, and achieving our mark."

Mackay's Moral: Act the age you want to be, not the age others expect.

"Apparently, fifty is the new unemployed."

Quickie—
Moonlighting: The Wisdom of Having a Second Skill

In turbulent times and in an era where job and career changes are so prevalent, it pays to have multiple personal skills. It used to be that a person simply stuck to a single professional profile. Not any longer.

This pattern is abundantly clear in the world of professional sports. Los Angeles Dodgers manager Joe Torre, for example, was a broadcast-booth presence for the California Angels between manager jobs.

How many Metropolitan Opera chorus members worked as (singing) waiters until the breakthrough role finally arrived? How many Hollywood stars unloaded trucks or drew sodas while they performed, often uncredited, roles in B and even C films? In an article titled "Actors Moonlighting on Horror Flicks," DVD columnist Michael H. Kleinschrodt points out that marquee stars like Casey Affleck, George Clooney, Cate Blanchett, and Halle Berry all worked on the scary screen.

When planning your moonlighting, it's generally best to develop skills that have some relationship with each other, but not necessarily for professions that are likely to suffer in the same flat economic period.

In a *U.S. News & World Report* column, Karen Burns advises, "You have a job. Good news! But you don't like the job. Or it doesn't pay a living wage. Or it doesn't offer health insurance. That's bad news. The secret to successful moonlighting is simple: Job B needs to provide what Job A lacks." She admits, "Long-term moonlighting can wear you down. But until the economy improves and/or you find that One Good Job, two jobs that complement each other may be the answer."

Chapter 19

Electronic Résumé Screening:
Use Language That Computes

Get a hold of an April 2009 article in *Fortune* called "Secrets of the Résumé Gatekeeper." It could save your career life. That's because your career survival is increasingly in the grip of tough guys, not with a chip on their shoulder . . . but with a chip for a heart.

Companies are being hit with a barrage of résumés that make Hurricane Katrina feel like the kiss of a gentle ocean breeze.

How are they responding?

How did you think they would respond?

They're screening out the clutter and using software programs to do it. Until you jump the hurdle and prove you are a meaningful applicant, your résumé is about as unwelcome as the latest batch of pollen on a hayfever sufferer's windowsill.

Reporter Beth Kowitt chronicled the saga of Al Campa. He heads up marketing for Taleo, which their Web site says does "on demand talent management."

Campa was looking for a product marketing VP and had gotten five times the normal load of career paper—a total of 250 résumés.

Instead of reviewing each career profile, he used "the candidate-screening program made by his company, and he narrowed the pool down to 20 . . . Great for Campa. Not so great for the 230-odd applicants who didn't make the cut." And by the way, Taleo sells this program to a bevy of Fortune 100 companies.

"When a résumé is submitted, the software parses, scans and breaks out the applicant's levels of experience. It summarizes some of the key elements for the hiring manager, who can also filter and define criteria." If such selection programs are on the loose today, expect that new and vastly improved versions will be manning the personnel beat in the months to come.

How do you become an "ace candidate" in the sensors of Robby the Recruitment Robot?

- Be specific and clear about your credentials.
- Use terminology to describe your experiences that is generally well understood and accepted within your profession.
- Don't "send out résumés blindly . . . [T]his 'spray and pray' technique is not an effective strategy," says CEO of career management firm Chandler Hill Partners, Sarah Hightower Hill.
- And write to "make sense to both the software and a human reader." At some point, you will need to win the hearts and minds of real human beings. If your résumé comes across as letter-perfect for a code specialist at CIA headquarters, there are few jobs for which you are a perfect fit. Most of them, as you can guess, deal with machines, not people.

Mackay's Moral: A smart résumé breaks the code of automated screening without breaking the backbone of real-world experience.

Quickie—
The Acid Test for Hiring

Ask yourself: *How would you feel having this same person working for your competition instead of for you?*

How often have I opened the morning paper or clicked on a trade journal Web site to a competitor of ours who has hired the ultimate tiger—street-smart, perfectly groomed, and hungry.

Then I think back about the time when *we* interviewed this same choice talent and:

- The vetting that exposed serious résumé omissions and chronology conflicts.
- The "popcorn" track record of one career burst after another, but no sustained success for his department after the guy was out the door to a different firm.
- The impatient, bossy attitude toward waitstaff on more than one restaurant outing that exposed insensitivity to people.
- A walled-in mentality that tried to resolve even the most delicate and potentially explosive conflict through an e-mail blast rather than a patient phone call or an impromptu meeting.

How often have I said to myself, "There but for the grace of God . . ."

Chapter 20

Headhunters:
Making Yourself Delectable

Teresa Mazzitelli, founder of The Mazzitelli Group, has been an executive recruiter for thirty-three years and has placed nearly 800 people at almost all levels in every job sector. Over twenty-five years working with MackayMitchell Envelope Company alone, she has helped us locate and hire thirty-seven team members, including my right-hand man, Greg Bailey.

Petite and scarcely over five feet tall, Teresa has earned the moniker "Bulldog" at MackayMitchell for her spunk and dogged persistence. Some years back, she helped us land one of our top sales people even though it took eighteen months to reel him in. Our revenues have sparkled ever since, due to her command of bringing us talent and his unrivaled marketing expertise.

Recently, I had a chance to chat with Teresa about what was afoot in the dark jungle of headhunting during the downturn of all downturns. She offered some tips, not only on how to survive a trip to the headhunter, but to come back with the old bean screwed on even better than before.

You're a recruiter who has worked with us for a long time. It's clear you know a lot about the culture and values of MackayMitchell Envelope. Do candidates tap into your reservoir of knowledge? Do they usually ask you penetrating questions about a company's culture and how they will fit in?

Harvey, ninety-nine percent of the searches I do are for passive candidates, i.e., people who aren't looking for a job and who are happy to stay right where they are. These are, to be sure, very desirable candidates, and it takes a lot of persuasion to entice them to move.

Passive search candidates usually ask discerning questions about the culture and values of any company they might consider leaving their present job to join. Remember, they don't have a compelling reason to leave and usually have convincing reasons to stay where they are. It's important that an individual really appreciate the implications of a career shift in a thoughtful way. Culture, values, how they fit in. These are very, very important questions.

Let's play out this same scenario another way. Assume you've been axed, there's a job vacancy, and you're lucky enough to pry open the door for a job interview with a recruiter. Let's say you don't ask any tough questions about the company, the culture, the values, and how you would fit in. Aren't you broadcasting an impression that you are desperate for a job? Doesn't that weaken your chances of landing the job, no matter how badly you may need it?

You're right. You may be out of work and worrying where next month's rent is going to come from. Nonetheless, the last thing you want to radiate is that you're a desperation case. You should always be asking substantial questions when your future is at stake, no matter how economically pressured you might feel.

Determination, resilience, character. That's the stuff we want to lasso for our clients. In adverse times, these traits attain towering importance. Not having them telegraphs you have little confidence in your long-term future.

How tough is it to attract passive candidates today compared to the recent past?

I have to admit it's not easier. The best people with good jobs and prospects have become somewhat more cautious, just as companies are managing their businesses in a more careful and conservative way. Employers and candidates alike feel that present circumstances are somewhat beyond their control.

What kind of job-loss situations are you seeing in the real world? Is this economic downturn really different from the past?

At a community breakfast recently, I was seated—it could well have been by design—between two managers from different companies. Both had recently been "reorg'ed" out of a job.

The guy on my left was caught in a situation that deserves comment. He was an IT director who reported to the chief financial officer in the company's C-suite. The CFO had significant experience in information technology. As the economy got tighter and budget pressure grew, the more the two positions seemed to duplicate each other. Day by day, they looked more and more the same to the top team doing the expense reviews. Naturally the IT guy got squeezed out.

I think that's an important example for your readers: If your skill mix is a lot like that of the person directly above you or below you and the economy tanks, watch out. Somebody's job is in peril. The difference from past downturns is that we're seeing many more of these situations today.

At your breakfast encounter, what was the other guy's story? And what did you learn about how they were taking their personal situations in both cases?

The one on the right was shaken to the core. His situation was a little different, but he had still been re-engineered out the door. This fellow was reeling in disbelief that he could have been whisked out of a job after decades in his profession and eight years with that particular company.

The guy on the left—the one who was caught in the duplication squeeze play—was about the same age. He was exuberant, enthusiastic, and ready to do new things. "My wife and I were talking last night. 'You know,' she said, 'maybe we really should go and open up that bed and breakfast on Nantucket.'" But if the right IT opening came along, I'm sure he would equally well consider that.

Two different attitudes. Night and day. Glass half full or glass half empty.

Now, which of these guys do you think is going to land on his feet?

A question about the kinds of questions a recruiter asks: When I read interview reports about candidates, they will often elaborate on the reasons people made job changes years and sometimes even decades ago. Why is this important?

We look for the motivating factors people use in making career decisions. What were the reasons behind their choices? It tells us about their decision-making abilities, how and what interests them . . . ultimately, are they a good match for your client?

In your business, your radar about human beings has to be pretty sharp, doesn't it?

Good recruiters rely heavily on a well-tested selection program. It has a three-letter ID code:

G-U-T

Good companies want to attract what I call *impact players*. Every candidate is a mystery, and someone like me is out there using educated gut instinct to peel the onion. That's how you judge if that person has the right stuff.

Doom prophecies are everywhere. Serious hand-wringing is in season world-wide. Everybody is worried about the future. It's OK if you reflect that anxiety when you talk to a recruiter, isn't it?

Everybody has natural concerns about their mortgage and paying for their kids' education. But don't let that apprehension take center stage. Genuine personal confidence is still a formidable human trait. Perhaps it's the decisive one in landing a job.

Harvey, a candidate has to believe he or she is very good at his or her core competency. It's hard to sell yourself if you aren't honestly convinced you bring genuine value to a new employer. You know the old adage: "Worry looks around. Sorry looks back. And faith looks up." Companies are in the market for candidates who inspire well-placed faith.

Is it smart for a candidate to conceal "skeletons in the closet" from a recruiter? After all, a recruiter works for the potential employer anyway, and he or she will just dish the dirt directly to the human resources director.

My advice: Take recruiters into confidence on blemishes. After all, everyone has them. Skilled recruiters are experts in Vetting 101. We can't take candidates on face value, because our clients expect vetting—fact-finding—to be a big part of the service we provide. It's too easy for applicants to put a misleading spin on their résumés or to allow selective memory to overtake objective reality. When I look at a résumé, the first thing I ask myself is: "What's missing in this picture?" Recruiters know every human life has its ups and downs. Often, they can help you present a flaw in an honest but diplomatic way.

Also, it's best to be up-front and authentic in an interview with a recruiter. Recruiters don't like surprises, and we also want to see how you'll hold up in front of our client if you make the "short list." No need to make it an Oprah moment, but recruiters are smart enough to detect if something is eating at you, and even more . . . if you're trying to cover it up.

For example, I had recruited a "star" that had excelled throughout her career as an arbitration attorney for her blue-chip employer. Talk about a high-pressure job! Sitting across the bargaining table gave her nerves of steel. You can imagine my surprise when midway through our interview her demeanor changed, her answers lacked cohesiveness, and she seemed generally spaced out. I'm thinking, oops, not the right referral for my client.

After digging deeper, it became crystal clear—she had just suffered a personal loss and had more than understandable anxiety. Her uncharacteristic behavior became plausible after she opened up. Recruiters "get it," and can be an invaluable asset to prep their candidate for the client interview.

Will a good recruiter camouflage a candidate's truly serious shortcomings just to place a body in a slot to pocket the placement fee?

Not if they're smart, Harvey. Self-interest motivates professional recruiters to act ethically and responsibly. That means being forthcoming and candid about the candidates presented. Recruiters want long-term relationships with their client companies, and there's no better way to torpedo that trust than by placing a bad hire. It diminishes the quality of the team. Each new addition should help lift the standard of competency and values of the organization you've been engaged to help.

Are networking skills better today than they were five to ten years ago? What role do Web sites like Twitter, Facebook, and LinkedIn play?

Candidates have many more tools at their disposal today, and professionals who manage their careers effectively know how to use these tools well. But even though computer networking seems more efficient, don't lose sight of what really influences potential employers to have a memorable impression of you. Will it be a glossy presentation in Facebook or a face-to-face encounter?

Let's say you go up to a CEO or a top-level executive after he or she has delivered a speech. You approach the podium beaming a genuine smile of appreciation and say, "May I give you my business card? If there might ever be a time we could sit and visit, I would value learning more about why you made some of the memorable decisions you described so well in your speech."

Which impression is likelier to register and to get your foot in the door—the e-mail . . . or the heartfelt handshake plus?

What's the #1 piece of advice you would give a person who chooses to have a presence in a social networking site like Facebook?

In Facebook entries on the Web, I'm surprised at how few people feature a bold, clear statement of what their core professional competency is. Giving that matter prominence in itself shows you are a serious-minded person.

A recruiter reacts favorably if a person maps out their presence on the Web strategically, choosing to be visible on meaningful search engines and to avoid frivolous ones.

Do you use sources like Facebook to create a roster of candidates for a search?

While I rarely use Facebook, for example, to assemble a candidate list, Web resources like Google, Facebook, and LinkedIn are increasingly important in the vetting process.

So these Web exposures aren't just risk-free fun-for-alls?

Don't celebrate your missteps in digital media or social networking sites. Think of yourself as a personal brand. Look at the damage Olympic Gold Medal swimmer Michael Phelps did to himself after a camera caught him using a bong in 2008.

That image ricocheted around the Web like greased lightning. Banner headline in BusinessWeek: ***"Michael Phelps' Kellogg Deal Goes Up in Smoke." While we may not all be able to butterfly like Michael Phelps, isn't anybody who wants to pursue a meaningful career in somewhat the same spot?***

Yes, you can easily damage your economic value. More important, you can mar how your personal values are perceived. We're all grooming a personal brand. How many negative hits can you and your wallet afford to take by doing careless things?

The Web has made communication so much faster. Is speed now the most important standard by which people's communications skill is judged?

The opposite may in fact be true. Be cautious about clicking the 'send' button for any e-mail addressed to a person who could influence your career or job prospects. People assume, incorrectly, that everyone makes allowances for reckless ideas or even bad grammar or misspelled words in an e-mail. That just isn't so. Snail mail may have been slow, but the process of sending an old-fashioned letter gave people time to reflect and review before it was sent down the chute.

Last, let's talk about the baby boomers. Have you run into cases of people in their early sixties who were cruising toward retirement? Then—at the end of 2008—they were whacked with a double wallop. Overnight, their 401k

cratered ... and in just a few weeks they lost their jobs. What are people in this kind of predicament doing?

I've encountered many people in this sort of fix. Such a person might take on the job of being a temporary senior executive. Just last week, as one illustration, I placed an interim chief financial officer. This solution can be great for companies who can't really afford to staff a long-term senior executive in a key position at this time. They may turn out to be hired full-time once the company conducts a permanent search.

Compared to other recessions in the last twenty years, I would say the average temporary senior executive is far "grayer" than in the past, and certainly matches the baby boomer age profile. Also, in this recession, people are becoming more pragmatic than was once the case. They are more entrepreneurial and adaptive—willing to accept learning new skills or taking on jobs that tap different skill sets—being creative about "reinventing" themselves.

Once the pendulum swings back—and we know it will—companies are sure to return to long-term talent acquisition, but temporary tours of duty may be just the ticket for displaced baby boomers today.

Mackay's Moral: G-U-T is the foremost organ of natural selection.

RE-EMPLOYMENT: YOUR EXTREME PREPARATION GUIDE

"On the other hand, my weekends are seven days long."

Chapter 21

The Mackay Daily Planner
for the Unemployed

So many people looking for jobs think something mystical will occur. The gods will either smile down upon them or not, and there really isn't much we can do but wait for the phone to ring.

They act like Melvin, who went to church every day for years and would kneel down and pray, "Please, God, let me win the lottery." Same prayer, every day. He never asked for anything else. Suddenly, one day, as he knelt praying, there was a clap of thunder, a bolt of lightning, and Melvin leaped up and yelled, "God, God, is that you?" A voice came back, "Yes, Melvin. It's me."

"Oh, thank you, God," says Melvin, "I knew you would hear my prayers. I knew you were going to let me win the Powerball Lottery."

"Melvin, Melvin, do me a favor . . . meet me halfway. Buy a ticket."

Moral: You have to make things happen. You can't just wait around all day and pray you're going to get a job.

A friend of mine, a New England recruiter, likes to ask this question, "Well, what did you *do* today?" She tells me she eliminates more prospects on the basis of their answer to this question than any other in her arsenal.

Think of the ways you can answer.

For example, there's: "After I dragged myself out of the sack, I flipped on TiVo for the latest dose of *30 Rock* and *CSI: Miami*. I think Tina Fey has the best deadpan look in videoland, and I intend to use it when the employment manager says something thick at my next interview. Hey, and who can beat David Caruso for cool wearing a pair of shades? Sunglasses of justice! Wait till I use that super-dude pose when I stride into an office reception area.

"Then, I shuffled into the kitchen and wolfed down a couple of MoonPies. No calls on the answering machine. Boy, that's a bummer. I wonder if I have it turned on right. So I caught up on my research. The bush telegraph on the Gigwise site dished up one outrageous take on Amy Winehouse. Really a hoot.

"I like to keep active, so I grouted some tile in the bathroom. After that I debated whether I should get my hair cut today or wait until the unemployment check comes on Thursday. Tinkered with my résumé. A couple of more rewrites and it should be a winner. I think I saved the last draft right, or did I? My friend Waldo had a couple of swell licks in his curriculum vitae, so I pasted the same paragraphs into mine . . . just for style, of course.

"My iPhone is *so* cool, and you're going to freak out when you see the picture I took with it of my big toe painted up to look like Dumbledore. I just posted it on YouTube. Then I called around for an hour or so until I was able to bum a ride over to your place. Well, here I am."

Or, you could answer Ms. Nantucket this way:

"Pretty routine day, I guess. Between seven and nine o'clock I jogged, showered, read the *Financial Times*, and tracked the key business links on the *Drudge Report* aggregation, scrolled through Monster.com for the embedded software engineering openings, and added some possibles to my list of prospects for my e-mail roster today. Between nine and eleven, I worked on my database and met my quota of making five renewed contacts a day. Between calls, I knocked off a couple of follow-up and thank-you e-mails on my notebook.

"By then, it was getting near lunchtime, so I threw some yogurt into a brown bag, met Angie and Paul for a stroll through the park. We're all on the job market. The three of us role-play interview questions for forty-five minutes two days a week. Then it was back to the laptop for IT-programming trade journals and a great lecture on TED by the oceanographer Sylvia Earle. Next I took a read on Malcolm Gladwell's latest piece in the *New Yorker*. I also reviewed the prospect company's latest earnings release—stellar!—and was impressed as well with their new computer literacy initiative in Central America. And, Ms. Interviewer, here I am."

We all know which answer you'd never give and the one you'd like to. The question is, *"Which way do you really spend your time?"* And which lifestyle has the best chance of getting you back to work?

Mackay's Moral: "How we spend our days is, of course, how we spend our lives." —Annie Dillard

---

Quickie—
Million Dollar Baby!

Hilary Swank has won two Oscars—the first for *Boys Don't Cry* and the second for *Million Dollar Baby*. She was also canned before her success blossomed. Following her appearance in sixteen episodes of *Beverly Hills, 90210*, she was written out of the series. Her apparent reaction to the setback was: "If I'm not good enough for *90210*, I'm not good enough for anything."

Most young actors would have just retreated into depression and self-pity. Swank didn't despair. Instead, she reportedly trimmed her body fat down to 7 percent. Her perseverance created the trademark svelte Swank shape. The training not only landed her the role in *Boys Don't Cry*, I'm sure it also helped convince Clint Eastwood that she had the right physical tone and tenacity to star as Maggie Fitzgerald in *Million Dollar Baby*. For this film, she had the discipline to train in a gym almost five hours a day and to bolster her clout with nearly twenty pounds of muscle!

Beverly Hills, 90210 was not the first time she tasted a setback. Swank grew up poor—spending part of her childhood in a trailer park. She and her mother even lived for a time in her mother's car.

She also savors the power and self-discipline of competitive sports. Growing up, Swank was a gymnast and a Junior Olympic swimmer.

It's hardly a surprise that Hilary Swank was chosen for the title role in the recent film *Amelia* about the legendary Amelia Earhart. This breakthrough aviator had a kindred cockiness about her and once said, "Never interrupt someone doing what you said couldn't be done."

Let Swank's *90210* experience be an inspiration to you—I don't care if you're eighteen or eighty. Use an intelligent, disciplined, and medically sound plan to get yourself back into shape after a setback, especially in your career. The rewards could put your name in lights.

Chapter 22

Getting a Job Is a Job

1. **Get a routine and stick to it.** Getting a job is not a nine-to-five job. It's a sixteen-hour-a-day proposition, from the moment you get up until the moment you go to sleep. With that kind of workload, you need a daily schedule to manage that routine and organize your time. No employer is around to police your time management, and that means the control burden falls squarely on your own shoulders. This doesn't mean you're being sentenced to endless rounds of self-punishment and drudgery. If you're going to be at your best, you've got to have some fun, too, so make room for a little downtime.

Start the week unofficially on Sunday night. You'll want to scribble out a short list of things to get done the next week and check it against the list you had the previous week.

Set goals. To put them to work for you they must be:

Measurable
Identifiable
Documented
Attainable
Specific

And they need to be examined regularly.

Note the first letter of each word spells Midas, and I call this approach giving goals **The Midas Touch** because it turns goals into gold.

How many new contacts did I make last week? Did I stretch out geographically into new areas? Explore new job descriptions? Improve my presentation or appearance? Grade yourself, and don't be too narrowly focused. A week without getting a job is not a week of failure. You may have accomplished other goals last week, things you've never had the time for or put in the effort to achieve in the past.

Think of what you are doing as a new do-it-yourself skill, like crafting a fine piece of woodworking or raising and grooming a bonsai plant. Why? Because you are going to need to use the same job-finding skill set twelve to fifteen times in your working life. You can and will become expert at it. So good and efficient, in fact, that you will be able to methodically get a new job in your off-hours while you actually have one during the working day.

2.   Get back in shape. Companies have always hired according to subtle, hidden values. We like to believe that discrimination in the marketplace has been largely eliminated. Not so. Even though we have legislation that forbids hiring on the basis of race, religion, age, and gender, there are still millions of Americans who have no legal protection against job discrimination. Prejudice against overweight people seems to be the only form of discrimination that hasn't been made illegal, and it's practiced with a vengeance. All things being equal, studies have shown that the overweight have a much poorer chance of getting a job than people who are not overweight.

Under any circumstances, take huge pains with your grooming, hairstyling, and wardrobe. And not just at interviews, either. Looking good is the rule every time you poke your nose outside the door. If you're serious about getting a job, you're going to be visible in a number of ways where your appearance will be observed and can work for you or against you. This is yet another reason for keeping visuals of the mugging, cavorting you off social Web sites like Facebook.

We're not all perfect tens, but there's a lot we can do to catapult ourselves up the scale. Appearance has always been 30 percent nature and 70 percent cunning artifice, so we can all be at least sevens if we try.

3.   Read. Until newspapers and magazines go out of business or they install pay walls on the Internet—and that may never come to pass—your problem is not going to be a scarcity of information. I used to recommend reading the local paper and the *Wall Street Journal* for starters, but that may have been fitting advice for an era when Jeeves was buttering your muffins and pouring your coffee. The *Wall Street Journal* and *Financial Times* charge for their services, but a subscription to the *Journal* in particular is well worth the investment, since it is so influential across the board in business. A good argument can be made that if your recruiter or your prospective employer takes a daily read on the *Wall Street Journal*, so should you. You can also use Web sites like Bloomberg.com and the *New York Times* to get a ton of business news.

As to job listings, today, according to Wikipedia, "Monster is the largest job search engine in the world, with over a million job postings at any time and over 150 million résumés in the database (2008) and over 63 million job seekers per month." Then there are the Craigslist entries. Again I turn to mighty Wik: "The [Craigslist] site receives over one million new job listings each month, making it one of the top job boards in the world." The local classifieds? What are the chances that your next job will be a local find? If *not* moving is key for you, there are regional Web sites springing up every day that can help you focus your search.

The Internet has redefined our information diet. In this creepy, crawling cyberspace world, you better be snacking on three levels of the food chain: breaking news—especially in your business and professional specialty; career opportunity postings; and high-nutrition management journals and mind-stretching essays and lectures.

It's not uncommon for an interviewer to ask the "friendly" and "casual" question: "What have you been reading lately?" Have a good answer. Current business books and e-zines, trade and technical journals in your field, thoughtful books of any kind, fiction or nonfiction, qualify if you can discuss them creatively and analytically. Be able to recite your bookmarks on Google Chrome or Mozilla Firefox. By the way, I hope your search engine is at least as good as either of those.

One still-employed job seeker took his efforts at changing careers so seriously that each evening he was frozen in front of his screen for hours to bone up for the next day's interviews. His little daughter couldn't understand, and one day asked, "Mommy, why does Daddy stare at those dumb articles all night? I want him to teach me how to play Guitar Hero!" Her mother explained to the tot, "Well, darling, you see, Daddy has so much work to do, he has to log on and finish it at home." "Well," responded the daughter, "why don't they put him in a slower group?"

4. Make those contacts. Keeping your network alive means casting a wide net. Dive into your files and give yourself a quota of, say, five contacts a day. Sort your contacts between e-mails and phone contacts.

I know people who send mass barrages of the same e-mail to twenty or thirty people at once. That may make sense in a personal emergency or when you are communicating within your family or a close-knit group of friends. Others are likely to see it as an affront, that they are just one in a supporting cast of countless others.

Make your phone calls brief, especially in the "AE age"—that's the next era after AD and it means After E-mail. More and more people don't want unexpected or extended calls unless there is a very good reason for them.

E-mailing or phoning, your agenda is obvious: What do you know that I don't that might provide me some work? It never hurts if you can carry your own weight and provide the people you're calling with some information that may be of value to them. You might mention a hot sale they may not know about or some even hotter business gossip you may have picked up during your job hunt, like a major executive shuffle.

5. Do your homework. Stay on top of new developments in your field, and that's saying a mouthful these days. There may be an art director somewhere who doesn't use or know how to manage computer aided design, but the market for hieroglyphics is slim! An increasing number of art directors have degrees in multimedia design or computer graphics. Creativity is important, but so are precision and ease. Now is the time to take those courses you never had time for, anywhere and especially online. And be sure you find a way to mention how you are clicking on to new skills during your interviews.

6. Know the company you keep. Before you interview, check with anyone you know who knows about the company: employees, customers, bankers, vendors. But most of all, learn the art of good Googling! Before, you needed to chase down facts like a Mickey Spillane gumshoe. Today, you swim in oceans of detail, and the new skill is how to prioritize what to look for and how to piece it together.

Point #1: You want clues to the company's reputation. Is it a leader in its industry? An also-ran? How does it compete? Does the company emphasize price? Quality? Service? Innovation?

Do you have any special strengths in any of these areas that you can bring to the table? If you do, don't forget to mention them during your interview.

Don't forget the flip side. If the company is in the technological dark ages, emphasize what you can do to help stage a cost-effective, low-pain, fast-acting renaissance. If the business is a service laggard, and you were once the assistant czar of service who helped redeem another company's customer relations, it may be high time to play that card.

Point #2: You want clues to the company's values and style. Be aware of the huge trend toward niche marketing, which is the concept of dividing the marketplace into even smaller segments in order to concentrate on a clearly defined target audience. Because of niche marketing, there are a lot of companies with highly idiosyncratic corporate styles, developed as a result of their adapting to the styles of the niche markets in which they sell their products or services.

Niche hiring has been a predictable outcome of niche marketing. You're going to find the best chance of getting a job—and of being a success—in a company where you fit in.

In 2007, Elinor Mills did an interview for CNET News with Stacy Savides Sullivan, the chief culture officer for Google, perhaps the most coveted employer in the world. Tune in to some of her comments:

- On the culture: "One that is team-oriented, very collaborative and encouraging people to think nontraditionally."
- On the kind of question a job candidate might be asked: "This is just hypothetical, but it could be 'How many bread boxes could you fit in an airplane?' or something like that. That's certainly not going to show if somebody is adaptable or flexible, but it's certainly going to show someone's thought

process and reasoning, the way they can rationalize a true answer to something. Obviously, there's no right answer."
- On the kind of social behaviors that are popular in the company: "We've done Google-wide ski trips since 1999. Different groups go up and we spend the night and there's a lot of team-building and bonding."

Those three items have nothing to do with the degrees you have, the schools you went to, the years of experience you've stacked up; but they have a great deal to say about the kind of person who would succeed at Google.

Then there's the aggressive, rake-it-in avarice of a host of Wall Street firms. That light-your-cigar-with-a-$50-bill glint of the recent go-go years is gone-gone.

Checking out company culture on the Internet is a piece of cake these days, though I can't resist sharing a vintage corporate culture classic.

Years ago, no male employee at IBM dared to wear anything but a white shirt. One day, the boss, the legendary Thomas Watson, came to work in a blue shirt.

"What do you think?" said one of the underlings to another.

"Better not try it," said his buddy. "It could be a trick."

7.   **Thank you. Thank you. Thank you.** Did you have a little chat with the receptionist or with a secretary while you were waiting for one of your interviews today? Write down that name and send a thank-you note recalling the conversation. Of course, you can e-mail your appreciation, and that counts for something. But, disregarding the fact that I hawk envelopes by trade, a handwritten note really bursts through today's electronic clutter. It'll help differentiate you from the pack when you call that firm, and it won't hurt your chances of having those calls put through, either. And, of course, the interviewer and anyone else you may have met at the company are musts on your list, as are any of the contacts you made during the day. For the past forty years I have strongly recommended you mail your thank-you notes back to the interviewers the same day.

I can't begin to tell you how many people I have advised to use this tactic who have told me how it knocked the socks off the interviewer! It was one of the main reasons they were strongly considered for a job opening—and in some cases, actually landed the position.

8. Keep notes. I harp on this point because it's so vital. You're going to want to have a record of *all* your day's meetings and calls, so when you follow up later, you know what was said, what personal information might be useful in your next conversation, and what your strategy is for your next contact. If you think I'm a nut about keeping records, let me remind you that this is the first generation that really has gotten out of that habit. Until recently, everyone wrote everything down. When Napoleon wanted to tell Josephine how much he cared, he didn't say it with flowers or send a Candygram, he wrote a letter (and used an envelope).

Why is post-interview debriefing so vital? We forget 50 percent of what we hear in four hours. Entering your immediate comments in your notebook is the only way to keep reliable records of the experience.

No matter who you are, no matter what you do, you need a system for keeping track of people. When I started in business, I kept a well-worn business card file that I thumbed through on a daily basis. When the backs of the cards were so covered with smudges and chicken scratchings that they became unreadable, I developed a system on paper where I could make regular notations to my customer files. That evolved into the Mackay 66, which you may be using now or have already read about. My #1 piece of advice in this book, head and shoulders above the rest, is to master the Mackay 66. You can get the Mackay 66 form free at my Web site: **www.harveymackay.com**

Whether it's a daily diary, an old address book, a Rolodex, or most likely a computerized contact management system, you need something to keep you organized. Start now and keep track of everyone you meet, making note of when and how you met them and what you learned about them. If you are unemployed, you'll be doing part of this from memory, putting together a log of everybody you've ever known who you think can help you. If you are employed now, you have a great opportunity to start your contact file. So get started. And never quit.

9. Volunteer. Get involved in a cause that means something to you, whether it's politics, the local soup kitchen for the homeless, United Way, Alumni Fund Drive, Save the Whales, Disabled American Veterans, or helping Alzheimer's victims—what have you. I'm very active in St. Vincent de Paul, for which I have delivered speeches to the homeless and helped raise funds.

There are four strong reasons for volunteering. First, when you make this sort of contribution, you're keeping actively busy during an emotional downturn in your life. Good for the head.

Second, you're improving your job-hunting skills. Volunteering involves marketing, selling, time management, public speaking, fundraising, creativity. What could be more targeted to your needs than learning, practicing, polishing your strengths, and overcoming your weaknesses? I would *never* have learned to sell if I hadn't been a volunteer trying to raise money for countless causes.

It's the best sales training boot camp there is, it's free, and no one, that is, *no one*, wants to do it, because no one wants to hear ten trillion "no's."

Are you uncomfortable speaking in public? Volunteering can provide you with the experience you need. Before I became involved as a volunteer in building support for a domed stadium in Minneapolis, I'd have been lucky to get asked to introduce the introducer at a PTA meeting. I ended up making close to one hundred speeches a year during the seven years we fought for that project. Now, speech making has become the gravity center of my professional life.

Third, depending on the organization and the role you take, volunteering will put you in contact with some of the most important people in your community. They'll see you do your stuff. (Do I hear you tickling the keys on your notebook already?)

Fourth, and not least in importance, you'll be doing your community a service you can be proud of. And if volunteering pays off in no other way than this, it's well worth the time and effort. It's good for the soul. Potential employers know that people who do volunteer work make loyal and dedicated employees, so get that volunteer service into your résumé, and, if you can, make offhand mention of it in your interviews, but don't boast about it.

10. Get ready for tomorrow. Clothes in shape? Appointments confirmed? Schedule set? Sign off. You've had a busy day.

Mackay's Moral: It bears repeating: Getting a job is a job.

Chapter 23

Want to Become an Entrepreneur?
Better Be One First!

I first met Roger Schelper on the raised hardwood court of Williams Arena in Minneapolis. He was then a member of the University of Minnesota Gophers basketball team. (Roger also did track and field.) Aplastic anemia took Roger off the Gophers b-ball team in 1969. Aplastic anemia is the result of the bone marrow not producing an adequate number of red blood cells. This devastating disease can be triggered by exposure to toxins, and Roger had sprayed a goodly number of backyards with chemicals as a young entrepreneur.

Let's talk about people choosing to experiment with being entrepreneurs after spending most of their life working on someone else's payroll. After I wrote *We Got Fired!* back in 2004, I was shocked at the number of people who wrote me how this book encouraged them to follow their dreams of starting their own business. People might lose their jobs and decide to give the "entrepreneurial thing" a shot. They might invest their entire life's nest egg on a fling—a high-risk play.

Take yourself. Acting and thinking like an entrepreneur had been second nature for you since you were a kid.

Harvey, I was very stubborn. From the time I was about ten years old, I wanted to be my own boss. My dad worked for Pillsbury, a big corporation in its own right back then, and we were transferred all over the Midwest. I wanted the kind of continuity of being rooted somewhere for my kids. These were my inspirations.

In the late 1960s, it didn't look like you were going to be a whirlwind entrepreneurial success story . . . In fact, the tea leaves said you were going to die.

At the time, bone marrow transplants were unknown. The doctors said I had six months to live, and I wouldn't accept that. I was doing faith healers, transcendental meditation, megavitamin therapy, and ten- and twelve-day juice fasting to detoxify my system from the chemicals I had absorbed from spraying yards.

So character and determination helped you beat a death sentence. That same spunk helped you succeed as a pizza entrepreneur and cofounder of the Davanni's chain.

An entrepreneur has to have a passion . . . and be stubborn and determined. You have to believe that nothing anyone will throw in your face will stop you. Aplastic anemia played a role in this.

The stubbornness was there. I developed the passion for food as I went along.

You went on to get your BS in business administration from the U. of M. in 1972, but you had already been involved with entrepreneurial start-ups back in 1971.

I worked in retail in the Twin Cities with a start-up chain named Nutrition World. It specialized in vitamins, supplements, and health food. I got into the health food business to learn how I could heal myself. As I said, bone marrow transplants weren't an alternative back then.

Nutrition World may have been a start-up, but you were a make-it-happen kind of guy long before that.

I grew up paying my own way from the time I was eleven. I wasn't looking for any help from anyone. As a kid, I had eight or nine regular lawn clients in the summer, and eight or nine snow shoveling customers in the winter. I carried two paper routes. I knew you had to give service. To make money, you had to price yourself properly.

While you were taking night MBA classes at the U. of M. in the spring of 1975, you started out on a brand-new venture. The economy was in the ditch. Gas prices at the pump had doubled. On top of the recession, the nation was still reeling from President Nixon's resignation in 1974. One heck of a time to start a business, wasn't it?

I was too young to know any better.

So you just struck out on your own?

I had three partners. Two of the guys were friends of mine in high school. One of my partners was Bob Carlson, the son of a well-to-do manufacturer who owned Minnesota Rubber. Mick Stenson's father was a successful owner of his own sales company. The fourth guy in the mix, Pat Woodring, was poor like me and came from Batavia, New York. He was married to a member of the Pontillo family, which pioneered pizza in upstate New York. Mick and Bob wanted to invest, and Bob had a particular interest in bringing New York pizza to Minneapolis/St. Paul. As a group, we decided to introduce Pontillo's to Minnesota. I was designated as the point guy to do the legwork and get the idea going.

What on earth gave you the conviction that you could enter a specialized ethnic food market like this?

Our market analysis was based on common sense. People of my parents' age weren't familiar with higher quality pizza unless they grew up in New York or New Jersey. In those days, pizzas were almost all cracker-crust products, flattened out by a sheeter onto a screen. Shakey's was one of the big players in the Twin Cities back then.

Selecting an attractive, unoccupied marketing niche was an important part of your plan, wasn't it?

Our New York pizza product was unique. There was nothing like it in the Twin Cities. The foundation of our pizzas was freshly made "live" (yeast-risen), hand-pounded, hand-thrown dough prepared in batches several times daily and rimmed on the deck. We baked in brick ovens like they do out East—and still do. We use Sicilian Romano and the best mozzarella you can buy, which is Burnett's in Wisconsin, twice world champion. We also distinguished our pies from New York City pizza and identified our product as "Western New York's Finest."

Submarine sandwiches were known in Minnesota, but authentic Philadelphia-style hot hoagies were not. The oven-baked hoagie is a sandwich named after Hog

Island when this was a shipyard during World War I, and many of the workers were Italian immigrants.

When you opened your first location, site selection must have been a major decision. For restaurants and retailing, it's location . . . location . . . location.

We decided to find a spot near the College of St. Thomas in St. Paul, which was also located near Macalester College and William Mitchell Law School.

I had done some reading on real estate and knew that an operation like ours had to be located to avoid barriers. The freeway was a barrier and so were the Mississippi River and downtown St. Paul. But the Highland-Macalester-Groveland neighborhood was still a rather big trading area with pretty good income levels and an attractive density of potential college student customers. The competition wasn't heavy because there weren't many B-1 zoned corners in this district. The corner of Grand and Cleveland was one of the few.

OK, you had a unique marketing concept and a good location. What was your philosophy on start-up and operating controls?

We put together an eight-hundred-square-foot, thirty-two-seat shop in the course of two and a half months. I did the contracting—the grunt work—which included running errands for the skilled craftsmen, some of whom were college buddies. We opened on an embarrassingly small shoestring budget. Keeping your going-in costs down is a very important survival factor in launching an entrepreneurial business.

The first shop started out staffed with five kids, and I worked eighty to ninety hours a week. The business had a small bank loan, and I said I wouldn't give myself a raise until it was paid off. We opened our doors in October 1975. By the summer of 1976, we paid off the loan, and I gave myself a raise from $600 to $800 a month. With the hours I was working, I finally made it over the minimum wage hurdle! In 1977, we opened the second store in Riverside by the University of Minnesota, Augsburg College, and a large hospital complex.

Was that tightfisted attitude ever smart! I know this from my own experience. So many wannabe entrepreneurs start their business behaving as if they were already success stories. Mackay Envelope Company would never have gotten off the ground without grueling hours and relentless expense control.

Harvey, I now teach classes in entrepreneurship. The first lesson I drive home: Because 90 percent of all entrepreneurial ventures fail in the first five years, you need to do something you love.

My mother thought I was nuts. "You have two college degrees, and you're going to make pizzas?" I told her not to worry, I'll be fine. Years later, she was pretty convinced I had made the right decision.

If you decide to go to work for yourself, what is the single most important decision you have to make?

I knew how to make ends meet and to make a bottom line no matter what it takes. I tell kids who consider being entrepreneurs: Go into something you love. That's the #1 test. If you don't, you won't be able to put in the necessary hours to make the venture work.

You now have twenty-one pizza shops, one coffee shop, and a wholesale bakery— nearly a thousand employees and annual revenues of more than $30 million. What happened to your partners?

Mick Stenson remains my current active partner. Bob is running his grandfather's and father's rubber business. While Bob is an investor, he has never been an active partner. Yet, he has provided great guidance and help getting credit early on. Years later we bought out Pat Woodring and Tony Pontillo, who also had a stake in the business. So it's just the three of us now—Mick, Bob, and me. We changed the name from Pontillo's to Davanni's in 1983.

Was it important that your partners shared the same values you did?

Having entrepreneurial backgrounds helped us be more realistic and disciplined about our expectations. I really like retail, and I really like people. My other two partners are both sales oriented, and they like people, too. We all have good business sense and are fiscally conservative.

When you look at the business you and your team have built, what do you think is your most important asset?

We have a very strong corporate culture. Anyone in the Twin Cities who has had contact with us—as a supplier or has had a youngster working in the firm— will tell you that Davanni's has one of the best corporate cultures in the Twin Cities and that it's a pleasure to do business with us. We have an incredible number of people who have been with us for two or three decades. That kind of loyalty is staggering for our business. Two weeks ago, we had a general managers' meeting. Our twenty-two managers have over 412 years of experience with Davanni's—that's more than nineteen years of service with the firm for the average manager.

You have stressed the importance of attitude for an entrepreneur. Determination demands confidence, but that conviction has to be reined in, doesn't it?

You have to keep your ego in check and your debt levels down. Don't overexpand. So often a new restaurant concept will enter the market and right away it's announcing it will go to six or ten units . . . thirty by the end of this year and two hundred by the end of 2010. It grows itself into a noose. You can't expand without operations, systems, and controls to absorb that growth effectively. You don't open a shop and immediately get profitable.

Let's say you were thinking of opening a business during today's recession. What's different now compared with 1975?

My advice would be to open a business with minimal staffing levels. We have between nine hundred and one thousand employees. The government has gotten so deeply involved in this area, it's discouraging. In the old days, a potential employer could ask you, "What do you think about this kid?" I might once have answered, "I wouldn't hire him. He shows up late and doesn't work very hard." Now, you're really restricted to, "Yes, we can verify he was employed here once."

I would keep my employment roster to a minimum—OSHA, government regulations, age discrimination, sex discrimination, pay discrimination. Our nation is harvesting what the politicians have sown. Make it easy to sue everybody. That's one reason that so many businesses have been driven overseas.

Roger, that's a pretty strong view, and some people might disagree with it. On the other hand, it could also be a plausible explanation as to why many companies are so anxious to eliminate jobs . . . and a motivation for employers to shift jobs overseas in that the regulatory climate abroad is not as demanding

as it is here. One last question: What would you likely have done if Davanni's wasn't a success?

If Davanni's hadn't worked, I would have tried something else. I was determined to establish and run my own business.

Mackay's Moral: Entrepreneurs who make it are usually born entrepreneurs to start with.

Chapter 24

The One-Stop Job Shop

Sally Flaig, a regular reader of my column in the *Hartford Business Journal*, was laid off from her job in March of 2009. She wrote to me that she was looking at different options including starting over in a different industry. I was impressed with the professionalism of Sally's job search. She attended local networking job search group meetings and does volunteer work with various groups including Habitat for Humanity. She sent out about two hundred résumés since March and has heard the message "you're overqualified" with "too much sales experience and not enough marketing." Sally has since accepted a position with the American Red Cross.

Sally also offered a very practical suggestion on a source of help readers of this book may want to consider. Sally writes:

> *The Department of Labor has actually been an enormous resource . . . The workshops are extremely productive and there are now programs that actually assign a job counselor to you for personalized service. I am enrolled in the WIA program (Workforce Investment Act) and will be meeting regularly with a job developer for help with my search. Additionally, there is federal money available for retraining, enhancing current skills, or acquiring new skills that, again, make a more attractive candidate.*

According to a Department of Labor spokesperson, "the Department of Labor began funding states to implement One-Stop Career

Centers . . . around 1994." With nearly "3,000 delivery points nation-wide," the department notes these centers offer help that ranges from: "self service assistance to more intensive staff assisted services to training services. Self service is provided through well equipped resource rooms with computers, copy machines, etc. as well as software to help with résumé creation and lots of Web sites on which to get career information and search for jobs, including the state's job bank or job matching system."

These programs also offer help with retention and up-skilling. This includes "training services to incumbent workers" and "supporting employee retention by offering services such as transportation, childcare assistance, and mentoring programs."

Many people would never have thought of turning to the federal government as a career planning resource. Well, times have changed, and a real effort seems to have been made by Washington to change with them.

Looking for a connection? To find the closest One-Stop using a zip code search, go to www.servicelocator.org.

Mackay's Moral: Your Uncle Sam is aching so badly to have you back on the tax rolls, he's chipping in some cutting-edge help to put you there.

Quickie—
Rebirth Certificate

A computer software expert is a software expert. Not exactly. There is, for example, a Certified Associate in Software Testing offered by the Quality Assurance Institute or a Foundation Level Certified Tester accredited under the Auspices of the International Software Testing Qualifications Board. There are all kinds of certified software experts.

Responding to a column of mine in the *Washington Examiner*, Alexis Chng-Castor, marketing coordinator of the HR Certification Institute, pointed out the increasing importance of certification in the human resources field. Certification is a "résumé sorter" that gives a candidate an extra edge in tough economic times.

There are countless certification paths and options:

- Learn what certifications are typically required for job openings you are hoping to fill, and *why* the certification is deemed important to your job skills. (Also, learn if a certain certifying organization is preferred over others in the field.)
- Talk with people who have gone through the certifying program and exams to learn what the biggest challenges and difficulties might be.
- Be sure your present certification is not out-of-date. High-technology fields change rapidly. What kind of continuing certification should you be undergoing to keep your credentials current?

While great managers view people as people, emotionless companies who reengineer individuals into and out of jobs tend to view folks as products. If you want to stay on the shelf, it doesn't hurt to flash a shining seal of approval.

Chapter 25

Use Your Head,
but Follow Your Heart!

In 1972, University of Minnesota football head coach Cal Stoll asked me to help recruit a promising young quarterback from Parkside High School in Jackson, Michigan. The name of this prize package: Tony Dungy.

Tony was everything. He starred in three sports—baseball, football, and basketball. In his early teen years he even was recognized by *Sports Illustrated* in its "Faces in the Crowd" section. He was a student body president at fourteen, loved and admired by fellow students.

Why was I asked to help land this dream addition to the school and the athletic program? Perhaps because of my perspective as a former varsity athlete and then president of the University of Minnesota Letterwinners Club. From the day I was born, I have always been mesmerized by all sports—from Ping-Pong to football. Then there's my dedication to my alma mater. Were I to accidentally cut myself, I'm sure I'd bleed our school colors of maroon and gold. Later, I became the national president of the Alumni Association. (The U. of M. Alumni contingent is a legion of formidable size. Today it has more than sixty thousand dues-paying members.)

So, off I flew to Jackson for the first of my two visits to the Dungy home. (In those days, an alumnus, or any interested party for that matter, could make unlimited recruiting visits to a prospect's home. Today, you can't have any contact with a prospect whatsoever.)

When I arrived at the Dungy home, I was well prepared. I had done my homework and was geared up to win. As I teach our sales force and always practice myself: There is no such thing as a cold call, and this was as warm a call as you could get. I had CAT-scanned and done an MRI on Tony, as well as his wonderful mother, CleoMae, an English teacher, and his highly respected father, Wilbur, a professor of physiology. I knew that education was the first priority in this deep-valued household.

The Dungys welcomed me with open arms. They were great listeners and equally well organized, asking questions that were both substantive and keenly perceptive. As highly touted as Tony was as an athlete, education was foremost in the family's mind, not football. The philosophy I maintained: The school does not make the kid; the kid makes the school. In other words, Minnesota could provide everything Tony wished for and dreamed of both on and off the field.

All the schools Tony was considering, I have to admit, had the same assets and advantages as the U. of M. Ultimately, it all came down to trust and chemistry. He was comfortable with Coach Stoll and trusted that Minnesota would deliver on important extras such as summer jobs and staying in touch with his parents to keep them updated on his progress.

When I returned from Jackson, I remember my report on my first face-to-face with Tony consisted of an eight-point description: outstanding student, happy, healthy, challenged, committed, focused, goal oriented, and absolutely loves football.

Tony chose Minnesota over another Big Ten school and started playing for the Gophers at age seventeen. He played in eight games as a freshman, and before his career ended he sparkled as an outstanding quarterback who set a number of school passing records. Following both the 1975 and 1976 seasons he was second team All-Big Ten quarterback. Those same years he was also All-Big Ten academic.

Of course, what Tony achieved on his own was foremost, though many people played key roles in supporting his success, as Tony would be the first to admit. Nonetheless, on countless occasions during Tony's glorious four years, I would refer to him among friends as a "son." I was so proud to be in constant touch with him and to watch him grow. Today, I only regret I didn't save CleoMae Dungy's letters to me during

Tony's four years. They were inspired writings loaded with lifetime philosophies and goals she had prayed for along with her husband, Wilbur—goals that Tony would embrace and that enhance his belief system as a motivational leader and humanitarian yet today.

Tony graduated after the customary four years. A move to the pros postgraduation seemed a certainty. In 1977, the NFL had twelve rounds of drafting, and there were twenty-eight teams in the league. Tony was realistic enough to know that he wouldn't be chosen for a quarterback slot, but such an intelligent, accomplished, and diligent athlete was sure to make it on someone's roster—in all probability, as a defensive back.

In the end, 333 players were selected in the 1980 draft. Tony Dungy wasn't one of them. The results might have been devastating for Tony. It was beyond comprehension that all the teams passed.

Time for a midcourse correction!

Time for a summit meeting at the number one restaurant in Minneapolis, Charlie's Café Exceptionale. The luncheon meeting was a long one—two and a half hours. I reassured Tony this was not the end of the world. He would be a surefire success in the business community. "Don't lose confidence," I reminded him. Of course, the silver lining was the lull between the end of the college football season and the NFL draft. It gave Tony a window of opportunity and he was smart enough to dig his well before he was thirsty. While Tony had one eye on the big prize of being scooped up by an NFL team, he also had some job interviews in corporate America, just in case the draft didn't work out.

On his own, with no help from me, Tony landed a dream job at General Mills, headquartered in Minneapolis. I was ecstatic and asked him when he was going to start.

That's when Tony dropped the atomic bomb on me.

"Harvey," he said, "this is the reason I wanted to meet with you and ask your advice on a real dilemma I have. You remember Tom Moore, our offensive coordinator?"

"Yeah . . . great guy, great coach," I replied.

"Well," Tony went on, "he is now with the Pittsburgh Steelers' staff.

Tom Moore not only assured me a tryout as a defensive back, he's quite confident I'll make the squad. I'm really in a quandary and not sure exactly which way to go."

This was a piece-of-cake decision. I shifted into high gear and spent the next hour haranguing Tony on the advantages of General Mills. Before the lunch, having gotten a whiff of the probable topic, I had even contacted a high-level executive to see what he thought of Tony. The General Mills exec got back to me. I will never ever forget his very words: "Harvey, we are so high on Tony that we expect him to be one of the top minority executives here at General Mills within five to ten years."

Of course, I told this to Tony, but it didn't begin to faze him in the slightest. His heart was set on making the Pittsburgh Steelers, no matter the cost. And the Pittsburgh Steelers were smart enough to sign Tony as a free agent defensive back. After just one season, Steelers head coach Chuck Noll recruited him as a defensive assistant coach, working for NFL legend Sid Gillman.

Over the next several years, he held defensive coaching assignments with the Kansas City Chiefs and the Minnesota Vikings, turning the Vikings defensive unit into the finest in the NFL.

Tony's drive to become an NFL head coach was unstoppable. In 1996, he was named head coach of the Tampa Bay Buccaneers—a team that was a laughingstock when he signed on. At Tampa Bay, his discipline and strategic sense built a team that regularly appeared in post-season playoffs.

Repaying the team's extraordinary advances under his watch, Tony was *fired* in January 2002! Tony has learned to take such setbacks philosophically. In his book *Quiet Strength*, he says, "I am a firm believer that the Lord sometimes has to short-circuit even our best plans for our benefit." I hope all of you jobless readers who feel the world is unjust are digesting this story carefully because two extraordinary things happened next . . .

The first was that the Buccaneers won the 2003 Super Bowl. They did so because of the outstanding organization Tony left in place before he was booted out for being too conservative with his offense. NFL teams aren't built overnight. Increasingly, managers in every profession and industry are being evaluated on how strongly their organizations continue to perform after they have left their jobs.

The second took place on February 4, 2007, when Tony was head coach of the Indianapolis Colts, a position he had assumed in 2002. Tony became the first African American head coach to win the Super Bowl as his team downed the Chicago Bears.

Tony retired from pro football early in 2009. Think about it: No one wanted him badly enough to draft him for the pros. No NFL team would accept him as a quarterback. And he left the game with a new record for consecutive playoff appearances by a head coach and the unmatched achievement of a Super Bowl victory!

I've had an opportunity to be in touch with many student athletes over the years but couldn't be prouder of the inscription that Tony wrote to me in his first best-selling book back in 2007: "Harvey, Thank you for all your help and support over the years. This would never have happened without you."

Oh, by the way, there's one more event in this saga I must share with you.

On November 17, 2002, Monday Night Football matched our Vikings with Tony's Bucs in a pivotal game in Tampa Bay. A lot of marbles were on the line, and the air was electrified. I follow every Viking pass and punt and have been quite close to all of the previous owners, including then owner Red McCombs. Red had graciously invited me to watch the contest in the visiting owner's suite with his family, and I accepted.

Before the game, I hustled down to the sidelines to greet Tony for a quick hello. There he stood—arms crossed, face expressionless, with the calm certainty of a Greek god. Tony looked at me, twisted his neck and circled the whole sell-out stadium crowd of 68,857 and said: "Harvey . . . sure glad I didn't listen to you!"

There are some valuable lessons here:

• **Don't ever give up in the aftermath of a setback.** In fact, look hard for the ways in which rejection can make you be more committed and effective in what you are determined to achieve.

- **Accept detours if they contribute to your ultimate goal.** The fact that Tony couldn't break down the barriers to being an NFL quarterback didn't derail him from becoming an outstanding NFL head coach. He converted his experience as a defensive player and then as a defensive coach to hone a foundation for his head coaching skills. It's an attitude Tony has famously expressed when he said, "We are learning how to win another way."

- **Most important of all, follow your heart.** Tony could have safely opted for an executive career. He would surely have succeeded at it. But he persevered and chose his own dream—not just excelling, but shattering the yardstick and becoming the new leadership standard for his profession.

Mackay's Moral: March to your own heartbeat, and your odds of commanding life's playing field soar.

Chapter 26

Adjust to What You Aren't:
Résumé Fine Tuning After Setbacks

When you're at a job interview, pay particular attention to how your résumé is read and physically handled by an interviewer.

- If the description of a particular phase of your career or some other section of your résumé is constantly being questioned, you almost certainly need to improve the statement. Listen carefully. It's not enough to know that something is troubling people. You need to find out *what in particular* is bothering them.
- Do readers find it hard to follow the organization of your résumé? Are they constantly jumping between pages or paragraphs when they read it?
- Do interviewers find the language used to be hard to penetrate? In an interview, are you constantly being asked to restate what you are saying? In particular, do they take your description of a position and restate it in terminology that uses more mainstream language?
- Is the information clearly laid out and presented in an appealing and inviting way?

If you lose a search, it never hurts to try to get a copy of the résumé of the person who won the job. Perhaps a recruiter will be willing to share it with you. If you have that chance, look for clues in both the credentials and the presentation of information in the résumé.

The great dilemma is that you are unlikely to find out you have a poor résumé because—if it's bad—you won't get an interview in the first place. There is an absolutely terrific Web site on how to write a résumé. It's presented by Rockport Institute, and the address is: www .rockportinstitute.com/resumes.html.

Among the dynamite points on the Web site:

- "Your present résumé is probably much more inadequate than you now realize."
- "The résumé is a tool with one specific purpose: to win an interview."
- "It is a mistake to think of your résumé as a history of your past . . . write from the intention to create interest, to per- suade the employer to call you."
- "Research shows that only one interview is granted for every 200 received by the average employer . . . Ten to 20 sec- onds is all the time you have to persuade a prospective em- ployer to read further." (Rockport points out—and chisel this one into your memory—most résumés are *scanned* and not *read*.)

And, the *Amen!* of the advice is:
"FOCUS ON THE EMPLOYER'S NEEDS, NOT YOURS."

Mackay's Moral: Remember the purpose of the résumé. It's to enable you to resume work.

Quickie—
How Not to Waste Your Time on the Internet

In 2006, *PC World* presented an article on "The 15 Best Places to Waste Time on the Web." I recommend you scan it. Do you recognize any features that resemble your own daily use pattern of the Internet? Without employment, Internet diversions can consume your entire day!

The Internet is wonderfully powerful. It is also dangerously seductive. Many Web sites give you the illusion that you are being productive while you are doing nothing less than chowing down useless brain candy.
Some particulars:

- Game sites like Pogo.com draw people in with the prospect of winning money, but the reality is most will just end up anteing up an annual membership fee. Sites like Moola.com screen a commercial video before you can play. Games are doubtless the worst time abusers.
- Celebrity gossip—What a trap! What does Lindsay Lohan's detoxification or Hugh Jackman's adoption plans matter to you?
- Rotten Tomatoes and IMDb are great sites for anyone who likes films. Spend too much time watching the movies they discuss and I guarantee they'll never be making a biopic about your life.
- Then, of course, there's YouTube and Craigslist. Do yourself a favor and tape a little warning card to the side of your notebook screen. It will remind you to ask uncomfortable questions:

Then ask yourself
How will this Web site help me get a job?
How will this piece of information make me more employable?
What am I now learning about my profession or industry that is new and important?

Chapter 27

Expose Yourself in the
Privacy of Your Own Home

Do you remember how, just before your boss "lost confidence in you" and set your keister on the cobblestones, you and your mate invested in a videocam?

You may have bought it to document little Johnny sucking his thumb, but why not use it to make adult videos? No, not the X-rated kind—the kind that can help you find a job by sharpening your interview skills.

Square one of every executive makeover these days is an expensive video training course to polish personal poise before venturing on the speaking circuit or a media blitz. Well, the most important pitch you're ever going to make is to your potential new boss.

Put modern media and management science to work for you and think Home Depot: do-it-yourself. It won't match a professional speech course, but it won't set you back hundreds of bucks, either. And the experience can brighten more than your smile.

This is not a game, and some rules will help keep your mirth in check:

- First, you need two buddies. I don't recommend asking either a spouse or a relative. Preferably, your pals should be people your age and career level. It would be best if they were in the same business or profession, because you want people who stalk the same jungle you do. They can rough you up with relevant questions. Consider doing this round-robin and exchange roles so they can benefit from the same training.

- One friend is the cameraperson. The other is the interviewer. No need for attempts at Academy Award–winning special effects. Just have the cameraperson focus on you—especially your expressions—and have this person stay as invisible as possible. The less you fixate on the camera, the better.

- You're not playing it for laughs. Get all your stand-up shtick out of your system in the first five minutes, and get on with it. Your video may have a light production budget, but this is serious stuff.

- Watch for involuntary gestures like pursing your lips or yanking your tie when someone asks you something disagreeable. People confronted with an unpleasant question often sharply turn their head away or suddenly look at the floor. Visit a Web site on body language before you roll cameras and you can be on guard for some of your classic giveaways.

- The pix shooter should try to capture when you hesitate, tighten up, avert your eyes, or laugh something off. A cameraperson who knows his or her stuff can even zoom in on you when you do. The goal is to beef up your own awareness of *gesture under pressure*.

- Brief the interviewer thoroughly on the firm he or she is supposed to represent. So your pal can be an effective questioner, the interviewer should try to project the firm's business reputation, hot buttons, and how it does business. Do this in a straitlaced, matter-of-fact way. A caricature of the firm you're simulating does you no good.

- Map out the kind of questions you expect the interviewer to toss at you, especially the tough ones, but don't script them. You want the mock interviewer to be a credible questioner.

- Ideally, give the interviewer a list of questions drawn from actual interviews. Include some that stumped you and have them shake up the order so you don't know what to expect. Tell them to save the nastiest queries for those moments you seem smuggest and most self-confident. Don't forget to have them pounce on holes in your résumé . . . or that boss who you allege jackknifed your career. After all, where do you think the recruiter or the personnel maven is going to go?

- This is an agility test, not a recall quiz. Don't memorize.

- Be brief and clear. Think media sound bite.

- Don't just answer questions. Ask intelligent, constructive ones as well. Your Larry King-for-a-day may not be able to answer them, so just dissolve their response. This will help develop your readiness to take a swing at a choice fastball and belt it out of the park. Recruiters say that candidates are often chosen for the perceptive quality of the questions they ask as well as the sharp answers they give.

- Record about fifteen minutes or so. Then stop. Now you and the film crew should all view the instant replay. Get your team's honest input. Where do you come across as real, enthusiastic, and competent? In which moments do you sound contrived, long-winded, defensive, or clumsy? Replay the video a couple of times. If you can sit through the umpteenth rerun of LeBron James highlights, you can bear watching yourself a few times, even if you miss the easy layup now and then—especially if it helps you land a job.

- Do a second interview—this time, a little longer one. Maybe the cameraperson and the interviewer switch roles. Even switch roles with the interviewer. Nothing can be so instructive or tough to take as another person seriously trying to project how you come across. Remember, these are your friends, and dosing out high-potency medicine like this without sarcasm isn't easy, so be sincere in your thanks. Quit before your concentration wanes.

- Grab a pad or go to your laptop and note the ten most important impressions and the five most challenging goals for improvement while the spills and chills of the experience are still fresh.

- After your real interview is over, compare the questions that were asked with those you prepared. How many did you actually field? Which did you dodge? What were your biggest surprises? When were you most in command? It's always best to seize and build on your strengths. Showcase more of them by segueing your answers to additional and relevant achievements. Drop them in with a low-key, casual touch.

Simulating interviews is an exercise worth repeating. Amateurs practice until they get it right. Professionals practice until they can't get it wrong.

Mackay's Moral: *Survivor* and *America's Next Top Model* are not reality. This is reality television. Your reality.

Quickie—
Encore! Encore!

David Buck is a highly imaginative guy who is resourcefully addressing an emerging need of overwhelming importance: the career shift that will become commonplace for adults at midlife.

David earned his BA from St. Olaf College and went on to receive an MBA from the University of Chicago. His "first" professional life was spent in the real estate world—leasing shopping mall space and then working in development of mixed locations that combined retail and residential.

In his midforties, David started reckoning with an inescapable fact of life: It's too short. "How can I leave a meaningful personal legacy?" he asked himself. David met Jan Hively, PhD, who founded the Vital Aging Network. She said to David, "You are no different from seventy-six million other baby boomers who are now looking for more meaningful work." David took this as a challenge—how can people help each other to move toward meaning in life and work?

Together, David and Jan started developing in the Twin Cities a new social network called SHiFT, which continues to grow. SHiFT offers new member-inspired programs including forums, interest groups, SHiFT Circles, and a Time Bank for sharing skills. The organization is also working on a new project called Midternships: Internships @ Midlife™, where people can take their interests and transferable skills into an internship experience.

SHiFT recognizes the "new arc" of most people's working lives—they get it. If you want some good ideas for your community or want to join in a grassroots community tailored to midlifers in transition, check out SHiFT (www.shiftonline.org).

Chapter 28

The Age of the Agile Exec

Tierney Remick is global market managing director for the executive search firm Korn/Ferry International. I first contacted Tierney when I wrote *We Got Fired! . . . And It's the Best Thing That Ever Happened to Us* in October 2004. She is a leading authority on executive search, especially at very senior management levels. Since she shared such astute advice before, she was a "must" encore performance for this book. Take heed, all you wannabe CEOs. The advice and observations Tierney offers about C-level job candidates relate to the traits companies are looking for in up-and-coming managers at all levels.

When we last spoke, "sixty percent of all CEOs ended up getting fired." In the present recession, have CEOs and other C-suite execs fared better or worse than five years ago?

The absolute turnover has declined but we anticipate it will rise again in 2010. The boards of directors have now had an opportunity to look at how leaders manage through crisis since many of them were elevated into their positions during times of high growth. They will be focusing on whether the same CEOs can drive a business longer term. These crisis dynamics will also affect other members of a top management team. Top managers are being assessed for their decision making, focus, and prioritization.

Are there any new career strategies top managers are using these days to get their careers back on track?

Top managers have had to demonstrate a certain amount of what could be called executive agility. Managers have to be able to prove that they can manage highly competitive markets, turnaround situations, and restructurings as well as periods of high growth. This is what separates the fabulous leaders from the mainstream.

These leaders need to be intelligent people by definition. That includes financial intelligence, business intelligence, and emotional intelligence. And a sense of balance in these ingredients is required.

Has the downturn changed how successful managers manage?

The emotional intelligence element is going to be more important going forward. Are you aware of the impact you have on the people you are trying to lead? Are they willing to follow you? Do you know how to leverage people's motivation? This includes knowing how to use inspiration as well as empathy.

Retention of talented employees will become one of the leading factors that distinguish a great leader. The next generation of the workforce is multicultural, very global, and highly mobile. These employees don't believe a particular organization will be their ultimate career destination. As a leader, the challenge becomes retaining and engaging talented resources for as long as you can.

Individuals in restructured environments are dealing with much larger spans of control. This has made influence leadership critical, not motivating people through the direct use of authority.

Tolerance for ambiguity is increasingly important. How do you manage when you aren't really sure there's a light at the end of the tunnel? The media may say we're coming out of the recession, but from what we see, there are still companies cutting back, and consumers have changed their spending habits, thus affecting the pace at which we may be coming out of this recession.

Is worldwide networking playing a greater role in senior managers finding jobs?

Internet networks are not necessarily more important in placement. There are a number of networks such as LinkedIn and Facebook. LinkedIn is a business network that allows people to access folks in companies in a pretty efficient way, if, for example, you want to submit a résumé. While Facebook is a social network, many small companies use it because of its broad connectivity.

Many of these networks are being used by the more junior level of the population. Add in phenomena like Twitter and blogs, and the Web has created a lot more connectivity. I'm not sure these networking links get you placed any faster, but they do connect you to a broader audience. As one illustration, you can reconnect to college classmates faster and restart dialogues.

An important note: These networks may offer connectivity. However, while you're using these networks, so are a million other people. A year or two ago, one or two names a day may have surfaced to me through the Internet. Today, I receive dozens of names that way each day. So network fatigue is setting in.

Has the Internet made it easier for recruiters to screen candidates?

For an executive recruiter, it's both harder and easier to screen a candidate. In the search world, information gathering—finding organization charts and where people are on them—has been commoditized. It's now public domain information. But it doesn't mean you can necessarily screen the candidates better—you just have more information about them and what they have done.

So, the successful recruiter has to offer a lot more than what can be easily learned on the Internet? That's something for a candidate to keep in mind. An excellent executive recruiter has to come up with talent that is both uniquely skilled and well qualified. What kind of traits do these new executive gems have?

The real value today's recruiter offers is to identify and assess for the specific leadership traits, skills, and competencies that organizations need. This is the kind of assessment you can't get off a Web database. At Korn/Ferry, we have moved toward the idea of the value proposition offered by a candidate—an idea which comes from the world of marketing. We still do traditional searches but we start by looking at organizations and ask what their business strategy is and what they are trying to accomplish. It's not just I want a VP or president. How do you get the right quarterback to lead the current team against the relevant business strategy?

Do these top talents accept the inevitable turnover of people? Do they regard human beings as interchangeable, easily replaced parts?

The CEOs who really "get it" view human talent as an investment. Those who don't view it as a cost. That attitude will be the distinguishing characteristic of an executive winner today. It comes back to the idea of whoever can retain the best talent the longest is going to win on the all-important human capital investment measure.

It's widely known that English proficiency has increasing importance for managers abroad who are not native-born English speakers. Is it also of growing importance for American-born managers to have a command of at least one other language than English?

For U.S. companies, English is critical, as it is for European-based multinationals where English is the common language. Increasingly, in a global business environment, you want your English speakers to have another language as well. If you look across the landscape of CEOs in large global 500 companies, English may be the principal language, but there's an important multicultural sensitivity that comes from having additional language fluencies.

You once told me that getting fired should be a "learning experience." What new kinds of lessons are fired executives learning today—experiences that weren't that common five years ago?

It's still important for people to regard firing as a learning experience. An awful lot of people are recognizing they aren't alone. The economic downturn has eliminated whole layers of management, not just individual jobs or poor performers. Much rests on how individuals explain their departure and how they identify and articulate their opportunities going forward.

Have you seen cases of senior managers trying to squeeze into jobs with a smaller income, a diminished title, or limited advancement possibilities? If a manager decides to pursue this course, do you have any tips on how to do this successfully?

This has been one consequence of the massive restructurings of the past five years. For some managers, a smaller scale job has been an inescapable reality, though not necessarily a negative one. A manager may be tied to a certain locale or a particular industry that has undergone massive consolidation. Also, some people were actually in stretch positions before the recession. For whatever reason, the job didn't work out, and they've been willing to go back and leverage their core strengths.

You might see a president or group executive (not a CEO) move back into a divisional or functional role. People have made conscious choices, such as joining a smaller company with better growth potential. There are a number of smaller companies out there that are able to invest and expand at a faster pace. They are also less political and less hierarchical, and that appeals to certain managers. As a recruiter, I don't necessarily see accepting a smaller responsibility or moving to a smaller company as a negative. I want to understand the why, the rationale behind it. How did a person contribute? Whether a person's title changes is a less important issue.

How about computer and techno-literacy levels? I would assume these expectations have grown even for the most senior managers, e.g., are they all armed with notebooks and BlackBerrys?

You have to at least be aware of the technology. You need to understand what technology your employees use, how they communicate with each other, and how decisions are being made electronically. It may not affect you personally in the way you lead your daily life. But you have to have enough familiarity to be able to determine when technology is truly an advantage for your business.

Tierney, are you saying that it isn't automatically to a manager's or a candidate's advantage to say he or she is all for always being at the cutting edge of technology in the way a business does things?

E-mail allows for rapid communication, but it doesn't allow for actual dialogue. It can reduce interaction. You don't get into conversations with others. Technology interactions can sometimes create more conflict and chaos than more genuine personal communication, achieved by picking up a phone or walking down the hall or down the stairs. E-mail may be efficient, but it isn't necessarily the right way to solve the problem.

Emotional intelligence is a factor in deciding if an executive knows when to use face-to-face contact and when to rely on electronic communications. A really successful top manager is always asking such questions as: What's the best way to lead the environment and to lead people? How do we tailor the communications so that we are actually creating a culture?

When we last talked, you stressed an incoming exec should have a clear agreement as to what he or she is expected to achieve. Has the economic turbulence of the last two years created new challenges in this regard?

Goal setting is important, but I would look at it from a slightly different angle. There has to be what we call great alignment. When you walk into a new role in a new company or in your own company, are you and the prospective manager in agreement about the nuances of what needs to be done?

On a personal level, executives who are looking for jobs need to understand what they choose to do to recalibrate their careers. As you evolve, you learn what environments you work best in to be successful.

With the trend toward continual re-engineering, is there a benefit for senior managers to develop multiple specialties? What core skills are companies looking for in top managers these days?

There are certain areas of specialization—especially in science and technology—that are truly unique and provide great opportunity. It goes back to the agility observation earlier. Specialization in an executive is fine if it truly allows this person to create added value for a particular organization.

The classic generalist has a downside of being a jack-of-all-trades. Great CEOs need to be very, very good in a couple of areas and surround themselves with people in other areas who are stronger than they are. The functional areas they should excel in will vary by situation, but several traits are mandatory:

They need to be strategic visionaries.

They must be able to organize the business against the strategy and to lead through their key direct reports to make things happen.

In a public company, they have to manage the key external constituencies such as the analysts, banks, and shareholders.

The irony is, what enables a manager to become CEO is having demonstrated great operational and commercial effectiveness. But these skills aren't necessarily what will make them a great CEO. What makes an exceptional CEO are the abilities to organize the business against a meaningful vision and to formulate and articulate decisions.

Are women senior executives encountering any special issues in today's economy?

Today's emerging workforce is a multicultural, multigenerational workforce, but we have gone backward in America on some issues. We don't yet have the new diversity of thought always represented at senior manager and board levels. This disconnects top management from the people they are trying to motivate. Asia probably has the most dominant female executives. There are likely more female CEOs in Europe than in America—many of them generational appointments in family-dominated businesses.

What would be the most important single tip you would offer job management candidates on résumé preparation?

Since executives are more mobile, the challenge is to demonstrate sustainable success for a business once they have left one job for another. It's one thing, for example, to have been head of a division, but did you actually lead it to operational success? If you're moving every two years, that can be more a reflection on you, the executive, than the company. There isn't enough time to really leave an imprint, a legacy. Either you made poor choices in choosing the companies or you haven't been able to successfully execute. Bottom line: You're leaving before they get to you first.

Mackay's Moral: Positions go to people who deliver stellar value propositions.

MOBILIZE
YOUR NETWORK

Chapter 29

Job Hunting Is a Contact Sport

When Britannia ruled the waves, the British used to send battleships steaming up and down the harbors of lesser powers as a way of ensuring that their opinions would be respected. It was called "showing the flag." Usually, it spared the British the trouble of kicking sand in the little guy's face.

Making others aware of your presence is still an effective job-hunting and job-holding tactic, and you can use it without firing a single shot.

In fact, if you *don't* have a presence, that sends signals in itself, especially on the Web.

Assume that you will be Googled by any potential employer. Maybe you're not at a level where you have given a major speech or written an article for your industry or firm, but you should look for opportunities to develop your presence on the Internet. Perhaps you write something for a volunteer community organization or your church. Maybe a distinguished mentor of yours has passed away and the Web site dedicated to him or her asks for people who have known or been influenced by this person to send a tribute that would be posted on the Web site. As I indicate elsewhere, the Web is not an adolescent playground—a cyber "Animal House"—where you highlight goofball antics to impress your pals. It's serious business, and the sooner you treat it that way, the better it will serve your career.

More and more jobs are being filled these days by headhunters, politely known as management recruiters. It pays to make yourself known to them. If these potential gatekeepers could be influential at some time in your career, shouldn't you be digging your well before you're thirsty and trying to lay some groundwork with them?

Here's how to make contact and to make the contact pay off:

1. Make your annual convention or trade show appearance more than a junket. Headhunters swarm over these like flies on a warm, melting Klondike bar. This time when you take the trip to Las Vegas, stay out of the casinos and pay attention to the name badges so you can learn who the specialists are in your field and introduce yourself.

2. Use the career-change columns in your industry's trade journals. If someone has jumped ship from one company to another in order to fill an important position, chances are a competent pro may have had a hand in the move. Take the newly placed person to lunch or arrange to toast each other on a stroll in the park. Do the "a friend of mine is considering a career change" number, and if he or she opens up, find out if there was a headhunter and who the headhunter was. Now you've got a reason to . . .

3. Congratulate headhunters on their own career advances. Give them a call. Drop them a note. No one ever got angry at a well-earned compliment. They have egos, too. And they're likely to remember someone who took the trouble to reach out and touch them.

4. Be visible. Keeping a low profile is for guys ducking bullets. You want the world to be aware of your progress. Just completed an advanced management training course? Been promoted? Broadened your responsibility? Who's going to know if you don't tell them?

When you toot your horn, don't save it for a few lines in your annual Christmas letter right after the paragraph about Johnny's two new molars. Develop your own e-mailing list. Include headhunters. Scan and send out the newspaper clipping or the news release. If there isn't one, write a short e-mail announcing how pleased and happy you are with your new credentials. The information you send is going into files that could be as important to you as your credit report, and always makes a lot better reading.

5. Be a resource. Now that you've got a headhunter's name on your contact management system, make sure your name is on theirs. Make it known that you'll be happy to assist them in their searches, coming up with names of possible candidates or companies. By helping them for now, you've helped yourself for later.

6. Take a chance on romance. Even if you're secure in your job and not seeking to make a switch, you may change your mind if the right opportunity comes along. If a recruiter offers you a discreet interview with someone who has expressed an interest in you, consider exploring the jungle. You could be pleasantly surprised.

7. Never, ever treat a recruiter rudely. Recruiters have very long memories. The recruiter you dump on today could be the person you're calling tomorrow or next week for help in finding a job. Do you think that person will be eager to return your call after you've banged the phone down in his or her ear, or given him or her a brusque buzz off to an e-mail inquiry? (On the other hand, be careful how you respond to a cold e-mail inquiry from someone you've never met. Are you really sure who will be getting the message on the other end?) There's always another candidate. Burn your bridges and you're going to be looking for a life raft.

Mackay's Moral: Your goal in the contact sport of job hunting is scoring a TD . . . not getting sacked.

Quickie—
Don't Lose Your Face in Facebook

BusinessWeek reported the classic story of a Big Ten university grad who was selected for a coveted summer internship. When the firm did a last-minute check of him on Facebook, it found his entry boasting about his "marijuana smoking habit." The same article commented on a young woman who "turned down a job at a Boston law firm, after initially accepting it, [and] the testy e-mail exchange between her and a senior attorney at the firm ultimately found itself in thousands of in-boxes across the globe."

It's never a good idea to play fast and loose with your identity on the Web. Doing so during a job search is the absolute zenith of stupidity.

When you present your identity on the Internet, learn to be your own policeman and public relations agent. Ask:

- How will what I say about myself enhance my ability to get the job I want?
- Am I saying something that may seem cool or awesome for the moment but will look catastrophic or asinine on reflection?
- When I e-mail a person, do I know him or her well enough—and do I know who else may be receiving his or her e-mails—to be dead sure that my communication is confidential?

Remember that the more interesting your story is and the more colorfully you present it, the greater the urge will be for someone to publicize it.

Your goal is to become somebody's employee, not everybody's celebrity gaffe.

Chapter 30

Mackay's Deadwood
Network Pruner

Should you grow your network throughout your life? Absolutely.

Should your network grow untamed and unpruned? Absolutely not.

A network should be regarded as a robust and diverse garden, not an equatorial jungle. A thriving rain forest may be good for the ozone layer, but it's not the best model for cultivating a personal network. As artist and author Lou Erickson once said, "Gardening requires lots of water—most of it in the form of perspiration."

When you're faced with a watershed event like a job or career change, it's a good time to reassess your network. If your network is a sprawling maze, it's very hard to give regular attention to your highest priority contacts. It's also easy to waste time on people who do little to further your career or enrich your life in any meaningful way.

As you spin through your personal contact list, ask yourself these questions:

What were my last three contacts with this person? What happened as a result of the interaction? How did I or the individual benefit from the contact?

Remember that it's perfectly OK to have a series of one-way contacts with certain powerful individuals—or their gatekeepers—who may someday be of great benefit to you. It's also justifiable to keep in contact with people whom you are helping out. It's less defensible to spend a lot of time with people who are constantly asking for favors, who are not individuals you have a personal commitment to helping, and who don't reciprocate in an evenhanded way. The horticulturist Luther Burbank maintained, "A flower is an educated weed." You are well advised to keep your network balanced toward members well educated in traditional terms or in the hard knocks of life.

Draw a mental map. Which other people have I met through this contact? Is this individual continuing to introduce me to worthwhile new additions to my network? Have I kept my "account" current by giving this individual new personal leads, information, etc.?

Has my list of network contacts kept pace with my life? Is it up to date with my latest job and career changes? It's very easy to anchor a network in a comfortable crowd of old school and neighborhood buddies. This may make you feel good from a loyalty standpoint, and it might produce a surprise benefit when an unexpected situation arises, but it's no way to run a railroad. Not if that railroad is supposed to be your high-speed network to achieving your life goals.

It's often useful to separate your network into two groups—active and inactive. There are people who are clearly part of your day-to-day professional and personal life. There are also people who you may not be in touch with for several years who could still quite plausibly be part of your world in three to five years. Before you toss the entry that Jacques likes Tiffany glass, or the note that Geri is mad about the New York Mets, consider logging these entries in the inactive file. With the storage capacity of modern laptops and notebooks, there's no shortage of space to keep these records. You just have to make the time to keep them well organized. Also, spend an hour, at least once each year, scanning the inactive file to see if someone has suddenly come back to life as a premium contact, due to changes in your life or career.

When you assess your present network, consider adding five or ten names—"my top ten"—that you would die to have as part of your present network. Who in your present network could help establish those contacts? Also, what are your personal goals in three to five years? Which people would likely be part of your network if you were to attain those objectives? I call this *aspirational networking*. We all work with a fixed amount of time for networking. For most of us, it should be a bigger slice of our time budget, but it is what it is. It's just that most people do a poor job of managing their networking time. If you concentrate on upgrading your network, less important contacts will either merit fewer interfaces or may entirely deactivate themselves.

If you're facing a job search, then you need to identify a select group—perhaps ten or fifteen people—whom you can count on to ride out the storm with you. I call this my personal top ten. Perhaps one or two are recruiters. It's likely several are former bosses or career mentors. Maybe another couple are industry association contacts you made at firms that may now be job prospects for you. One could be a powerful CEO in your community whom you befriended in a volunteer project. It would be wise if one is a skilled communicator who can help you sharpen your résumé and prepare answers for interviews. Getting a job is more of a team effort than one usually thinks, and it's up to you to recruit that team from within your network. By the way, all the team members don't need to know about the other players, but you certainly need to have a clear grasp of who they are and how you are relying on them.

In case you think that the social skill of networking is superficial compared to your "hard" professional qualifications, bear in mind what management expert Peter Drucker once said: "More business decisions occur over lunch and dinner than at any other time, yet no MBA courses are given on the subject."

Mackay's Moral: Sow your network well, and you will sew up deals when you need them.

Quickie—
Network to New Work

Lennette Wood, a column reader from Oxnard, California, wrote me to share her job-bridging success. Other readers may benefit from Lennette's creative and effective solution. "I was the Membership Director for the Oxnard Chamber for two years," she writes, "enjoying my job when the signs of the economy started affecting my membership and my salary. The office reduced the work days to four days a week."

Undaunted by the cutback, Lennette let "a few fellow chamber members know that I would be available to rep their product or service one day a week." Her contact paid back a better return than she expected.

"This networking with about four people led to two job offers," she says, "but not part-time . . . full-time. I chose the one that was the safest in this turbulent economy and have been so happy with my decision." Lennette is a self-described "Cinderella story in a down economy." Her experience is vivid proof of the power of networking. "I left the chamber in good standing and now many members of my chamber whom I once tried to help with leads or networking have helped me." Lennette has now become the marketing representative for Coastal Occupational Medical Group.

Many people have built up reservoirs of goodwill they don't realize they have. When you face a setback, do what Lennette did. Examine your own balance sheet of credits and debits, identify which credits could help you out of your present predicament. Then tackle the challenge with a positive attitude. The results may surprise you.

Chapter 31

Bass Are Still
Where You Find 'Em

Fishfinder #1: There is more than one person who could be your boss. It pays to know who the other guys and gals are.

If you're the principal electronics engineer for a municipality, it behooves you to know the senior public works officials for at least three other towns in your region. If you're a delivery truck driver for the corner dry cleaner, commit yourself to meet three other dry cleaning owners who do home delivery in your neighborhood.

Why? *Because today's competitor can always become tomorrow's employer.*

If you drive a dry cleaning truck, you've got something current non-bosses, who are those potential new bosses, want very, very much: customers so loyal to you personally many of them can't even remember the name of the dry cleaner you're working for now.

As far as your customers are concerned, they're employing your services, not the name on the truck. Disloyal? Who'll cry for you in the front office if you're downsized out of a job?

Just remember, be discreet. Don't talk to a "competitor," i.e., someone who isn't in fact a branch of your present outfit trading under another name.

Years ago, in the early days of black-and-white television, the most popular show in Minneapolis was called *Masterpiece Theater*. It was strictly local, ran on Sunday nights, and featured nothing but old movies. The sponsor was a local dry cleaning establishment called G&K Cleaners and the "host" was the owner, a fellow named I. D. Fink. In those days, there were no restrictions on the length of commercials, and those for G&K Cleaners were interminable.

Every ten minutes or so, the movie would be interrupted with what seemed like a commercial of equal length consisting of Fink explaining some arcane feature of the dry cleaner's art in intricate detail. Fink was considered an extraordinarily dry speaker to begin with, and the subject was, if possible, even more so. I mean, who cares what they do when they dry-clean your pants? The kicker was, unbelievably, these commercials worked. People loved them. And business poured in. In fact, G&K got so big that, in order to disguise its almost total monopoly on the Twin Cities' dry cleaning industry, it ran some of its operations under different names. One day, folklore has it, Fink gets a call from an irate customer. He's watched *Masterpiece Theater* for years, believed every word Fink told him, and what happens? His shirt comes back with a spot still on it. He's had it. He's getting a new dry cleaner. Nothing Fink says helps. The customer slams down the phone. The next week, the ex-customer's new dry cleaner appears at the door. It's the same driver as before. Only this time, there's a different name on the truck. It was that special rare case.

Remember two things about the Fink Gambit:

First, be sure when you cast your line not to hook yourself in the seat of the pants. There are companies that operate the same businesses under different names. Be careful you don't apply to one while you're employed at another. That hint of dissatisfaction with your current job could be hazardous.

A second thing to store in your tackle box: Don't give up on a huge chain just because you've gotten turned down by one branch. While these chains try to use uniform hiring standards, individual managers are still individuals. Many candidates will apply to one store, one service station, or one dry cleaner in a national franchise operation and assume that a turndown means that the entire chain won't hire them. Well, that's not necessarily true. Supply and demand vary from branch to branch and from area to area and so do the attitudes and quirks of the person doing the hiring at each particular location.

The identical principle works in management: If you're a financial analyst, even if you're skunked at the regional headquarters in Georgia, the company could be biting at the same firm's headquarters in Florida.

Fishfinder #2: You have a job? Lucky you. Work hard for yourself. Work hard for your family. Work hard for your future. But don't forget to work very, very hard for your out-of-work friends. *Send leads to those in need.* Call them every two or three weeks to bolster their spirits. Lest we forget, the iron law of human relations remains:

"Be nice to the people you meet on the way up, because you might meet them again on the way down."

Mackay's Moral: Those who'll remember you when you get the pink slip are the ones you remembered when they landed in the ditch.

Quickie—
Ageless Alumni

Many people think university career placement offices are only for recent graduates. A 2009 article titled "Rah, Rah, Résumé!" by Jan Hoffman in the *New York Times* dispels that myth.

Syracuse University recently provided a 1976 alumna with the names of "graduates in related fields" and helped her fine-tune her résumé.

Other colleges offer older graduates such help as "panels of alumni experts, professional affinity networks, personal coaching and job listings." Schools like Lehigh have revamped their placement services to be much better equipped to support "midcareer professionals."

Why does this make sense? Colleges and universities sit on top of the most valuable job-search gold mine in the world—personal networks. Some alumni may be out of jobs, but most are not. And the college experience tugs huge heartstrings of personal loyalty to rally around fellow graduates. And the more people an institution of higher learning can place, the more people in its network available to help place other alumni.

Then there's the upside for the institutions. Some of the people who are helped are alumni who have broken off ties with their alma mater for decades. When they get career assistance, they often respond generously in terms of a contribution to the school or remembering the institution in a legacy.

As you go down your network checklist, don't overlook your alumni affiliation, no matter how many reunions you've missed.

Chapter 32

The Octopus Exercise

As I mentioned earlier, during the course of a lifetime, you're likely not only to make twelve to fifteen job changes, but at least three to five career changes as well. By my lightning calculations, it appears that for every two or three times you change jobs, you're also going to change careers.

Take a sheet of paper or call up the graphics drawing program on your laptop.

Draw a small circle in the center.

That's the body of the octopus. My picking an octopus is no accidental choice. This animal is one of the smartest invertebrates around. It's even said they can open screw-top bottles. Also, as I write this, I am in Rome, Italy, and I had a less-smart octopus for dinner last night.

This octopus body represents the skills and knowledge you use in your present job or in your most recent job. It's your operating system and core database governing your drive to reach out and grab onto other jobs.

Now, draw a series of lines branching out from that central area. These represent jobs different from the one you have now, but jobs for which you could conceivably be qualified if you had to shift careers.

For instance, let's say you're the rental agent for a major property management firm in your town. You've been at the business for five years, and your general knowledge of commercial real estate is pretty good. What other jobs could you reach out for?

How about site locator for a major retailer in power malls?

Negotiator?

Default evaluator for a firm that has bought up high-risk mortgages?

Physical plant and property manager for a major manufacturer?

Real estate auditor for an investment trust?

Rental investigator for a municipal or taxing authority?

Specialist in automated HVAC and security controls for property management?

Instructor in commercial real estate at the college?

Appraiser for a local bank or housing authority?

That's nine arms. If you're knowledgeable in commercial real estate, you could probably build an octopus with eighteen arms.

Keep in mind that many of the most desirable jobs around today didn't exist ten years ago, so lift that lid and think outside the box about jobs that *could* exist in five years that people could think would be wacko today.

Mackay's Moral: In octopus networking, tenacity matters as much as tentacles.

Chapter 33

Matchmaker, Matchmaker,
Find Me a Job!

The advent of social networking suddenly made it possible for people to reach thousands and in some cases millions of contacts to fulfill very specific personal needs for products, relationships, and—most of all— jobs. This is a brand-new marketplace. How do you manage it to get the best results?

To be sure, job seekers have to be very creative in this shrunken economy. The Internet offers a seemingly huge sea of opportunity, but there are lots of one-person kayaks paddling in it. For every job you have applied for, there are dozens . . . or hundreds . . . or thousands of other applicants with the same target. Your paddling skill won't make the difference; building a personal lifeline to a potential employer will.

Google a job, scroll through the classifieds, or dash directly to Web sites of the companies where you most want to land a job. Job-site listings are increasingly controlled by keywords that screen applicants in or out. What is the system short on? Two-way communication. It's like cyberspace Cinderella. What employer wants to waste time squeezing on a shoe that won't fit, especially if there are hordes of other contestants breaking down the doors?

Savvy users know how to play the system, to choose keywords in packaging their résumés that trickle through the human resources filters. The hiring manager's heart swells, convinced he just found Cinderella, not a pumpkin. In the interview, he discovers the applicant is better suited to writing fiction than delivering results.

Serious job seekers are leaning toward a new group of more personalized and intelligent sites. These sites are designed to match users to the exactly tailored requirements of specific opportunities. One such site, Bintro.com, uses semantic technology that recognizes, extracts, and categorizes your work to figure out what you really mean . . . and what companies need. It understands natural language and industry-specific terminology.

I like the personalized approach it takes in connecting job hunters with the perfect job. I also like that it's a free service for both candidates and employers, and its privacy policy includes a guarantee that it will never resell or barter your name or other information you submit on the questionnaire.

How should you utilize these new sites? Sell your skills, but don't hype them. Also, present a cohesive Web identity. Be a unified, positive, employable person on the Web—consistent from site to site in every place you have a presence.

Create a LinkedIn page and a Facebook page, because most people who are interested in hiring will Google you or go to Facebook to scoop up information about your background and experience. Keep in mind that this is your professional persona and restrict it to information you would share with a potential employer.

Remember, all information on the Web leaves a permanent record. Whether on your personal site or a friend's, your behavior outside work can wind up in pictures or videos that can sabotage your job prospects.

Catalog what you have to offer a prospective employer and then seek out groups and meetings online with people who can benefit from your knowledge or experience. Plenty of sites with user groups offer such virtual and physical meetings. They're great ways to get involved in a nontraditional way, meet people from your industry, and also discreetly call attention to your competence while you chat with your peers. Another great way to put forth your need and expertise is to create a blog that is specific to your background—and have the discipline to steadily feed it new insights.

A lot of job seekers have hefty experience in areas that are no longer in demand. Don't despair. You can emphasize hobbies, personal interests, and volunteer work to build a second career. For example, an out-of-work banker might be an enthusiastic shutterbug and take a step toward turning that passion into a part-time job while seeking out something more permanent.

It may be time for you to make what was a passing attraction a front-and-center skill. An entry-level writer or freelance graphic designer may not be able to find a job in that profession, but why not build a portfolio and donate the time and output to a nonprofit organization? A small gesture—it may seem—but you'll help others out while you get valuable exposure.

In the years to come, Web sites and Internet presence will define your job candidacy as much as a résumé does today. Whatever service you use, just remember one thing: Never stop putting yourself out there. And, for the sake of your career, make sure the person you present on the Web is one who others would want to hire.

Mackay's Moral: The Web is volatile territory. The trick is to glow, not to incinerate yourself.

Quickie—
One Sweet Tweet

The Web site PhysOrg.com serves professionals in a variety of sciences and technical disciplines. In April 2009, Etan Horowitz reported on this site about Brittany Ward, an account manager in her early twenties in Florida. "Just minutes after she was laid off from her job earlier this month, [she] pulled out her cell phone and typed a short message. 'Needs a job.'" And "when she hit enter, more than 2,000 friends, family members and strangers learned of her plight via Twitter and Facebook."

She got plenty of supportive responses. There's an emotional efficiency factor in Twittering. Ward said, "With Twitter, all of a sudden they hear the story, and you don't have to keep repeating it." For many people, the faster they can put an end to this phase of job loss, the quicker they can move forward with the positive part of finding a job.

When I visited TwitterJobSearch, it boasted posting "22,315 new jobs in the last seven days." Visit www.twitip.com/leverage-twitter-for-your-job-search/ and read some excellent tips by Miriam Saltpeter of Keppie Careers. Three pieces of advice really resonated with me:

- Come "up with your 'Twit-Pitch'—what you have to offer in 140 characters or less. [It] will help you clarify your value proposition."
- "Brand yourself professionally. If you are planning to use Twitter for a job search, set up a designated profile and account. Choose a professional Twitter handle."
- "Think about what you can do for others. Don't blatantly self-promote. Instead, help promote others. 'Retweet' (pass along information someone else shared, giving them credit)." This, Saltpeter maintains, is the best way to build your own Twitter network following.

"Last tweet?"

Chapter 34

Don't Be Blackballed
by Your BlackBerry

In a 2009 *New York Times* article, author Alex Williams recalls how a Dallas "college student sunk his chance to have an internship at a hedge fund . . . when he pulled out a BlackBerry to look up a fact to help him make a point during his interview, then lingered—momentarily, but perceptibly—to check a text message a friend had sent."

"A third of more than 5,300 workers polled in May by Yahoo HotJobs, a career research and job listings Web site," according to Williams, "said they frequently checked e-mail in meetings. Nearly 20 percent said they had been castigated for poor manners regarding wireless devices."

"Students bring their cell phones or they're on them when they walk into a meeting," business etiquette consultant Gail Madison told me. "I had one student who was calling on a cell phone while texting on another at the same time. My hair just about caught on fire!"

In meetings within companies, many attendees now use their BlackBerrys or iPhones to conduct a running commentary on the session. The BlackBerry messages will often be jeering raspberries at the presenter. "You'll have half the participants BlackBerrying each other as a submeeting, with a running commentary on the primary meeting," according to the Williams article. "BlackBerrys have become like cartoon thought bubbles."

When your interviewer plays with his or her smartphone in your presence, it's none of your business. If I had a multimillion-dollar prospect talking with his infant grandchild or playing a video game while I pitched my company, I'd find a way to let that slight roll off my back. I'd only be worried if someone with that kind of attention span and obvious disregard for people would be around next year to renew the contract.

The *New York Times* article quotes Nancy Flynn, an Ohio consultant, on a seriously incorrect opinion held by many: "People mistakenly think that tapping is not as distracting as talking . . . In fact, it can be every bit as much if not more distracting. And it's pretty insulting to the speaker."

If you're on a job interview, the rules are clear, and there isn't a lot of wiggle room to make them any looser:

- Turn off your smartphone before you go into an interview.
- Do not be seen talking on your phone when you go into an interview.
- Do not be seen reaching for your phone as you leave an interview.
- Don't boast about the amount of time you spend talking or texting on your smartphone during the day.
- Try to find a way to point out that you discipline your cell phone and Internet time for productive results, and then actually do it!

Companies are increasingly aware of the huge amounts of time people waste on the latest gadgets. They want employees who have the self-discipline to use these tools wisely.

Two more afterthoughts: A wacko ringtone on your phone may wow your friends, but it can paint you as a goofball if it goes off someday when you and your new CEO are unexpectedly riding fifty floors in the same elevator.

Lastly, Gail Madison recommends checking the outgoing message on your cell phone. If it says "Yo, dude, you've reached Hot Mama"— it's time to retool.

Mackay's Moral: Companies want to hire pros who are linked into the latest technology, not junkies who are hooked on it.

Quickie—
Twitter: Risk and Risqué

The headline for a Twitter article by David Phelps in the *Minneapolis Star Tribune* offered a caution: "put a lid on tweets" before starting a job search. Phelps reported on one PR agency candidate who "tweeted herself directly out of a job interview." The agency said "she was negative and critical of other agencies" in her tweets and other Web hits. The agency was concerned what sentiments she might voice about them or their customers.

In June 2009, Twitter received widespread praise for sparking political change in Iran by instantly publicizing demonstrations. It pulled focus to the "Angel of Iran"—a young woman whose slaying was videotaped by a bystander. Twitter can be equally powerful in derailing careers in image-conscious companies. Let's face it. In today's harum-scarum economy, would you rather hire tact or temerity?

Social networking sites—such as Twitter, Facebook, and LinkedIn—are now checked as carefully as résumés once were. In the Phelps article, Amy Langer, a placement firm cofounder, says, "It's becoming part of the vetting process." That's because social and business networking are now tangled up in one very visible maze. When you tweet an awesomely bad partying photo of yourself on a social site, you can easily crater your career on the professional side.

We live in a stressful world. There's a big temptation to share your inner feelings, trials, and zany ballistic moments. Just because your pals do it, why follow those lemmings off the cliff?

Risks are everywhere. In the Phelps article, one female exec "suffered serious career damage when a boyfriend posted a seminude picture of her on her Facebook page." By the way, turn the tables and play the vetting game in the other direction. Before you get involved with your next boyfriend, be sure to vet him on the Web.

FILL IN THE BLANKS

Chapter 35

Plugging Holes in Your Résumé

Food Network chef Robert Irvine trained on Britain's Royal Yacht *Britannia*, served on the kitchen staff of the West Wing of the White House, and was executive chef for several cruise lines. Pretty good credentials. Good enough for most people. But not good enough for Robert Irvine.

He aerated more fluff in his résumé than a three-star Michelin chef whisks in a soufflé on a good day. For example, he said he was a knight commander of a royal order, that he had a degree from the University of Leeds, that he had been a chef in the White House proper, and that he had been directly involved in creating the wedding cake for Prince Charles and Lady Di. A 2008 article in the *St. Petersburg Times* revealed he had none of these latter credentials, and Irvine was replaced as host of *Dinner: Impossible*—only rejoining the show in 2009, with a heftily corrected bio.

In 2001, George O'Leary became head coach for the University of Notre Dame football team. Days afterward, incredible inaccuracies in his résumé appeared in the press. He claimed to have a master's degree from a school that never existed and contended he had three letters in football from the University of New Hampshire. The facts: He hadn't played in a single game. His résumé padding prompted the school to ask for his resignation.

In 2006, the Minnesota Vikings hired Fran Foley as VP of player personnel. According to the *Minneapolis Star Tribune*, Foley's résumé "described his coaching jobs at three schools—Colgate, the Citadel and

Rutgers—as full-time assistant coaching jobs, when in fact he was a graduate assistant." He also exaggerated "his college playing career at Framingham State College." Incredibly, according to the *Star Tribune*, Foley "ascended to a position in which he will be responsible for hiring and firing the people charged with assessing the talent and character of the players." Needless to say, Foley was quickly replaced.

Also in 2006, David Edmondson resigned as CEO of RadioShack when the *Fort Worth Star-Telegram* learned that college degrees he claimed to have in theology and psychology were bogus.

Our ability to read résumés has advanced eons from what it was ten or twenty years ago. Before you engage some flack to puff up a career that wasn't, consider these options:

- **Leave periods blank that you can't account for rather than bluffing.** If you don't want to write about it in the document, be prepared to describe the lapse in person. Even better, have one of your references ready to explain that this was a difficult time in your life. Companies are largely less worried about what you did—provided it wasn't a felony— and far more concerned if you are likely to do it again.
- **Don't put a shine on lateral moves or demotions.** They felt you weren't ready. You disagreed. They downgraded your job. You had no say in it. Corporate people know best of all that corporations don't always have a clear or kosher motive for what they do.
- **Work from the present backward.** You aren't trying to prove you lived a flawless life, birth certificate forward. You're out to prove you're a competent and qualified human asset today.
- **Don't ever lie about academic, military service, or professional certification credentials.** Somehow and some way this disinformation will find its way back to you. Furthermore, don't ever let well-meaning people overstate your background, even when it seems innocent and justified.

Mackay's Moral: Few things explode more easily than an overly inflated résumé.

"I'm fifty-three, but I have the résumé of a much younger man."

Chapter 36

Imagination:
There's Just No Substitute

An elderly man living in Phoenix calls his son in New York and says, "I hate to ruin your day, but I have to tell you that your mother and I are divorcing. Forty-five years of misery is enough."

The son gets all excited and responds, "Pop, what are you talking about? You can't divorce Mom after all these years. That's crazy."

"It may be crazy," says the old man, "but I am going to tell her on this coming Thanksgiving Day! It will be the last one we spend together!"

Frantically, the son calls his sister in Chicago and she explodes: "Like heck they're getting a divorce. We're both going to fly to Phoenix tomorrow and talk some sense into Dad! I don't care if it is Thanksgiving!"

Then she calls her father and shouts at him over the phone, "Do you hear me? Don't you dare do a thing until Brother and I get there tomorrow." Then she hangs up.

The old man hangs up his phone and turns to his wife. "OK," he says with a smile, "they are coming for Thanksgiving and paying their own way. Now what do we tell them for Christmas?"

That's what I call creativity at its best. Studies show there's no link between intelligence and creativity. However, we can *all* become more creative if we put our minds to it.

Creativity certainly helps in finding jobs. I say, don't be boring. Don't be predictable. Don't be just another candidate. Stand out. Be different. Use a little creativity.

Here are some examples of people who used creativity to land a job:

- A person who had been out of work for four months saw an ad for her dream job with a local TV station. The standard tactic, a cover letter with a copy of her résumé, netted absolutely nothing. So, she launched a more imaginative campaign, which included letters from the fellow she was going with, from her lawyer, from her eighty-year-old mother, even from her priest, who wrote, "I'm enclosing this in hopes that you will hire her. It's depressing to look at her sad face, and besides, we haven't had a donation from her in months."

- A candidate for a teaching job with the Minneapolis Public Schools sent a singing telegram praising her skills. "When people sell themselves in a creative way, it does attract attention," said the person who hired the candidate.

- An advertising applicant won a job at an ad agency when he sent out a creative mailer touting his services. When the cover was opened, the inside page showed a photo of the candidate standing next to a sign that read, "I'm the One."

- A contender for the marketing director position at an arena where professional basketball is played sent her résumé and cover letter in a sneaker with the comment, "Now that I've got one foot in the door, how about the other?"

As you can see, one of the best strategies is to separate yourself from the pack. The part that makes the difference between getting the job and being an also-ran is giving the interviewer what he or she doesn't expect. Be pleasingly unpredictable. Be entertainingly original. In short, shock 'em.

One young person I was mentoring slam-dunked his interview for a marketing slot with a major company by showing up toting his own PowerPoint presentation. Did that help the interviewers visualize him working for them? You bet.

Some years ago I attended the graduation ceremony of my daughter, Jojo, at the University of Michigan. Seated up in the rafters, I watched thousands of seniors parade across the stage. Suddenly the crowd started roaring, as if Michigan had just defeated Ohio State in football. Instead, a female graduate had walked across the stage with a placard on top of her mortarboard. In huge letters were the words, "I need a job." I don't know if she landed a job with her ingenuity; however, people were falling all over themselves to give her their business cards.

As my friend Pat Fallon, chairman of Fallon Worldwide, one of the great advertising companies, says, "Imagination is one of the last remaining legal means you have to gain an unfair advantage over the competition."

Mackay's Moral: Really smart people know creativity often beats knowledge.

Chapter 37

Psychological Evaluations:
Shrink to Grow

In the last dozen years, major league sports have added a new spectacle to the events calendar: Draft Day. This element has become huge, and fans gather by the thousands in local sports arenas to watch TV coverage of middle-aged men in suits fumbling with Ping-Pong balls, making solemn-sounding announcements, and scribbling on blackboards. Who's getting whom? Who's trading? Who's standing pat? Who's expendable? Who's untouchable? What kind of talent is in demand, in decline? Who got snookered, who snatched a prize from under everyone's nose? Who's winning, who's losing? No one *really* knows because you can't tell the final score when no one gets the ball until the following season, but it's a great game for any fan who enjoys lots of controversy and strongly held expressions of opinion.

Most of the Draft Day hype and hope focuses on athletic skills, but sophisticated player personnel executives, who are responsible for these multimillion-dollar decisions, know they have to factor in other elements. They realize that the performance of their choices will depend as much on the personal qualities as on the raw physical talent of the choices.

Personal qualities are a lot tougher to get a handle on than the numbers for the forty-yard dash or the vertical jump. Is this player committed? What is his value system? Is she coachable? Will he be a team player? Will she be able to overcome her shortcomings? Will he choke? Does she quit? Has he established sound training habits?

Sports franchises are built on the answers to these kinds of questions.

So are businesses.

For forty years, I have relied on industrial psychologists to help me sort out the complexities of a hire. According to the American Management Association, the number of U.S. companies using psychological testing is growing rapidly.

Fortunately, for us business types, it's a lot easier to get your subject to test when he's a forty-five-year-old salesperson than a nineteen-year-old athlete—even though with the athlete you may be risking $10 million or more on the results. Just imagine the fan reaction if you were able to get one of these kids to test for you and you came up with something like, "We decided not to draft Mr. All-American because, even though he can shoot the eyes out of the basket from thirty feet, he has an unresolved conflict with authority figures."

Whatever the results, I never let the industrial psychologists make the decision for me. Their information is just another tool in the hiring process; it's just another arrow in my quiver.

But it's also a tool you can use to your own advantage as a prospective employee, in two ways.

If you're out there beating the pavement for a job, I recommend you get yourself to an industrial psychologist and get tested—on your own.

I'm not going to kid you, it's not cheap. It will cost you at least several hundred bucks, but the oral and written exams will uncover strengths you never dreamed you had (and a few weaknesses to work on also). If you're being let go, try to talk your employer into paying the tab as part of your outplacement package.

Remember, you're at a crossroads in your life. The next job you take could determine your future for a long time to come. Isn't it worth your while to know whether you're heading in the right direction? If there is ever a time to change careers, to rethink your goals, isn't this it? Fate has forced you into this situation, so take advantage to find out about yourself and what you're good at. Don't do it on the cheap. Go to a firm with an excellent reputation so you know you're getting a sound evaluation from someone who's a lot less biased about you than you are.

Another use for this information: You now have in your hands the kind of report that 99.9 percent of other job seekers—your competitors—

don't have. It contains information every interviewer is trying to learn about a prospect before making the hiring decision. Armed with this psychological profile, you now have your own personal Good House-keeping Seal of Approval. It's a way of providing potential employers with the valuable information they want.

Does it show that you are a less than perfect human being? Of course. Not to worry. We all are. What it also shows is that you have areas of strength, as well as creativity and imagination in your job-seeking skills. And that may be just enough to resolve the decision in your favor.

Mackay's Moral: Know thyself to get thyself hired.

Chapter 38

Shrinks: A Skull Session

Brad Swanson and Bill Kirkpatrick are industrial psychologists. Both are PhDs, have decades of experience, and are principals of SKS Consulting Psychologists in Minneapolis. MackayMitchell Envelope Company has enlisted them time and again to help make management staffing decisions.

- Want to know how this year's crop of citrus sizes up? Ask the fruit dealer who's groping those Jamaican Uglis every day.
- Who's going to be the next Seabiscuit at Pimlico? I'd make book on the best handicapper in Baltimore.
- Which young mezzo will be belting out *Carmen* at the Met next season? Check out the music critic at the *New York Times*.

Have a yen to know what's going on in the heads of recruiters, human resources directors, and candidates in this time of woe?

Talk to the folks who are out there squeezing those noggins every day and helping to decide which are ripe and which are rotten.

Here's what I learned from Bill and Brad on a recent visit.

Some people are compelled to downscale the job they take. Some actually seek to do so. Does this work?

BRAD: We have seen people accept jobs with lesser stature and jobs with lesser pay. Sometimes, the latter option has been the result of group action, when

162

employees pool together and decide they have to cut their salaries. Often, though, this direction comes from above. More and more, such adjustments are becoming acceptable to people because it's a practical solution. Those affected are returning to a survival mode. Not surprisingly, many are just grateful to have a job.

BILL: I just talked to a man who used to run a large cooperative and decided to apply for a much lower level position in a manufacturing plant. He discovered he had a health issue that was related to his workplace for the cooperative. After medical treatment, he could have returned to his former job, but a replacement had already been hired. He decided to apply elsewhere for a lower level position so he wouldn't have to relocate his family. This particular potential employer didn't choose him, contending he was overqualified.

Even though a person may genuinely be prepared to accept a downgrade, companies are often suspicious of candidates whose credentials overqualify them for a position. They're afraid he or she won't be motivated even though, as in this example, the person may be perfectly willing to accept a job with lesser scope for any of a variety of reasons. This sort of applicant needs to present a clear and convincing case if the employer is going to trust the person's intentions, especially when the pool of available high quality candidates is so large these days.

What about temporary executive positions?

BRAD: We term those "survivor jobs," and in some cases they make a lot of sense. These positions can serve as a "filler" until a desired job is secured, and they can also be satisfying and fulfilling in themselves.

Because every hiring choice is a more important and impactful decision given tight budgets, are people relying on your input more heavily than in the past?

BILL: Companies are being more cautious and careful about whom they hire. Economic conditions are certainly making firms appreciate how critical it is to make sound hiring decisions. There is also a body of qualified unemployed available people who have lost work through no fault of their own. Employers want to take advantage of these circumstances to get the foremost talent they can.

BRAD: Sometimes reorganization programs have unintended consequences. Recently, a large national retailer offered an across-the-board buyout program in which employees could take a severance package. A lot of good people accepted it, knowing they were capable and confident they could find jobs. Some of these people used the money as a grant to fund a personal sabbatical. Some used it as seed capital to launch their own entrepreneurial ventures. Ironically, this retailer then had to go out and fill some of the jobs created by the vacancies resulting from their workforce reduction program.

BILL: Striking out on one's own and taking such a severance package is something done by really talented people who are confident they can land on their feet.

Confidence is always a pivotal trait for a job seeker. Is it even more so in the present job climate?

BRAD: Confident people can certainly take advantage of today's environment. Confidence—and not arrogance—has always been a positive attribute, and it is more valuable, maybe even necessary, in a down economy.

BILL: Another trait of rising importance over recent years is flexibility, especially a willingness to adapt to change. There are clear personality characteristics that speak to that capacity.

How does flexibility factor into the palette of top-priority traits that are sought after today?

BILL: The world marketplace is changing rapidly. Flexibility is clearly reflected in those aptitudes needed for successful global involvement in many ways.

Has flexibility also grown in importance because organization structures evolve and transform themselves so quickly and so often these days?

BRAD: You have to be ready to shift easily.

BILL: This is part of a long-term trend that has been underway since the mid-70s. The trend toward flexibility is tied into the increasing significance of collaboration within companies and the shift away from hierarchical structures.

An aptitude for teamwork and peer-group leadership is a real plus?

BILL: Surely these two skills are critical in a down economy, but I'm not sure that the down economy is the sole or specific reason for their importance. In other words, these aptitudes are a real plus in any economy, up or down.

Step back from the present economic context for a moment and talk about the model for the classic stereotype of the successful business person. Has that ideal also evolved in recent decades?

BRAD: Certain industries like security firms and advertising had profiles that were strongly male-dominated forty years ago. This has surely changed.

BILL: The prominence of the dominating individualist has receded. The one-man show à la early Michael Jordan is disappearing. Companies prize team effort and group involvement to a greater degree. The world is too complex for a one-star show to hack it. Too many pieces of the puzzle have to fit together. A facilitator who can integrate all the pieces becomes more important.

BRAD: Firms want thinkers who can bring all these components together. You need to think and link more broadly and beyond the scope of your particular technical function.

BILL: Another force behind this has been the shift in economic output from manufacturing to information and services.

Has the greater presence of women in senior positions also stimulated the growing preference for collaborative thinking?

BILL: Women as a group have an advantage over men as a group. Collectively, their style and orientation are less ego driven. They tend to welcome and include people. They listen better and are more oriented to draw contributions out from others.

BRAD: This still varies by industry, and it is most pronounced in those industries toward which women have gravitated such as advertising, where the account executive role needs to be more a liaison, a collaborator, a facilitator.

BILL: One thing is certain: The Rambo prototype is surely not as effective as it once was.

What have you learned about mentors and grooming successors in this new environment?

BILL: Women generally tend to be more nurturing, and that marks the prevailing training and development style today. Women ask for assistance more naturally.

BRAD: Men try to be too self-reliant. Women also tend to seek out mentors.

Are people more agile networkers today?

BRAD: Absolutely. You certainly have to be a networker to get a job in this economy.

BILL: That gold retirement watch your dad or grandpa got? Nobody's dangling it out there anymore. Because changing employers is now routine, each person is expected to take responsibility for staying in touch with the market and identifying where the next opportunities are to be found.

Comment on the huge surge in social networking on the Web with sites like Facebook and Twitter. Has this changed the image of the computer nerd as a socially acceptable type?

BRAD: Bill Gates de-nerded the nerd.

BILL: There are undoubtedly a lot of digital network tools available. Interpersonal contact—pressing the flesh—remains important. While some people may have a carefully groomed Web image or résumé, meet them live and they may lose their luster.

BRAD: Technology has helped people broaden their network.

BILL: It's now the case that networks have become a principal—perhaps *the* principal—way to find jobs. Networks, more than ever, are also the way that recruiters find candidates.

Piggybacking on what you say about people having larger networks because of the digital tools: Heaven help those folks who have not made networking a priority and used every available device to enlarge it intelligently.

BRAD: Having a scrawny, undernourished network shows up very fast when you talk with someone. And having a vibrant, growing network is an attraction that recruiters and employers look for. It's a sign of personal strength and vitality.

Lastly, let's talk about people who are nearing the end of their working careers. Job changes happen a lot more often, and they are taking place for people in their late fifties and early sixties more than ever before. Are older workers more self-aware and realistic today?

BRAD: That's definitely true. And if they are being realistic, they have to recognize the need to adapt and stay current. If someone in his fifties doesn't demonstrate flexibility these days, that person stands a good chance of being let go. Companies can no longer afford people who can't adapt. There are very few jobs left where you can just say "I'll do it my way" or "that's the way I've always done it."

BILL: The dinosaurs are giving way, just like their ancient analogues. When there was plenty of food out there, they thrived. When the environment evolved, they refused to—or couldn't—change their ways fast enough.

BRAD: Companies won't put up with dinosaurs anymore.

What's your broad-brush opinion: Are people in general more positive and optimistic than they were ten or twenty years ago?

BRAD: To an extent, the tendency to be optimistic or fatalistic is a genetic trait; but no matter how you're inclined, you have to be realistic, too.

BILL: Another key variable is how much you feel you are in control of the circumstances governing your life, which psychologists refer to as locus of control. A blue-collar worker may feel much less able to influence his or her prospects than someone with a broader skill base and more influential contacts. At every level, however, there has been an undeniable surge in anxiety.

Mackay's Moral: Shrinks don't test for failure. They test for fit.

Quickie—
Take Pride in Stride

In 2009, Lawrence Summers became President Obama's chief economic adviser. His previous roles include a stint as treasury secretary in the Clinton administration and president of Harvard for five years.

After Harvard, Mr. Summers was out on the job market in 2006. You'd think his résumé might have earned him a bye if he were applying for a job at a finance firm, albeit a top-tier one.

Not so.

In 2006, he expressed an interest in joining D. E. Shaw & Company, one of the highest rolling hedge funds around, as an adviser to investment strategists. According to the *New York Times*, "As part of Shaw's rigorous screening process—the firm accepts perhaps one out of every 500 applicants—Mr. Summers was asked to solve math puzzles. He passed, and the job was his."

There's a lesson here.

Good enough on paper is not nearly enough these days. The best employers want to know if you are as good as your history might suggest. And your prospective boss wants guarantees you will be good enough to do *exactly* what needs to be done.

Did Lawrence Summers smart over being made to fill out an entrance exam?

I imagine the almost $5.2 million the *Times* says he earned in just his second year at Shaw was the kiss that made it all better.

Chapter 39

Mackay 44
Interview Prep Checklist

Timing and Advance Planning

1. Scheduling—try for the time of day you shine best.
2. Get a good night's rest the day before.
3. Try to work out in the morning. It will help improve your alertness and relax you.
4. Create a contact sheet for each company with names, phone numbers, e-mail addresses.
5. If a recruiter is involved, have a premeeting huddle about positioning for the interview.
6. Review your own videos of your simulated interviews.
7. If any forms are needed, complete them neatly in advance.

Apparel and Appearance

8. Shine shoes, check fingernails.
9. Get a haircut or a style . . . bring a comb.
10. Choose a suit with shirt and tie or blouse.
11. Coordinate accessories (including watch, umbrella if necessary, etc.).

Reading and Research

12. Read recent articles on the prospective company.
13. Research company Web site for their latest news and press releases.
14. Know the company's most recent annual and quarterly sales and profits.
15. Google people you'll be meeting for background on them.
16. Know how to pronounce names of people you will meet.
17. If possible, learn the names of the receptionist and administrative assistants.
18. If this is a second interview, review notes of past meetings.
19. Scroll through the day's business news so you have something to talk about.
20. Create a list of good questions you will ask the interviewer.
21. Check e-mails just before leaving for any last-minute rescheduling.

Take Withs

22. Portable phone (turn off before interview)
23. Portfolio or business case
24. Résumé copies (at least two)
25. Business cards
26. Blank paper or notebook and pens
27. Breath mints or spray
28. Your personal calendar if a follow-up meeting is discussed

Getting There

29. Plan on being punctual and intend to arrive several minutes early.
30. Check weather report in case you need to plan on extra time.
31. Google map and either pre-drive or investigate road congestion.

32. Investigate parking practices.
33. Identify the correct building entrance.
34. Anticipate going through security and having to wear a visitor badge.

If Meeting over a Meal

35. Eat something like a power bar or piece of fruit beforehand.
36. If possible, know the menu in advance.

Just Before Showtime

37. Do a once-over in the mirror for hair and clothing.
38. Pay attention to your posture.
39. Have a reasonable idea of appropriate, positive opening comments.
40. Put on a warm, relaxed smile.
41. Prepare for a dry, firm handshake.

Plan Follow-up Pre-Interview

42. Anticipate beforehand how and where you will debrief yourself.
43. Have stationery and postage ready for handwritten thank-you notes.
44. If a recruiter is involved, know how to reach this person after the interview for a debriefing.

Chapter 40

Footlights and Footwork

A job interview is not very different from a public speech. There is precious little room for blowing a line in either scenario.

Comedian Jerry Seinfeld has noted public speaking is the #1 fear. Death ranks second. "In other words," Seinfeld reasoned, "at a funeral, the average person would rather be in the casket than giving the eulogy."

David Leisner is a gifted guitarist and composer based in Manhattan. He is also an expert on a very important topic: stage fright. David shared some thoughts with me on the subject after returning from a successful concert tour to Sweden in 2009.

If you're facing a round of critical job interviews in the coming days and interviews scare the dickens out of you, do yourself a big favor and visit David's Web site that offers "Six Golden Rules for Conquering Performance Anxiety" at http://davidleisner.com/guitarcomposer/noname.html.

In certain respects, a job interview and a public concert have similar objectives for the candidate or performer. Both like to visualize resounding approval from the audience. The musician wants the approval in applause and ovations. The job hunter is happy enough with an offer letter.

However, the job candidate needs to be very conscious of signals from his audience—the interviewer—and must be open to adjusting his presentation during the exchange. I asked David if there is a meaningful way that a musical performer must also "listen" to his or her audience. One often hears of a dialogue between performer and audience in a live concert. Does this in truth happen?

"Most performers," David said, "are like me and get some signals from their audience. In a good way, that can help feed a performance. Others don't do well operating in that way. I don't have a clue as to why that's so. Some people are better off putting themselves in a cocoon and staying in a protected zone. If you get too many signals, you become too self-conscious. Too few, and you aren't really communicating in the most meaningful way." The same holds true for interviewees as well. A successful interviewee straddles the line between awareness and confident assertion. One of David's Golden Rules: "Do not second-guess any audience member's reaction to your playing."

David is fond of a view from the contemporary painter Thomas Nozkowski: "It's important to have the brush flow." Once it stops and a painter has to think about what he or she is doing, that generally spells trouble. The same is also true for outstanding athletes who achieve their best results in the batter's box or on the diving board when they are "in the zone."

"Basically, to find the flow, you have to get out of the way," David believes, and he thinks that is true for a job interviewee as much as a painter or a musician. "We put up so many barriers through self-judgments or worrying about what the other person thinks," David adds. "In an interview, you need to have some sense of what the other person is thinking, but not so much that it makes you self-conscious."

Another Golden Rule: "Be onstage, not in the audience. Be in the giving mode, not the receiving one." As a job interviewee, your foremost responsibility is to help the interviewer appreciate your strengths and to be enthusiastic about them, not to guard your answers so the interviewer won't discover what makes you tick.

Again and again, David circles back to the issue of self-confidence: "If I were to single out one element as having paramount importance, it's trusting in oneself. You've practiced as well as you could, and you have to go forward." You have to believe you're good on your feet. If you don't embrace that belief, I guarantee you that you won't be. In David's words:

Part of the conviction you need is that the spontaneous moment will work for you. In a concert or an interview, a common fear is that a certain problem or challenge will arise and we won't be able to deal with it. In advance of it occurring, we worry about how we will deal with this problem or that one. One of the secrets is trusting that you'll be OK at that moment if you're spontaneous, saying what you need to say as the moment requires it.

Many interviewees spend a lot of time worrying about how they will answer an especially tough question about their past or why they may have failed at a particular job. The side effect is that they may easily reduce the overall quality of the entire interview by 20 or 30 percent because they aren't focused on the issue of the moment.

Before concerts, David—who is fifty-five—still meditates on his Golden Rules to handle performance anxiety. I asked him what exactly that meant. Does this entail wrapping himself in a yoga position and chanting? David emphasizes that he means the "freest possible inter-pretation." Think about what you need to achieve and try to bring these skills and principles to a sharper level of awareness. "There are lots of demons just beneath the surface," he says, "just bring them to light and then squash them."

Lastly, I asked David if he ever has a hint of stage fright coming on during a concert and how he combats its emergence if it does. "To get back on track," he said, "I try to surrender myself to the 'forward flow' of what I want to achieve. In the moment you freak out, just keep going forward. This relies on trusting yourself and your natural talent."

While it's important to master stage fright, it's also key to look at challenges like job interviews and public speeches as opportunities, positive events with sometimes unrecognized benefits. Sora Song wrote an article titled "The Price of Pressure" for *Time* magazine in 2004. In it she cites a meta-analysis published by the American Psychological Association of "300 studies involving some 19,000 subjects." Such or-deals as "enduring layoffs" have significantly negative effects on almost all immune functions. Believe it or not, short-term stress situations like public speaking—and I would put job interviews right up there—can actually have a positive impact on our health. The investigation found that for people "asked to speak in public or do mental math in the lab, the tasks tended to mobilize their fast-acting immune response."

The legendary CBS news commentator Edward R. Murrow summed up stage fright with wonderful brevity as "the sweat of perfection."

Mackay's Moral: Edward R. Murrow said pros have one big edge: they "have trained the butterflies to fly in formation."

Quickie—
The Mother of All Questions

In August 2009, John Chambers, the CEO of IT giant Cisco, was interviewed by the *New York Times*. He was asked to share the questions he asked a job candidate. His most interesting one:

"Who are the best people you recruited and developed and where are they today?"

Everyone gives lip service to people being the biggest resource in business. Who doesn't sing the praises of smart hiring and management development?

Chambers is saying *prove it*. This challenge works for any level of management in any company.

Does Chambers' question apply to young people who are entering the job market? Why shouldn't it? If you ran the student newspaper or the debating society, how did you help develop the next editor or the chief debater who succeeded you?

If your next job interviewer doesn't ask you the Chambers question, and you have had stellar results in finding and growing people, make it a major selling point. And if you don't have a meaningful answer to the question, then make your own recruitment and development skills a #1 priority when you land your next job.

The people who build companies are the people who build people.

Chapter 41

In a Job Hunt,
Make Sure Your Ducks Are in a Row

In *Swim with the Sharks Without Being Eaten Alive*, I wrote that the biggest single mistake a manager can make is a bad hire. And yet this mistake is made all the time. If a human resources or personnel officer can claim a success ratio of 75 percent, he or she borders on genius because so much of the hirer's job is instinctive rather than scientific. Like real life.

A man and woman can date each other for years, but let them share quarters or marry each other and they will know more about each other within weeks than they knew during their entire previous history together.

Or let's say two married couples are the best of friends and have been neighbors for twenty years. One day one couple calls the other couple and says, "Hey, we've got a great idea. Why don't we go to Europe together for three weeks?" Result: When they get back there's a house on the block for sale. The two couples never speak to each other again.

An employer can interview a prospect for months, put him or her through every kind of boot camp drill, get to know his or her golf game so well the employer can tell within ten yards where the prospect's slice will land, exchange dinner invitations, check out the spouse's talents for the tango. Result: Six weeks after the hire, the employer is reaching for the Maalox Plus and looking for a replacement.

There is no single question, no magic formula to guard against failure in any enterprise involving human beings. We do the best we can.

The most common pitfall recruiters face is to be dazzled by personality. The 25 percent failure rate experienced even by ace recruiters is usually the result of confusing interview skills with job skills. We're all vulnerable to charmers.

The best way recruiters can protect themselves is to extend the process long enough to see candidates under as many varied conditions as possible. As we've seen, that doesn't always work. Here are a few more tricks of the trade candidates should know about:

1.   **Are your references what you claim they are?** Are you concealing some bad ones? Recruiters check references more carefully than ever these days. The Internet can expose in milliseconds what once took days of due diligence to uncover. The harder recruiters dig, the more they find. Don't fake it, whether it's school, employment, or personal references. Often, when recruiters are not satisfied with the first set of references, they ask for more. Sometimes, they already know the answer and are just testing to see how hard you will try to cover something up. If there are unexplained "gaps" in your job history, you should be able to cover them with some kind of constructive effort, like school, volunteer work, individual entrepreneurship. Thankfully, parenthood is increasingly acceptable. Also, consider a seemingly unorthodox tactic: Be completely candid with the recruiter in describing the smudge in your résumé and ask for *their* help in presenting it in a favorable way. Recruiters have seen more blemishes than China has computer chips.

2.   **Do you meet the job specifications?** Many job failures are the result of an imperfect match between the person and the position. A candidate eager for a job will say just about anything to demonstrate his or her qualifications. It's up to the recruiter to be focused, to have a clear understanding of *exactly* what skills are needed and not to be led off course by a winning smile. Listen carefully to the job requirements. If you don't have the training or background described in the job prospectus, be up front about it. Discuss whether you can still qualify for the position through on-the-job training or further education. Even better, describe what you are doing online to shrink your know-how deficit.

3.   **Do you know how to think?** Note how the interviewer's questions are geared to open your thought processes for inspection, not just

merely to elicit a mechanical response, like "I designed fifteen computer programs." What did the programs accomplish? To what extent did you involve users in the design process? How much did the programs help solve user problems? How many led to other, systems-wide streamlining in the company? Recruiters are looking for qualitative responses that substantiate quantitative claims.

4.   **What are your work habits?** Note how the interviewer wants to know where your ideas come from. Do you take all the credit yourself? How do you work as a team member? (This question has skyrocketing significance in thinly staffed organizations shouldering big workloads.) How will you fit in with the people you will be working with? Will they want to work with you or will they avoid you? When you answer a question, are you direct or evasive? Responsive or vague? Wordy or succinct? Here's where your interviewing skills are likely to match your job skills.

5.   **Are you truthful?** Whether it's references, accomplishments, skills, whatever button is being pushed, the interviewer is always looking for evidence of dishonesty, or, almost as bad, bragging and exaggeration. Don't even think about trying any of them. Getting caught here is a hit below the waterline and fatal to your chances.

Summing up: Be sharp, not slippery.

Mackay's Moral: Eels can be electric, but I've never seen one mounted as a trophy fish.

Quickie—
Rehearsing Job Interview Questions

- Always have four or five key messages in mind. An interviewer's questions may be at the top of his or her mind. At the top of yours should always be the impression, the energy, and the commitment you want to convey.
- Never be evasive, but try to constructively bridge to an answer that is responsive to both you and the interviewer.
- Don't confuse the carefully crafted words of your answer with the content behind the words. In short, don't deliver baloney. A smart interviewer will always demand meaningful and relevant responses.
- With each answer, always consider the next question that it might or does imply.
- Maintain evenhanded composure. A sudden shift of posture or glance can send a powerful signal of discomfort when a question arises. Have your interview rehearsal colleagues be especially attentive to question areas of this sort.
- Distinguish between a question that is lightly exploratory and one that is seriously penetrating. When an attorney questions a witness on the stand, he or she will often use a casual question in the hopes it might unleash an avalanche of unnecessary candor. Be on your guard.
- Encourage your rehearsal partners to sometimes seem disinterested or even negative. Even though an interviewer may be dedicated to finding out the last detail of your career and personal makeup, many people asking questions will feign indifference just to see how you react. Prepare yourself to perform before a "cold" audience.

Chapter 42

9 Motivators to Make Them
Want to Return Your Call

1. Scour the individual's personal, academic, and professional background to identify someone you might know who could have influence with your target. Have your intermediary make an advance call.

2. Find out whom this individual has mentored in the past and see if you know any protégés. Call your target and ask if he would be willing to offer fifteen minutes of career counseling because of his remarkable reputation for management wisdom.

3. Find out your target's favorite charity and pledge to contribute $100 to it if she returns your phone call.

4. Learn the individual's #1 not-for-profit community organization and offer him twenty-five hours of pro bono work in exchange for a job interview.

5. Investigate if the person Twitters or blogs and initiate some clever input on her Internet presence.

6. Discover the person's foremost hobby and offer up some truly unusual information that he would otherwise not have a chance to learn.

7. Read the individual's most recently published speech or article and send a letter as to why you found the talk convincing.

8. Diagnose a new product line introduced by a competitor of the person you are trying to reach and send a brief report

to your target as to why it creates an opportunity for this person.

9.   Talk with your target's administrative assistant and learn about *that* person's hobbies or other interests in the hopes that building a sincere phone relationship with the gate-keeper will help open the gate.

"I miss the steady paycheck."

Quickie—
Lubricate Gatekeepers to Oil the Gate

Gatekeepers, usually so poised under pressure, have human needs just as the rest of us do. Generally they are the Type B enablers of Type A driven bosses. Gatekeepers receive more than their share of annoyance from above.

When you are dealing with a gatekeeper, you would do well to remember the following:

- When you phone a gatekeeper, always ask if this is a good time to talk. You'll find that 50 percent of the time it isn't because he or she is either waiting for the boss or a priority call to come in.

- Avoid calling at high-demand times. Monday mornings, for example, are generally poor windows to reach offices dedicated to high performance.

- Listen. A gatekeeper can be your best source of information on a manager's decision-making habits and preferences. The gatekeeper may also give you important scheduling and availability information on the manager just in passing conversation. Don't overlook it.

- Be specific in identifying yourself and your purpose in calls and e-mails. These beleaguered folk have tons of information swimming across their desks. Be precise in identifying why you are calling. If it relates to a particular document, call it up on your computer before you make the call.

- Learn who the gatekeeper's backup is. Generally there is one, and this person often plays an important role in absorbing overflow work. I can't tell you how key this often overlooked tactic is.

Chapter 43

No Isn't an Answer . . .
It's a Question

Two guys are facing the firing squad. The officer in charge has just finished "Ready! Aim!" and is on the verge of "Fire!" when one of the men about to be shot yells, "Hey, wait a minute. First of all, this blindfold's too tight; second, you didn't offer us a last cigarette; and third, I should get a chance to say a few words, like 'long live the revolution' and things like that."

"Shhh," says the other guy. "Don't make trouble."

What do we do when the game is lost? We sulk. We pout. We grouse. We sow sour grapes. When we've lost out in a job search, it's "How could that company be so dumb to hire her instead of me?"

Hey, that's human nature. The only people I know who smile and hug the winner when they've lost are the forty-nine non–Miss Americas in the annual Miss America Pageant. I should know because I was a judge in 2001.

Here are two utterly unconventional but totally intelligent reactions to rejection.

Let's say you're an outside candidate for a job. There's a grueling competition. It takes weeks to resolve the search and you . . . lose. Call up the winner, congratulate him or her on the victory, admit the defeat stings, and then ask a favor. Ask that person if he or she would be willing to have lunch with you and to share anything he or she could that might help you use this setback as a learning experience and to prepare yourself for your next job search. You don't want to probe into why

184

you *didn't* get the job. You know the company chose wisely. You only want to better understand the makeup of a successful candidate.

I once met an electrical engineer from Spokane playing tennis in Arizona. He knew his ohms and volts as well as he did his lobs and aces, but he had spent a long, long time on the bench between jobs. Finally, he reasoned like an engineer and said to himself, "When an experiment doesn't work in the lab, what do you do? You research why." So, he got in touch with the last two victors in the beauty contests where he was runner-up. Both meetings were worth their weight in Whartons.

After each meeting, he debriefed himself as soon as possible. He noted the smallest details: How they answered questions, how they dressed, what their goals were, their educational and career experience, what they emphasized and de-emphasized. After following up with thank-you notes, he used what he had learned to fine-tune his own presentation and bring it into line with what the marketplace was buying. In his first interview after his meetings, with the right attitude and the current buzz straight from the winner's circle, he landed the job he holds today.

Firms that don't hire you will *never* give you a straight answer. They're afraid, and not without some sad experiences along these lines, that telling you "we thought your answers were evasive," or "your personal style seems incompatible with the boss you'd be working for" would expose them to the possibility of litigation or, at best, bad PR. But it's a different story when you talk to a successful job candidate. It's as impossible for the new hiree not to tell you why he got the job as it is for a lotto winner not to tell you how he picked the winning numbers.

Another very different reaction to defeat is to market the extensive research you have just acquired to a third party. Imagine that Company A has picked someone else in a contest where you were a candidate. During the interview process, you learned information that suggests that a rival—Company B—could have a real opportunity. Perhaps Company A is discontinuing a product line that leaves the market open to Company B. Maybe Company A is going to have serious problems managing a particular district because of pending staffing switches.

In the past, you might have approached Company B, and it could have told you it wasn't hiring. If you present your newfound information to Company B simply as rambling commentary, you are likely to be written off as an opportunistic chatterbox. However, if you map out a meaty business plan that is several pages long and includes how you could help realize this opportunity, it could be a very different story. If Company A hears about this gambit, its current management will almost certainly never hire you in the future. On the other hand, it didn't choose you, so what do you owe it? And who's to say that its current management will be in place two years from now? This tactic has risks, but what opportunity doesn't?

Mackay's Moral: A smart cookie converts "No" into "Know."

D-DAY:
PLAN THE ATTACK

Chapter 44

Bytes: Researching the Hands
That Will Feed You

What's the #1 way to differentiate yourself during the job interview? How do you make yourself stand apart from other highly qualified candidates? Your clothes, your handshake, your aura of confidence, and your professionally formatted résumé all matter a great deal. However, nothing counts more than how well prepared you are for the substance of a job interview.

Spending a few minutes studying a firm's Web site is hardly enough. You have to dig deep and learn what's important to the person interviewing you. What are the company's business objectives? How is it reacting to the latest industry issues? What is its competition doing to win new business? What is the background of the person you're meeting with, his or her personal values, and his or her business responsibilities and goals?

Sam Richter, president of SBR Worldwide and senior vice president/chief marketing officer at ActiFi, is a guru on being prepared. He is one of the better finds I have made in my business career. As one of the nation's premier experts on sales intelligence, Sam's *Know More!* training program teaches executives around the globe how to find information and then how to use it to gain an edge in sales, business development, and account management. I know the Sam Richter approach works because he has made three presentations to our sales force at Mackay-Mitchell Envelope Company, and our company uses his system. We enthusiastically support what Sam does. His expertise may be one of our best kept secret competitive edges. Beyond the business relationship, we have also become good friends.

According to Sam, the most important sales call you'll ever go on is your job interview, and I couldn't agree more. The same strategies and processes used to win multimillion-dollar business agreements, when employed correctly, can help you win your next job.

In Sam's award-winning and top-selling book, *Take the Cold Out of Cold Calling: Know More Than You Ever Thought You Could (or Should) About Your Prospects, Clients and Competition* (www.samrichter.com), he describes the reasons most buyers buy. At least in the first couple of meetings, buyers don't "buy" a company's products or services (note that the "sell" in those first one or two meetings is usually the opportunity for a future meeting and/or the opportunity to submit a proposal). Instead, buyers are buying the salesperson—this person's knowledge and ability to solve problems. Buyers are asking themselves, "Does this person understand me, my company, our unique issues, and how to make my job/life easier?"

This is even more true in the job interview. The buyer, the person conducting the interview, is already interested in your "product or service"—your résumé—or he or she wouldn't be talking with you. What the buyer really wants to know is: "Do you understand *my* and my firm's issues, and what relevant experience do you have solving similar challenges?" The interviewer is asking himself or herself the same questions as a product/service buyer.

When I meet with a job seeker for an informational interview, I can't tell you the number of times I've had people confide in me: "I've spent the majority of my career in the same industry. . . . How can I possibly compete in a new industry where I don't have experience?" My response? That's an excuse! Stop trying to sell your "product"—your résumé, which is nothing more than a listing of your past work history. Instead, focus on the other person and *his* goals. Your résumé should just be a guide for discussion. Use it to tell relevant stories. Remember, what the "buyer" wants is a relevant and experienced problem solver, so *learn about the other person's issues* and show how you can be the one to deliver solutions!

Sam has developed a variation of his *Know More!* sales training program title, *Know More! Job Interviews*, in which he discusses how to find information to ensure relevancy during the job-search process. In it, Sam contrasts two sample job interview opening statements:

Standard Interview: "As you can see from my résumé, I have 15 years of experience in the financial services industry. I have a career record of continual promotion; I've always received great reviews from my superiors; and clients consider me a friend."

***Know More!* Job Interview:** "I was doing some research on your industry, and it seems like a big issue your company faces is that government regulation is limiting the 'perks' you can provide prospects. Thus building relationships is tougher and tougher. Is that true? I thought so. As you can see from my résumé, I have 15 years of experience in the financial services industry, and none in the medical device industry. I'm a smart person so I'm guessing you can teach me what I need to know about the medical device industry in a few months. However, it would take you 15 years to learn all that I know about solving the exact business issue you face—building meaningful prospect and client relationships in an ever-increasing regulatory environment."

The standard interview puts the focus on the candidate's background and lack of relevant *tactical* experience. In the standard interview, the candidate actually guides the interviewer down the path of concluding that the candidate doesn't have enough industry expertise for the job. Unfortunately, it's the typical opening remark I've heard in hundreds of job interviews.

The *Know More!* job interview actually reframes the discussion. When the interviewer looks at the résumé, the natural thought process is to focus on the lack of relevant industry expertise. However, with the *Know More!* approach, a couple of things happen:

1. The candidate really impresses the interviewer with the statement, "I was doing some research on your industry . . ." Those eight words alone separate this candidate from 90 percent of the others who don't take the time to do their

homework. Immediately the interviewer wants to learn more. The focus is less on the candidate's industry expertise (or lack of it) and more on what the candidate knows related to solving specific problems.

2. The candidate gets the interviewer to think differently. Most likely, the interviewer is having an internal conversation going something like, "You know, this person is right . . . we don't really have anyone on staff skilled in building long-term relationships, and that's an especially tough competency to find . . . our industry isn't that difficult to learn, but trying to locate someone who understands how to build true relationships is a commodity that is really hard to locate."

In the *Know More!* job interview, the résumé is used as a guide to tell relevant stories. "Let me tell you about a time when . . . ," "We had a very similar experience that I helped solve when I was at . . . ," "I can completely relate to that issue, and in fact, I faced it dozens of times when I was . . ." The résumé is no longer a potential negative; rather, it leads the interviewer into asking questions where the candidate can completely be impressive with his or her knowledge and problem-solving experience.

In Sam's book, he states, "A cold call is not just when someone uses the phone to make a sales call on potential prospects." According to Sam, "Anytime you meet with someone—whether it is a prospect meeting or an existing client meeting—and you're unprepared, you're making a *cold call*. When you don't know what's going on in the other person's world, what they care about, what their issues are, what their personal likes and dislikes are, then you're cold calling." When you go on a job interview, are you going in *cold*?

The goal is to learn as much as you can in a reasonable amount of time about the other person and then figure out how you're relevant to something that interests him or her. As Sam puts it, "When you do that, you're going to have a *warm call*, in which you position yourself as credible, where you've captured the interest of the other person, and where you can ask great questions because you already understand a bit about what's going on in the other person's world."

A cold job interview isn't just cold at the start. It leaves you and the interviewer cold at the finish. A warm *Know More!* job interview defrosts the doorway. It turns practical research into an enticing opportunity.

In his book, Sam shows how to use free or low-cost tools to access information on companies, industries, and people. Whether it's effectively using popular search engines or accessing data via the "Invisible Web"—the 90 percent of Web pages that search engines don't access—the information that you need to know more, the data you need for warm interviewing, is out there if you know where and how to look.

To learn Web search secrets you probably never thought possible (and that, in fact, are a little scary), and to learn the magic of warm calling, visit "Sam's Warm Call Resource Center." While at the site, you'll find a continually updated list of business information Web sites and search tips, and you can download Sam's "Warm Call Toolbar" so you can access business information resources directly from your browser. (I bite my tongue as I share this tidbit. It's the risk you take when you relay a choice secret. I can only hope my competitors don't pick up Sam's book.) Although designed with the salesperson in mind, the Warm Call Center's principles can be applied equally well to the job-search process because it makes finding information prior to your job interviews easy, fast, and fun.

Following are just a few of the search tips you'll find in Sam's book. They will improve the efficiency of your Internet skills and help you to prepare for job interviews with more relevant background:

Google Timeline Search: Type the name of a company in Google. If the company name is more than one word, put the name between quotation marks (e.g., "acme corporation"). On the Google results page, just under the Google logo on the left side, you'll see a link that says "Show Options." Click on the link. This allows you to sort your Google search results using a number of criteria.

One of the options is labeled "Timeline." Click on the Timeline link and you'll see a graphic timeline by decade, with certain time periods blocked out. Click on one of the blocked-out periods and you'll see a graphic timeline by year during that decade, with the search results only showing information about the company from that year. Click a blocked-out year and you'll see a graphic timeline by month, with the search results showing information that is related to that specific month in that specific year.

How can you use this information? Imagine prior to a job interview you conduct this sort of search. You click on the current month and pull up press releases and articles. You reference this information during your job interview. For example, you might say, "I saw in your company press release from last week that you are . . ." or "I thought that article from last month where you were quoted was . . ."

As you're looking at the timeline, notice if some years or months are more blocked out than others. This means Google has a lot of information related to that time period. Click on that time period and see what you can find. Then, in the job interview, you're able to say things like, "I see that in 2003, your firm introduced . . ." or "I know that over the past few years, you've . . ."

Find out what was going on at the company in the past, and what it's doing today, and you can ask pertinent questions. Read the information carefully and relate what you find to experiences in your career. Then tell great stories about how you've handled similar situations.

LinkedIn.com: This social networking site helps you create connections at companies, learn about people, and ask for referrals. Once you're registered, invite people into your network. Your online network can grow quickly because as people accept your invitations, and as you accept theirs, everyone's network is shared. Once you've built up a good-sized network, you can use LinkedIn's advanced search to start searching for people by name, company, job title, and more.

"Each person creates his or her own online profile, so you can learn a lot about someone's background and interests. If you find someone you'd like to meet, you can request a referral from one of your contacts," Sam says. For example, Sam has more than fifteen million people in his network. Don't we all wish we could say that! "I can type in just about any company in the United States and if I don't know someone there, I probably know someone who knows someone there and I can use LinkedIn to facilitate an introduction," he added.

"If I was going on a job interview, I would absolutely search for the interviewee in LinkedIn prior to my meeting and I would learn about the person's career and educational history, his/her interests, etc." Sam elaborates, "I would also see if we have any shared connections, and I would either ask for a recommendation or referral before or after the job interview, and I might even reference our shared connection during our meeting."

Pipl.com: Pipl is a meta-search engine, meaning that it searches other search engines. Pipl also mines the "deep Web," meaning it looks for information that other search engines might not find. What makes Pipl special is that it limits its search results to people information.

"I use Pipl prior to any sales call, and it's the perfect tool for re-searching a person prior to a job interview," Sam says. "For just about anyone at the executive level, I can find some good information and use it to establish a connection." During a job interview, you can start out by saying that you've done a little bit of homework because you wanted to learn more about the interviewer prior to the meeting (this will impress the other person and it will help alleviate the fear that you're some sort of stalker). Then you can reference what you've found.

Be careful, because Pipl will find everything from a person's home address to political donations and even court records. But you'll also find Web sites where the person is referenced and even articles and documents where the person was quoted. Praise the other person for something he or she did that impressed you. Remember, the sweetest sounds a person can hear is his own name, and a way to endear yourself to anyone is to compliment her on her work and the recognition she's received.

Your Local Library: In his book, Sam notes we now all have greater access to more information than at any time in history. Even so, the average candidate is penalized by an information disparity. Big compa-nies with big budgets pay for expensive databases, where with a mouse click, they can instantly access company data, sort through hundreds of millions of industry journal articles, and locate current and archived newspaper articles from just about any paper in the country. Small companies and individuals who can't afford premium access are left out. Unless they have a local library card.

Most libraries pay for premium subscription databases that you can use for free. Want Dun & Bradstreet or InfoUSA (known as ReferenceUSA at most libraries) to research companies, their competitors, executive biographies, and more? There's a good chance your library subscribes to one or both of the databases. Want to see if the company where your next job interview is has been featured in a local newspaper, or see if the person you're interviewing with has been cited as an expert in an industry trade journal? Your library most likely has the information.

"Your library is an incredible source of business content," Sam says. "What's better is you can access most of these databases at no charge via your home or office computer, as long as you have a library card. Find your library's Web site (for a listing, visit the 'Warm Call Center' at www.warmcallcenter.com), choose a database from the online resource area, enter your library card number, and you're accessing many of the same high-end information resources that would normally cost you tens of thousands of dollars to use."

Another helpful hint from Sam: "If you have a job interview and don't know much about the company, use a newspaper database to see if an article has been written about the firm. In a newspaper article, you'll find information that is not necessarily on the company's Web site, including revenue and employee figures, and oftentimes an executive is interviewed where they talk about the company's direction, future products, and more. Also make sure to research the company's industry. Read a recent trade journal article discussing industry trends. Reference this information in your interview, share data, and discuss how you have helped companies facing similar business challenges."

With the amount of information available online today, there is absolutely no excuse for not knowing something about the company and person you're interviewing with before you meet or call. Remember that the person interviewing you—regardless of how nice—is not rewarded for caring about you. What he or she does care about is if you can help him achieve his goals. Do your homework and you'll establish your credibility, you'll differentiate yourself from most other candidates, you'll be able to ask intelligent questions that solicit meaningful dialogue, and you'll be able to share relevant stories.

Mackay's Moral: Web search skills are the platinum card of the knowledge economy.

Chapter 45

Early Birds Get the Worm,
Late Birds Get the Job

Gregory F. Packer is a regular joe. Nonetheless, he's been photographed in countless publications and media reports because he shows up first in line for celebrity event after event. "He is credited as being the first in line to purchase an iPhone at the Apple Store at Fifth Avenue in New York. He began camping in front of the store at 5:00 a.m. on Monday, June 25, 2007, 110 hours before the iPhone went on sale," says Wikipedia. For all his ingenuity in getting publicity, I don't recommend Mr. Packer as a role model, unless your job goal is to be a unique media icon.

From the time we were kids, we've been force-fed the idea that *first* is best. We seldom realize that it doesn't always work that way. Sometimes *last* is best.

The conventional wisdom is to be first across the finish line, first in our class in grades, first in line for chow, first for tickets to the Beyoncé concert, and first to be interviewed by a prospective employer. You never want to be the first candidate to be interviewed.

Advertising genius Pat Fallon taught me long ago that ad agencies that pitched new business first or early in competitive reviews almost never won the account. Those who were positioned sixth or seventh in a typical review had far better chances. Give any savvy ad agency an opportunity to select a time slot for a client pitch and it'll always take the last one, the one closest to the moment when the choice of agency is made. These people make their living understanding human nature. They know what makes people tick psychologically.

Clients tend to dismiss the first pitches they hear as they would preliminary fights on a boxing card—not to be taken terribly seriously. They're on the card to give them an opportunity to see what's out there, to try out their questions, and sharpen their reactions in preparation for the main event.

The same kind of buildup is used in assembling a concert program. You start with the aptly named "warm-up" acts. They're the appetizers. The headliner is the main course.

Want to see true creative ingenuity in action? Watch what happens when a prospective client tries to schedule an agency pitch.

"We wish we could take the Monday 8:00 a.m. slot, but all our account people will be having open heart surgery that day. They should be up and around by Wednesday afternoon, though."

With most openings, the company's job specs are likely to be vague at first, becoming clearer only after the employers have had the opportunity to interview (and argue about) a couple of candidates. You don't want to be the test dummy, smashed into a wall, so the company can design a better set of wheels for someone else.

My son, David, is a film director in Hollywood. He has pointed out a similar pattern in the selection of films and stars for Oscars. Those that win rarely make their box office debut at the beginning of a given year. The strongest contenders are those appearing at year-end. They end up with far better recognition and recall value in the eyes of academy members.

If you are going for a job interview, try to learn how many candidates have already been seen. If you ask, and the recruiter dodges the question, consider yourself to be among the first or second entrants, and be prepared with a good, believable reason why a later time would be better. Don't be above a little white lie that a conflicting business trip or prior engagement prevents you from doing an early interview. Particularly in this economy, people are so anxious about getting a job that they sacrifice this principle often to their own great disadvantage.

If you can't avoid being first, try to leave the interviewer with something to think about: "I know you'll be talking with other candidates, and it's hard to remember the first person you talked to, but I'm committed to doing everything I can to work for your company, and I'd like to be asked back for a second interview. These are challenging times, and I believe I can make an immediate impact in strengthening this business. When you bring me back in, I will give you a detailed plan as to exactly how."

I'm proud to have known the late Norman Vincent Peale, who told the story about the eager job applicant who sees a help-wanted ad and rushes down to apply. By the time he arrives, there are at least two hundred people lined up waiting to be interviewed. After waiting in line for some time, he bolts out, runs to the front, where a woman is ushering them in one at a time, and says, "My name is Bruce Madison, and you tell the people who are doing the hiring in there that I'm fifty-third in line and don't hire anyone until they've talked to me." He got the job, of course.

Mackay's Moral: The Bible is right, the last shall be first, but you don't want to wait till you get to heaven to prove it.

Quickie—
Pickiness Pays

Ron Kaufman, a friend and writer with whom I have shared a podium on occasion, provided some sage advice on what to look for in hiring. "If you want aggressive sales results, hire those with an energized 'can-do' approach. If you want to give great customer service, only hire people who will run the extra mile."

Sales staff applicants might be led on a scavenger hunt of sorts. He says to arrange for job interviews at one location, but leave a note there directing the applicants to another site several blocks away. Repeat the ruse at the next location, but move the interview a few doors down. Applicants who arrive energized by this process, rather than upset or complaining about the inconvenience, have demonstrated the stamina to pursue sales leads and succeed.

A friend shares the story of how he hired one of his best salespeople. He agreed to do a "courtesy interview" for the daughter of an acquaintance, even though he had no intention of hiring anyone. At the end of the interview, he thanked her for coming and apologized that he really didn't have the authority to hire her. Undaunted, she asked, "Who does have the authority to hire me?" She was hired because she didn't go down in defeat, an essential trait for any salesperson.

I am especially intrigued by Kaufman's approach to filling customer service jobs. He advises you to conduct interviews on Friday at 8:00 p.m. When the applicant arrives, ask for help packing a last-minute customer order before the interview begins. A prearranged "customer" should then call, and you spend a few more minutes on the phone. Watch the applicant's mood as all this transpires: Is he or she as patient as you are? That will tell you whether that candidate understands the importance of going the extra mile for a customer.

Chapter 46

A Winning Suit Trumps

During recent years, no firm came to symbolize the laid-back opulence of the economic boom better than Google. With some "workplaces that feature pool tables and volleyball courts," this Internet giant has bent over backward to woo top performers.

Then tough times came upon us all, including this mega search engine. "Google has also begun chipping away at perks," the *Wall Street Journal* reported in December 2008. "In recent months, it reduced the hours of its free cafeteria service and suspended the traditional afternoon tea in its New York office."

Just months before, you could get your foot in the door of many an employment office sporting a tattered sneaker. Talent was king. Overnight, job hunting became a buyer's market and employers turned downright picky about who will be offered a coveted spot on the payroll.

A crisp and businesslike appearance was back as an expectation on the part of many prospective employers. A *New York Times* article announced "The Return of the Interview Suit." It quoted Gloria Mirrione, a managing director of a financial services placement firm: "We are back to a time when every company expected both women and men to wear suits and we didn't have a Casual Friday . . . They are looking for a sharper style. I recommend a strong suit that says you are collected and ready to work."

Your DNA may promise unsurpassed success. You could have more drive than a six-thousand horsepower locomotive. You'll never get the chance to excel until you're on the payroll. More than any professional category in the business world, sales candidates are screened for good grooming.

The *Times* article highlighted some critical appearance details. For example, a solid black suit screams attention to dandruff flecks or gray hairs. White shirts should be "pristinely clean" and preferably new. Women's tote bags need to provide a professional-looking home for one's BlackBerry.

In other words, don't look like you're going camping. The clothes you wear—and they don't need to be expensive—say a lot about your discipline, taste, and social poise. That accepted, the most important thing you need to dress for an interview remains your mind.

Learn everything you can about the company and its immediate needs. Any company hiring in a tough economy is banking on its new employee making a key contribution immediately. Find out what that is.

Times author Eric Wilson suggested scouting a prospective employer's tastes and expectations before an interview. "The key is to research the corporate culture to learn what a potential boss might expect." I like that research to go well beyond appearance preferences. If your prospective boss is a golf nut or is crazy about symphonic music, be prepared to say something sensible about these topics.

Rob Donkers, a Canadian educator, recently e-mailed me that a young woman sewed up a job as a "software programming ninja" when she appeared for the interview in a Japanese warrior costume. For most jobs, though, the button-down look is the better bet.

When you enter an interviewer's office, zero in on memorabilia and personal touches:

- What books are prominently displayed on the shelves? Can you share a comment or two about an important lesson you learned from reading one of the authors?
- Autographed photos and civic or industry awards can be particular points of personal pride. If you can offer some authentic praise or admiration, consider making a passing comment.

- The individual's laptop, monitor, or other office equipment can open up a conversational opportunity.

A job interview is fundamentally a sales encounter. People buy from people they like. And people hire people they like. It's that simple. People like people who are genuine, pleasant, sincere, easy to talk with, and friendly. Good chemistry and people skills are crucial.

Have a clever story, quote, or anecdote or two in mind that you can slip into the conversation. Something positive and memorable. Billionaire Warren Buffett, one of the few of us who can afford to dress as he pleases, uses an unforgettable trademark line to take a poke at himself. "I buy expensive suits," he quips. "They just look cheap on me." In a flash, he makes himself accessible and unforgettable.

Follow up a job interview with a handwritten thank-you note. Thank-you notes are essential, especially when they mention how you will fit into the company's culture or help meet its immediate business needs.

Paying attention to how you look can help you get a job. For that matter, it can also help you keep one. With reengineering a constant fact of life, employers want to retain people who best present their firm's image.

Mackay's Moral: Dress like a mess and you won't see success.

Chapter 47

Speed-Reading
Reception Areas

In February 2009, Mary Printz passed away at the age of eighty-five. She was an answering service switchboard operator in Manhattan. Some of the calls she fielded may have been long-distance, but they were always straight from the heart. She became the confidante and communications nerve center to a host of Hollywood and Broadway celebrities. A human Google of her day, Mary Printz went on to be celebrated as the role model for the Broadway musical *Bells Are Ringing*.

Never underestimate the power of a receptionist. As I have often said, the occupant of this first-line position is one a CEO is well advised to interview and help select. In fact, as the number of secretaries and administrative assistants in firms has declined, the role of the receptionist has generally become far more influential.

These days, the receptionist who greets you is as likely as not a company's switchboard operator. Note his or her name. Listen for cues as to this person's hobbies and special interests so you can make small talk when he or she next directs your call. If there's a family photo on the desk, that can be another hint to a human touch.

Read the reception area as well as the receptionist.

Some companies will place recent articles about their business or their managers in the reception area. Don't overlook these. Also, many firms now stream video about their latest products on wall-mounted screens, and you would do well to pay attention to them.

Reception area trophies can be killer cues. The company softball teams may be internal legends, and you might suddenly remember how good a shortstop or pinch hitter you used to be. If you don't know the difference between a yellow MacGregor Fast Pitch Softball and a Worth Super Green Dot Slowpitch Softball, this company could be out of your league. Also, on trophies of a different sort: Ad agencies delight in showing trophies for creative awards they have won. Best you know which and why before you show up to admire the silver-plated loving cups.

How about phone protocol? Some companies regard reception areas as quiet zones and won't appreciate your engaging in a cell phone marathon as you await your interview.

If the company is a subsidiary of a large corporation, to what extent is corporate identity evident? If it's all but invisible, the business you're interviewing with could be fiercely independent of its divisional identity.

One company communications department candidate I knew was impressed to see every major business publication on the visitor reading rack of the firm with which she was interviewing. That is, every major publication except the *Wall Street Journal*. Keeping this in the back of her mind, she didn't mention the gap in her interview. During the discussion, she *did* learn that the company was having a feud with the *Journal* at that time. She was able to offer some tips on building a successful relationship with this key publication and mention her stellar list of contacts there. She believes this one educated, reception-area reflex guided her thinking and got her the job.

Observe how seriously security and access are treated. Are people generally understated and soft-spoken or are they extroverted and enthusiastic? Also, the employees who file by you are a fashion show of company dress code standards. Take note.

The furnishings of the reception area are frequently picked by the CEO to broadcast important signals about the company. Does this business pride itself on being cutting-edge modern, comfortably traditional, or cost-trimming spartan? A long gallery of CEO portraits full of cherished memorabilia often earmark a company steeped in history and tradition.

All of the above may be true, but be careful you are reading the right story. That means doing your homework before you land at the reception area. If a new management team or CEO has suddenly parachuted into the company with the mission of overhauling the business, all those carefully read signals may be signs of things that the company wants to change. You can bet that any new hires signed on will be recruited to help shake up tradition.

Mackay's Moral: A reception area can tell you as much about the workings of a company as a restroom can reveal about a restaurant.

Chapter 48

A Business Lunch Is No Picnic

"More decisions are made around dining tables than boardroom tables," says consultant Gail Madison, "but the business schools just don't tell you." Gail should know. She's brought in to counsel MBA job candidates from the premier business schools on matters of corporate etiquette. One association she esteems particularly is her work with the prestigious Wharton School at the University of Pennsylvania.

Generation Xers and Generation Yers—groups that are under the age of forty-five—have an especially tough time with etiquette. Before landing on the kids for this lapse, consider that their parents often share heavily in the blame. Gail calls them "helicopter parents" because they hover over their children and make every effort to keep the kids comfortable and insulated from social pressure.

Fledgling job candidates often learn the no-nonsense standards of big business on a most unlikely playing field: across the cutlery and glassware of a white-tablecloth restaurant. We're talking about the Yankee Stadiums of business.

Gail is a major-league hitting coach who has seen it all and knows every mistake and miscue a job candidate is likely to make over lunch or dinner.

Gail, how important is showing up on time, and how exactly should you greet your host or hostess?

Candidates will race in ten or fifteen minutes late. Why? They didn't pre-drive the route or anticipate road congestion. Worst of all, they come in complaining about the traffic or the weather, and this sets a negative tone. The last new staff member an employer wants to add is one complaining that circumstances were beyond their control. The clock is a very important measure to employers. If you show up a half-hour late, that's still grounds for termination in many companies.

Also, a late arrival can well throw you off stride, as you wipe perspiration off your brow or don't execute a firm handshake. When you're dealing with a person senior to you, you should keep in mind that that individual offers his or her hand to you first and then you are quick to respond. Don't call a senior job interviewer by his or her first name until he or she tells you that you should. It's a sign of respect, not of formality.

Do a polished appearance and power dressing still matter? Or, better asked, has power dressing made a revival?

After the handshake and initial eye contact, research says your new acquaintance will next take a peek at your shoes. Be sure they're shined.

Dress for the job or position you want, not who you are today. If people perceive you as an executive, you have a far better chance of being considered for a more senior job. There are exceptions. Some tech firms won't talk to candidates who aren't dressed in a T-shirt and jeans. But for these laid-back firms, the salespeople are still dressed in suits and ties.

There are very specific rules for power clothing. A navy blue suit still ranks #1 for men or for women. For men, white shirt with a tie having blue and red in it. A black suit is #2. Dark gray is #3.

Grooming matters. Hair that is unkempt or too long works against you. For women, hair that's down and flowing becomes a distraction. It needs to be pulled back. Distractions are a bad thing in the corporate world. Everything is tight and tidy. Looking provocative is out of place, and that includes piercings and tattoos. Every woman needs a little makeup. The three-day-old grunge look for men is, in my opinion, nothing short of catastrophe.

Gail, you have some strong opinions on what a candidate should do with managing the "props" on the table. Were I to sum up your tips, I'd say: Remember the table is not your personal playground. What you point out has indeed aggravated me as an interviewer over the years.

Harvey, the playground metaphor is well put. When you sit down, don't place your cell phone or sunglasses on the table. A guest adds nothing to a dining table. A purse, portfolio, or attaché case goes on the floor beside your feet.

Let the host lead. You start sitting down as your host sits down. You don't touch your napkin or anything on the table until your host does. When he or she takes a drink of water, then it's time for everyone to start drinking water.

So many younger people sit at a dining table as though they were hunched up over a computer. Sit up straight, feet flat on the floor. Don't cross your legs or flip your hair. Having your hands near your face or hair distracts many people. Don't lean on the table with your forearms. Don't fidget with or rearrange silverware, saltshakers, or bread plates. This can be a forceful distraction, and a quietly amused interviewer may start to wonder about the little theater you're staging: "What's going to happen next?"

Ordering can be one of the most hazardous minefields for a candidate, can it not? There are a lot of considerations, and you need to know the rules of the road or you can quickly veer off into a lamppost that can do your prospects real damage.

Don't order alcohol. If an interviewer asks you if you want a drink, it is often a test. Why do people drink alcohol? So they can sit back and relax. That's not how you want to be for an interview. You are there to demonstrate how professional you are.

Ask your host for suggestions on what to order. If he or she says, "We come here for the steaks," that may well be code for what the interviewer will order. If you select a chef salad, you're stressing difference.

If you can, order something user-friendly. Given a choice, skinless, boneless chicken breast—easily cut and mounted on a fork—with mashed potatoes and green beans is not tricky stuff. Beware of dishes swimming in sauce.

The host will ask you to order first. Even if you're uncomfortable with that, do it. Keep it simple. A host needs to match the number of courses with the number you order. If you order a five-course menu, he or she will be compelled to do the same. Think simple starter and entrée.

My single most important piece of advice: It's not about the food. Eat before you go—an apple or a power bar. You will be better focused. You won't be expected to clean your plate.

Handling serving personnel is another test to keep in mind.

Be kind and polite to the waitstaff. The interviewer isn't just checking out how you handle the silverware, he or she is also reading how you manage other people. Don't send your order back to the kitchen.

If it's not about the food, it must be about the conversation. How can a candidate help an interview move smoothly?

Smile. Don't be crazy silly. People like other people who are enthusiastic and positive. They also respect others who are in control of themselves. Your behavior should validate the following message: "I know the rules. I'm comfortable being a key player."

Make good, confident eye contact. That's a major measure of managerial strength and confidence. Hold someone's glance for two to three seconds before you look away briefly. Project that you are in control yourself, holding gestures to a minimum. Keep your voice in a steady moderate volume range. Be careful about ending every sentence with a question—many young people do. Constantly interjecting the words "you know," "um," "ah," and "like" broadcast insecurity and a poor command of the English language.

Regarding eye contact, one of the best tricks I've ever learned is to look at only one of the interviewer's eyes. This takes lots of practice but presents you as a person who is totally focused and engaged in the conversation.

During a meal conversation, small talk is more likely to be part of the interaction than in an office interview. You think the interviewee is obliged to be prepared for this, don't you?

There's small talk versus power talk. Small talk will inevitably be part of the conversation. Be prepared to elevate the game in a natural way that shows you are a serious player. Reference a front-page article you saw in the *Wall Street Journal* that morning or a book you just read. Have something interesting to say.

Because you're out of the office, your résumé may still be an important topic of conversation. Right?

Based on research, consider asking the interviewer before or after the meal is served, "I know you are extremely busy. Have you actually had a chance to read my résumé? This is not intended as an insult, but I know that résumés are often read by prescreeners, and you might not have had the opportunity to see mine." Here's a statistic that stuns just about everyone: 85 percent of the people actually doing the interview have not seen the résumé for the person they are meeting!

At which point, you should be ready to offer a crisp, clean copy of the document (have at least two) in the folder or case by your feet. Know your strengths really well and be prepared to point out how you would be a great fit for this company. As to weaknesses, be ready to identify them—and most important— what you have done to improve upon your shortcomings. Don't raise the questions of compensation, benefits, or vacation during the visit unless your host does.

While the dialogue is going on, are there any other behaviors to guard against?

There are many little tests that go on during corporate interviews, and a candidate needs to know they are happening. No matter how hot it is, don't take off your jacket or suit coat, even if your interviewer does. That can be a test as well.

Be conscious of your bearing. People who have been fired or engineered out of a job can gradually start slumping or give off signals of being defeated as a conversation progresses.

Make sure your cell phone is turned off before the meeting starts. That's another reason for arriving early. If it rings during the meeting, do not answer the call. Just turn off the phone. Or, better yet, don't bring your cell phone into an interview.

I've often maintained the most important dessert in an interview lunch is when the candidate asks the interviewer questions.

Is that ever the truth! Do your homework. When the lunch is over, the interviewer will probably ask, "Well, do you have any questions for me?" The comment not to make: "Nope, I think you've covered just about everything." Ask interesting questions. That means going beyond topics easily answered on a company Web site or the entry about it in Wikipedia.

The most important consideration in framing your questions? Personalize. Ask the interviewer, "What do you like best about working at Firm X?" or "What's the most interesting project you were ever assigned?" Engage the interviewer, and then be quiet and listen. This is the opportunity for interviewers to unfold what they are about. Don't shortchange them of this chance to talk about themselves or to weigh what you hear and determine if you're a good fit for this company.

If you don't attempt to pay the bill, is that considered rude and presumptuous?

Don't argue with the interviewer paying. It's clear in such a situation that the interviewing company pays.

On the other hand, not knowing basic table etiquette might have a hefty price tag.

Indeed, it can. An accountant was up for a six-figure job. He went through the entire interview cycle without any exposure to other managers over a meal. Since he was going to be responsible for entertaining clients, the company figured it would be smart for someone to take this numbers guy out to dinner to make sure he could navigate through a place setting. He never took his napkin off the table during the entire meal . . . He wasn't hired. He didn't have basic dining manners down. If you can't deal with the protocol of a basic table setting, how will you ever handle a business or entertain a client?

Yogi Berra said it best: "It ain't over till it's over." A business interview is far from over when you and your host part company.

One of your last questions to the host or hostess should be, "How would you like me to follow up with you?" Immediately after the interview, send a short thank-you e-mail, and then be sure to debrief yourself into your notebook after the lunch to record what you did badly, what you did well, and especially which questions you answered clumsily or which stumped you completely.

Within twenty-four hours, mail what's known as a "correspondence card." This is about three and a half by five or four by six inches. Several fine stationery companies make them. A correspondence card is a blank, heavy-stock, formal card with no printed message or decoration on it. You handwrite a thank-you note, briefly reinforcing one or two points you made at your interview and include your business card. You mail this in a hand-addressed envelope with a first-class stamp.

Students of mine counter this suggestion with skepticism: "If everyone does what you recommend, no one would be special." Based on history, only one half of one percent will actually do this, so you end up special, I reassure them.

I've shared national speaking forums with a business coach named Burt Dubin. Burt says he saved every handwritten thank-you note he ever got in twenty-four years of life in corporate America—all four of them. The handwritten note is still very powerful, as you have emphasized on countless occasions, Harvey.

By the way, even if you are unemployed, you should have an attractive, professional business card printed up. It's very important that it have a suitable job title for the kind of position you are immediately seeking, let's say "Insurance Actuarial" or "Marketing Analyst." If you are actively searching two or three somewhat different kinds of jobs, business cards are inexpensive to print these days, so have them printed up with different titles.

Even among experts, there are different schools of thought regarding the pros and cons of aggressively following up on an interview. You warn candidates that their insistence can make them look vulnerable.

It's OK to make one follow-up phone call after one week. If you don't hear anything, they just may not be that into you. Or they could be busy. Don't panic. Don't appear desperate—that is very negative and can undo all the good work you achieved in the interview. Wait it out.

Mackay's Moral: An interview lunch weighs how you butter your bread . . . and decides whether you'll be getting any bread at all.

Chapter 49

Art of the Ask:
It's Not Just Your Answers

Countless job candidates come to an interview beautifully prepared to answer questions. The mistake they make is they're not prepared to *ask* them.

At some point in every serious professional job interview, you're going to be asked if you have any questions of your own. This is not the time to ask about salary and benefits. Your tactics aren't to probe for information on your personal needs. This is the courtship phase. You're still a long way from any permanent relationship. You have to strike sparks, differentiate yourself, show your people skills, and be perceptive.

Do you know what kinds of job interviews your cold interviewer really likes? Answer: when he or she gets to recommend a candidate for the job. There are so many, many interviews where the interviewers don't. Successful candidates are the interviewer's handpicked selections, and interviewers root for their choices the way handicappers root for their horses.

Interviewers serve as the gatekeepers not only of the company's personnel but also of the company's values. They are there both to screen out candidates who don't fit and to be the first to tattoo "company" on the foreheads of those who do.

Give them the chance to do the fun part of their jobs—reveal the corporate soul:

1. **Ask about the company's values.** Nothing is dearer to a company than its values. If you can ask a positive question

that links the company's values to its performance, you've already gone a long way toward demonstrating that you're with the program. For example, "Last week I read in *Modern Envelope Reporter* that your quality program is knocking the industry's socks off, and your sales prove it. Isn't it pretty tough to maintain that standard of quality day after day?"

2. **If the company is one of the industry leaders, have them tell you more.** Successful companies, just like successful people, usually do not count modesty among their greatest virtues, and they're not immune to skillful flattery. Ask the interviewer how the company got to be so good at what it does. "What does the competition see when they look at you?"

3. **If the company's in the pits, ask questions that suggest solutions**. Companies in trouble are like people in trouble: They want solutions. They're looking for role models, action plans, and action people to help transform them into winners again. They're hiring because they've got some ideas about what it will take to put them back on their feet. They need the people who can help them execute those ideas, and provide some of their own. Ask, "Which companies in your industry do you feel you'd most like to resemble?" "How do you plan to achieve that?"

4. **Listen to the answers.** Don't make it appear that you're more interested in your own clever questions than you are in hearing and reacting to the responses.

5. **Be perceptive, not contentious.** Don't show off by asking for the interviewer to act as a company spokesperson and explain some embarrassing gaffe like an environmental fine. You're not there to sit in moral judgment. If the company's behavior has offended you, this probably is not the place for you to seek employment. Be an interested and respectful listener.

6. **Don't forget to read the walls and desks.** You may be talking to the consummate company person, but he or she

is still a human being. Is there a three-year-old's finger painting framed and propped up on the desk, perhaps next to a team photo or a Rotarian award on the wall? You should somehow be able to relate to one of these.

The late Victor Kiam ("I liked the company so much, I bought it"), one of history's great serial entrepreneurs, told of a young man who wanted to work for him at Remington. After looking over the applicant's résumé, Kiam said there was nothing available. Rather than ending the interview, the young man offered Kiam a plan. He would work for free for a month, betting his free labor that he'd find a position for himself at Remington. You guessed it—he found some problems during those thirty days, and devised a plan to solve them. He got a job.

Mackay's Moral: You may not be interviewing for a sales job, but you have to be a great salesperson to sell yourself.

Quickie—
One in a Hundred

Among financial services firms, few have been as successful as the North Star Resource Group, a firm with seventy thousand clients. Its chairman and CEO, Phil Richards, has taught business at the Carlson School of Management and lectured at universities in Beijing and Shanghai. He's written a book titled *25 Secrets to Sustainable Success*.

A 2007 Malcolm Gladwell article in *The New Yorker* reported that North Star "interviewed about a thousand people, and found forty-nine it liked, a ratio of twenty interviewees to one candidate." The candidates undergo a "training camp" where they act as financial advisers. That period lasts four months, and during it they are each expected to acquire at least ten real-world clients. "If someone can obtain ten clients, and is able to maintain a minimum of ten meetings a week, that means that person has gathered over a hundred introductions in that four-month period," says Ed Deutschlander, co-president of North Star. "Then we know that person is at least fast enough to play this game.

"Of the forty-nine people invited to the training camp, twenty-three made the cut and were hired as apprentice advisers." North Star figures it takes another three or four years to see if people really have the right stuff and hopes to retain about ten of those twenty-three.

Some of the very best businesses make book on these odds: Only one in a hundred of the people you see is likely to have the goods to be a star . . . and to keep burning bright. As a candidate, you might groan about having to march down this trail of white-hot embers. However, if you make it, think of the security of working with a firm this strong—and of the eye-popping clout that just being picked adds to your résumé.

Chapter 50

Post-Interview Homework

After a job interview, do you know what happens in the office of the recruiter, personnel manager, and boss you just visited? They close the door and take out an evaluation form or a recording device and pass judgment on your future. In other words, they do their homework.

I'm astonished at how few job candidates take their own futures seriously enough to record or organize their notes on interviews that potentially have such an impact on their lives.

If you're going to put your future and your fate in anyone's hands, it should be your own. You have your own evaluation to make, impressions about your performance and about the company.

Those of you who have read my first two books—*Swim with the Sharks Without Being Eaten Alive* and *Beware the Naked Man Who Offers You His Shirt*—probably know what's coming next. First there was the Mackay 66 Customer Profile. Then came the Mackay 33 for Employees and Managers. What else but the Mackay 22 Post-Interview Homework, which you fill out *after* all job interviews? All these forms are available free on my Web site, www.harveymackay.com. (Can you tell I like lists?)

Because I believe so strongly in my mantra, "Prepare to win," I've also prepared a questionnaire I call the Mackay Sweet 16, which you can also find on my Web site. This will help you get ready *before* you ever go to your first interview

You will find the Mackay 22 in the next chapter. Was I smart enough to use the Mackay 22 when I got my first job? No. I did, however, strongly suggest that my three children use the Mackay 22 when they launched their job hunts. They were each ultimately successful.

As for the Mackay 22 form, obviously you don't flip it out during your interview. Don't refer to it either. The job interview is a corporate ritual, and your role in this mating dance is not to take control but to react intelligently and creatively to the signals you get from your interviewer. Getting the job is always going to be your #1 priority, but getting the answers to the questions about the job is right up there as a close second.

Simple discipline. Basic questions. But for my money, simple and basic are the only way to go. This is so important, I'd fill it out even before I wrote the thank-you note to the interviewer!

Complete the following form as soon as possible after your interview, while the information is still fresh in your mind. (Research tells us that we forget 50 percent of what we've heard within four hours.) Then, use it as a reference tool as you move along toward getting the job you've always wanted.

Spend a second "packing your parachute" for the next outing.

The controller of the company at your last interview zinged you with: "Say, in the fourth quarter of 2008, Time Warner incurred a noncash impairment charge of goodwill and other assets at its AOL subsidiary. You don't recall what the number was, do you?"

"Not offhand," you muttered limply. After all, what's this? You're a marketing guy, not a finance guru!

Put all those hours of watching Regis and *Who Wants to Be a Millionaire?* to work for you. And I don't mean remembering Gaborone is the capital of Botswana. Go to the next interview armed with a phone list of "lifelines," and prime two or three of your friends in advance. When someone spears you with a gotcha question, you can be the perfect New Age team player and say, "That's a great question. I don't remember just now, but I know a guy who's a whiz on AOL. Shall I text him on my BlackBerry and see if he's there?"

Elsewhere in this book, I recommend not taking your smartphone to an interview at all. If you decide to do so, make certain it is turned off until it might be needed. The above opportunity is one of the few convincing reasons I can think of for taking your cell phone sidearm with you.

Mackay's Moral: What you gather from your first interview is invaluable for your second interview . . . and second interviews land jobs.

Chapter 51

The Mackay 22

Here is the crucial information you should gather after each job interview:

1. Date of Interview. Name of firm. Phone number. Address. Interviewer. Title.

   _____

2. Describe position being filled.

   _____

3. Last person left job because . . .

   _____

4. Position reports to: title. Who reports to this position?

   _____

5. Key duties of job.

   _____

6. If last person in job succeeded, why? If last person in job failed, why?

   _____

7. Chances to get ahead? Describe. Can you move laterally within the company to other departments requiring other skills? Describe. Does the company encourage educational and training programs? Describe.

_____

8. Would relocation be necessary now? In the future? Probable?

_____

9. Describe the "ideal" candidate.

_____

10. Important information about pay, benefits, etc. . . .

_____

11. When can you expect a decision? Was the interviewer specific? Vague?

_____

12. Five most important questions you were asked?

_____

13. Three most difficult or embarrassing questions?

_____

14. What three things did the interviewer seem to like most about you or your background?

_____

15. What reservations or concerns did the interviewer reveal? What did you say or do during the interview that you wished you hadn't?

_____

16. New company information you learned that you might be able to use later?

_____

17. How would this job/company be a good fit? How would it be a poor fit?

_____

18. Did you mention any references? Which ones? Have you alerted these people?

_____

19. How did the interviewer describe your potential boss?

_____

20. Is this the kind of person you would trust? Feel comfortable working with?

_____

21. Any special conditions under which you might be offered the job? Did you mention any conditions for you to accept it?

_____

22. Fresh from the interview, what would be the biggest attraction to you in taking this job? The biggest drawback?

_____

Chapter 52

The Second-Round Interview:
How to Get to the Finals

Second interviews come in all shapes and sizes.

In her book *Tearing Down the Walls*, Monica Langley describes how financier Sandy Weill settled on Robert Lipp for a leadership role at Commercial Credit. Lipp, who was then with Chemical Bank, had signaled Weill as to his availability to make a move, and a successful first interview had taken place. Shortly thereafter, "the Weills invited the Lipps to dinner . . . Knowing full well what was [going to happen], Lipp told his wife . . . that the evening would be the 'requisite dinner' to see if Sandy and, more important, Joan [Weill] thought the two men could build a partnership." For Sandy Weill, his wife, Joan, was an important assessor if Lipp and Weill could team up.

Social settings, far from being relaxed get-togethers, are often critical milestones where a candidate who has passed the first hurdle is eyeballed by a trusted adviser—someone who may not even play an official role in the organization. That's why it's so important to gather as much research as you can on important interviewers, their most influential counselors, and how they make decisions.

Generally, your warm-up for a second interview round should be even more rigorous than it was for the first series of contacts. The following pointers list some of the most important preparation pointers.

Carefully review your notes from the first interview round:

- What questions were you asked that were most difficult?
- Which answers did you give that sounded most contrived and inauthentic?

- What questions were you asked more than once? (That generally indicates the topic or concern is someone's hot button.)
- What further intelligence can you gather on people with whom you didn't seem to hit if off to see where you can build bridges?
- If there were questions you weren't able to answer in the first round, have you gone back and researched the answers?

Try to find out what other candidates have made the first cut and what particular advantages and strengths they may offer compared with you.

Definitely talk with your executive recruiter, if one is involved, and learn what you can about the company's reservations and attractions to you as a candidate. You need both to play to your strengths and to address your weaknesses.

Prod the recruiter to learn who are the most important decision makers who will determine if you will be hired or not.

In a second interview, you really need to shine. Many recruiters will ask you if you are a morning or afternoon person and will try to schedule key interviewers to fit with your peak performance hours. If the recruiter doesn't ask about this and this is a major issue for you, still do your best to have the schedule work to your advantage.

Study the names of receptionists and assistants from your first interview so you can recall them easily on your next visit.

Research the company to see what is new since your first visit.

Are there changes in the roster of interviewers for the second round? If so, why?

Develop a strong, clearly worded, and compact set of reasons why you want to work with this organization in this job and internalize them. Interviewers will be probing for your enthusiasm, commitment, and clear-headed reasoning.

As you look at the list of interviewers, think back about the previous conversations. Recall topic threads from your earlier conversation with each individual to 1. identify themes you can build on in the next meeting, and 2. assure people you felt your first conversation with them was memorable and engaging.

Give your terms and desired compensation and benefits further thought. Reflect as well on your career objectives and advancement expectations. It's likely someone will ask you more detailed questions about these topics.

Look at your notes from your other second-round interviews in the past with other companies. Some people clutch as the prospect of success increases. Others become euphoric and overconfident. When you *didn't* succeed in second-round interviews before, what were the reasons people gave you?

In Google, enter the following two terms in quotes: "Dean Tracy" and "Round Two Interview" and you should find the Web address for an important article by Dean Tracy, a California recruiter.

In it, Tracy uses the term *pain-points* to refer to particular stresses the interviewing organization may be under. They could be budget issues, staffing shortages, timetable pressures, or a number of other challenges. I would emphasize that you should be listening very carefully for pain-points in the first round of interviews. In the second round, you should be ready to offer tangible suggestions about how you can immediately help to alleviate pain in an organization.

Tracy also gives some excellent advice on how to prepare the three major ingredients of your "value proposition": "having a vision/overview for the job, establishing trust with clients and colleagues, and being able to identify and set goals and objectives."

Never forget you are a salesperson, and the product you are selling is you. You have already succeeded in convincing the prospect that she should consider buying your pitch. You're now at what salespeople call the closing stage. The more you can persuade the interviewers that they can be confident and at ease in picking you, the greater your odds.

Mackay's Moral: The closer you get, the harder they'll look.

GET HIRED

Chapter 53

Job Search of
a Twenty-Something

In June 2009, I learned about a recent graduate from Stanford who majored in international relations. This impressive young lady prefers to remain anonymous, and I have respected her preference. Her GPA was 3.6. Born in Minnesota, her father is an executive with a large Minnesota company, and her family moved often during her earlier years. I learned of her when I met her dad at a dinner party in Minneapolis. He related an incredible saga of how hard it is for even a talented, well-credentialed young person to find a job in today's market—and the kind of persistence and state-of-the-art networking that's necessary to cut the mustard.

I'll call her Ms. S. She started out as an English major at Stanford, intending a career in marketing, advertising, or public relations. While she doesn't have a degree in Spanish, she took courses in the language throughout her Stanford years and spent time studying in Spain.

Your first serious business experiences came through summer internships. How hard were these to come by?

After my freshman year at Stanford, I couldn't find a marketing internship. Firms were only willing to hire marketing majors for marketing internships. (Stanford doesn't have career majors.) That summer, I worked instead as a temp in the company where my dad works. I had contact with different divisions and did all sorts of projects. The next summer, I wanted to go to Africa and do something in the developing world. I applied to several programs Stanford offers in this area, but most of them were health care focused.

Rather than being stymied, you started to work the network you were developing.

That's right. I had met someone who was on the board of TechnoServe, a D.C.-based nongovernmental organization specializing in business planning and entrepreneurship in developing countries around the world. I mentioned that I was interested in doing international relations work in Africa. My TechnoServe contact gave me the name of another person active in developing countries. The program she represented doesn't normally take undergraduates. It places people who have finished their first two or three years in consulting and work for free before going on for their MBA. I convinced her I could still be of help to this program, and I was able to get a grant from Stanford to underwrite my involvement. I went to Swaziland in southern Africa.

I want to point out that Swaziland is no vacation paradise. It's one of the poorest nations in the world. More than half of the population lives on less than a $1.25 a day. The AIDS infection rate ranks #1 in the world.

Nonetheless, you worked with business consultants there, and it seems to have fueled an intense interest in consulting as a career.

What a really great experience! At the time, I had no idea of what consulting even was. The result: I became seriously interested in doing this as a career.

After my junior year, I wanted to find an internship in management consulting. This was the summer of 2008 at the beginning of the economic downturn, and internships generally were still hard to find.

I probably had twenty interviews with all sorts of companies.

I was able to land an internship with the San Francisco office of Mercer consultancy doing work related to human capital.

OK, you wanted an internship in general business consulting, but you settled for one specialized in the human resources area. So, you made an intelligent compromise. But even getting this wasn't easy, was it?

The offer for this internship came pretty late, and I believe my persistence in calling back had a big influence in getting the offer. I learned that you had to keep a prospect fired up. A tip my dad gave me was to keep calling back and following up until someone tells you to stop. Otherwise, he said, how will someone know you're really interested in the job?

Did Mercer like your work as an intern?

Mercer made me an offer to join it for a job after graduation, but I wanted to go into management consulting per se rather than human capital consulting.

So you were now about to enter the general interviewing stampede that happens in the fall of a Stanford student's senior year.

In autumn 2008, I interviewed with at least fifty different firms . . . and maybe more. I applied for every single job that was consulting related. The prospects included McKinsey, Boston Consulting Group, Deloitte, and Bain. These companies ended up not really recruiting new staff, at least not at Stanford. I also competed for investment banking jobs at the same time. As fall ended, I still didn't have a job.

You didn't have a job, but you were making lots of contacts, weren't you?

That's for sure. I got to know people at Cargill who had formerly been employed by consulting firms. And I met someone who was in marketing at General Mills.

Life throws a wrench in the works. According to your academic plan, weren't you now supposed to leave the States to spend time in Spain as part of your international relations studies? Continuing your job search from abroad was going to be no piece of cake.

I was on a Stanford program that put me in Madrid for the winter. From Madrid, I managed to continue my follow-ups by e-mail and long distance. During the winter break and before I left for Spain, I did several "informational interviews" over lunch or coffee to continue to learn more about different careers including consulting, marketing, banking, PR, and consumer products. At the same time, I kept looking for a break. At each interview, I would ask, "Do you have any contacts who might help me find a job?"

Did these executives just shrug their shoulders?

I ended up getting tons of names. While I was in Madrid, I set up an American phone number online so I could talk with people. I talked with people in all sorts of industries. Sometimes I was talking with people in sectors like grocery marketing. I knew that I didn't want to work in that area, but I always hoped I might learn the name of a contact in some area that interested me.

You, I can see, are a determined optimist. Did all this fieldwork pay off?

In the end, a couple of contacts helped a great deal. One of them was a guy who had worked for Booz Allen Hamilton. The former Booz Allen exec had heard I was looking for a consulting job. He put me in touch with a bunch of former coworkers at Booz & Co. and other top consulting firms. Some were a friend of a friend of this contact. Others were former employees of Booz Allen. I talked with them and actually did some job interviews in Madrid with Spanish contacts he had given me.

That point about former employees is worth remembering. Many companies could care less about former employees. But the prestige consulting companies like McKinsey and Booz consider their former staffers to be almost an alumni club. This networking fact is worth knowing because it's also true for prestige law firms, ad agencies, and other top service firms. Some offices even hold Christmas parties to which former staff members are invited along with current ones. The point is this: These networks never die because they are often such a great source for both future business and jobs.

So now you have the door open at Booz. What happened next?

I first talked with an exec in the San Francisco office, asking for an informational interview to learn more about the business. She agreed to do this. Then Booz ended up offering me an actual job interview in its Chicago office, but it said that I would need to cover the costs of transportation for the interview (normally taken care of by the interviewing company).

No doubt it wanted to see how seriously interested you were.

I flew to Chicago the day I got back from Madrid and made plans to travel to San Francisco as well, figuring it was to my benefit to talk to as many people as I could. A week or two after my job interview in Chicago, I got a job offer from Booz Allen.

Congratulations! This reminds me of one of my favorite stories about persistence: The stonemason hammers away at the granite for a hundred swings, and nothing happens. Then he delivers strike 101, and—voilà!—the perfect break. Who knows which blow will cleave the boulder?

So what was the most important single principle behind your success?

It was a drawn-out process, but the importance of networking is at the top of the list. Many of the job interviews resulted from talking with managers who were able to help me make contact with others. I turned over every stone I could just to see what was under it.

As you excavated through this stack of learning opportunities, weren't you learning a lot about how to present yourself?

After my internship interviews, I developed a sense for what things people would pick up on from my résumé and the kinds of details and anecdotes about my life that I should share. You definitely learn what you need to say. At Stanford in the fall of 2008, I often did an interview a day. My friends and I joked that my interview time actually exceeded the time I was spending on school and classroom work.

Did you also adjust the way you presented yourself?

During 2008, I changed my résumé—adding and dropping various things—at least six times.

Give us some particulars.

For several years, I was on the Stanford rowing team. Rowing crew showed a commitment to teamwork and hard work. That participation came up in interviews sometimes, but only sometimes.

Just before the Booz interview, I had added to the very bottom that I played the harmonica in a band at Stanford. My mom had casually suggested I put it on because it showed the less serious side of my personality and that I could be fun to be around.

At the four Booz interviews, the harmonica playing was the first thing they asked me about. I found that interesting because, although interesting, I didn't think it was a super-important fact about me.

Tons of résumés land in prestige companies like this, and it's important to show who you are in the real world. Are you the kind of person others would want to spend time with day in, day out, or when you're walled in at an airport? Consultants clock a lot of time in transit.

Running the gauntlet sharpened the facts you presented about yourself. Did it also affect your personal poise and how you felt about yourself?

I became both more relaxed and more assertive as the interviews went forward because I grew more comfortable and confident presenting who I was. It's hard for kids my age to tell people older than we are, "You need someone like me. I will do X for this company. This is how I will fit in." That's tough to explain with confidence, but after so many interviews, I had no problem doing just that.

You did a lot of aggressive networking to land this job. What did you learn about contacting people so insistently without annoying them?

I go back to my dad's advice to keep pushing ahead until someone says no. You can take that advice different ways. Some people can be really obnoxious when contacting people, but I discovered that, generally, people want to help you, especially if you are sincere in your questions.

Obviously, some people helped me a bit more than others, but I believe every person has a story he or she wants to tell, and I learned at least one thing from everyone I talked to. It could be a tip on how to interview or how to present yourself. If you're honestly curious, it doesn't come off as aggressive. People don't realize how willing others are to help you and how much time they will take out of their day to give you some advice.

In networking, you always have to deliver a quid pro quo. Was the benefit you offered often the gratitude of being an appreciative learner? Is that payment in itself?

Being a sincere and grateful person goes a long way. Another benefit to older people in firms is that they are sincerely interested in what's on the mind of today's college graduates. Candid input is useful to them.

People don't learn how to ask for help when they network until they actually help other people who ask them for tips.

I learned to try to help younger students who came to me and wanted help in tackling their job search. I may have helped them, but their questions also had a payoff for me. They helped me to organize my thoughts about my own experiences in better ways.

A lot of people are really busy. Put it out there that you are available in any way—via phone, e-mail, etc. Some are much less willing to help you than others.

When someone says it's easier to answer via e-mail than on the phone, you have to be willing to float along with his or her preferences.

How influential was technology in your overall search?

Incredibly. Right after you talk with someone, you need to send an e-mail to them thanking them for the experience, mentioning what you learned, and telling them you'll keep them posted. And you have to actually do what you say you will.

I created a folder on my laptop of all the people with whom I needed to follow up later. When I was in Spain, I used the Skype phone system to make free calls over the Internet. Skype made it possible for me to talk with people thousands of miles away. Many of them didn't even know I was in Spain because I had an American phone number.

A couple of career-oriented Web sites were also big helps. Doostang, for example.

Let's stick with Doostang for a minute. This is a career-oriented social network that lists a half million young professional people. The Online Communities Directory says Doostang is "open to alumni and students from globally ranked undergrad and MBA programs." Do these sites actually work?

I applied for internships listed on those Web sites and actually got interviewed. That surprised me. Doostang is more similar to Monster.com. Another Web site is LinkedIn.com, which I would say is more of a long-term networking site.

How about your general presence on the Web? If people had Googled your name, they would have found entries on you. I did, and learned you were part of the Stanford rowing team and that your favorite place to pull an oar was on the Potomac as you enjoyed historical monuments.

You have to present yourself in different ways. Having yourself pop up from a variety of angles on the Web has become a much bigger deal. In 2008, an interviewer actually e-mailed me background on me he had collected on the Internet. I was happy there were only good things about me online.

You seemed to have managed your personal online identity so that it wasn't frivolous.

I'm not a super-techy person. It's not that I've tried hard to portray myself in a particular way, but I've been conscious that people would be looking at my presence on the Internet.

You have to be an excellent time manager to immerse yourself in such a way.

No doubt. It pays to be a sharp administrator and understand that follow-through has to be timely. That could be one of the most important things. I imagine someone who is poor at time management is going to have trouble getting a job these days.

Time management is huge. In the past couple of years my network grew so large that I was getting e-mails from lots of people and it was hard to keep up. I got a BlackBerry last fall because e-mails were coming in so quickly. When I was at interviews all day, I needed to be able to check my in-box between appointments.

I made it a big priority to get a job by the end of the year. I scheduled my time around being able to talk to people. When I was in Spain, I spent a lot of time talking to people in different time zones in what was the middle of the night for me.

Lastly, you don't view members of your network in a one-size-fits-all way. You distinguish among people with specialized knowledge versus people who are bridges to other contacts versus pure-and-simple social contacts. You seem to have a clear idea of the roles various people play in your network.

You can't go into every contact with the same attitude. I became much closer with some people and felt I could be more candid with them.

I also talked with head partners of various consulting firms and CEOs of small companies. Those contacts were more professional. Before every interview and phone call though, I always prepared and wrote out a list of questions. Often, the conversation would just flow from one topic to another. If it didn't, I was ready with meaningful questions. That's important when you're dealing with people who are really busy. They appreciate that you've taken the time to map out what you wanted to talk about beforehand.

Mackay's Moral: To get to play in the majors, major in what matters in the modern world.

"I hate retraining C.E.O.s."

Chapter 54

Shriveling Your Way into a Job

"With more than three job seekers for every opening, more workers are having to take significant pay cuts to find employment," according to a CNN Money report in 2009. The resulting squeeze may be a tighter fit than snuggling into that black cocktail sheath you wore so winningly in your college days.

Any new employer willing to take you on will be skeptical of your intentions and your integrity.

Be prepared to demonstrate permanent lifestyle cutbacks. The new job shouldn't seem like a panic trip to a fallout shelter. Be prepared to show how you and your family are meaningfully reducing monthly expenses to live within a new budget. Perhaps the second car goes. Your stay-at-home spouse is now in the market for part-time work. Private education for the kids may be trimmed back to public alternatives. Yes, even the summer cabin may have to go. A new employer may look for strong reassurance that this is a realistic long-term adjustment.

If you felt out of your depth with your former responsibilities, this may be the time to admit it. Perhaps you didn't like the extra weight of management. Maybe you really were aching to a return to those days as a technician or backroom researcher. Companies know that people won't tolerate ego abuse long-term. If you convince them of a credible, revised self-image, that can be a major plus.

Position the move as a calculated transition strategy. Establish what your potential employer's expectations are. Maybe your new job prospect is only looking for a two-year commitment. Perhaps you will use the two years to train evenings and weekends for a new field of work. Or you only need two years more of employment until you can bridge to pension and retirement benefits. Your chances are much better if you and your employer share a plausible common plan.

A shower of companies—including some giants like General Motors and Citigroup—have downsized to survive. People should enjoy the same right that firms do, but they will only earn it by being tough and credible.

Mackay's Moral: Sometimes good things come in smaller packages.

Quickie—
What Personnel Types Prize

Retired auto executive and turnaround artist Lee Iacocca once said it was an advantage for a manager to get along with people "because that's all we've got around here." What was true for Iacocca is even truer for human resources executives. The HR honcho or employment manager—depending on the level of your job—is considered a company's foremost internal authority on selecting staff. If you don't cut the mustard with these often soft-spoken but usually hammerhead-tough guard dogs, what do you think your chances are of getting an offer?

Not all HR executives are alike, but most share some common traits.

- When personnel types hear anything that smacks of prejudice, gender bias, or good ol' boy redneckism, it rivals the sound of a .45 magnum ricocheting in an echo chamber.
- Personnel types at great companies like Medtronic have their eyes on one attribute above all others: talent.
- Human resources administrators have to complete countless files. Administration may not be the heartthrob of your career interests, but it's in your best interest to radiate respect and appreciation for the need for timely and accurate reporting.
- Companies with poor teamwork behavior are the dysfunctional families of business. The HR folks usually mend the fences, so you're an asset if you come across as a good neighbor who easily embraces company goals.
- Personnel types often have academic training in psychology, sociology, or industrial relations. For conversation, the *Harvard Business Review*, the C-suite feature on the Bloomberg financial Web site, and the Conference Board Web site are all excellent sources for top-notch human resources articles.

Chapter 55

Fly Under Fetching Colors

In the May–June 2009 edition of the *Conference Board Review*, there's an article with a dynamite rating somewhere between TNT and mega-blast. The title is "Talent Is Everything" and it's authored by three senior managers at a Deloitte research subsidiary. Here are four of the power points made:

- "Top executives may be asking many of the right questions, but they often lose sight of what appeals to and keeps hold of talent in the first place. Compensation and benefit packages are surely important, but the opportunity to develop professionally consistently outranks money in surveys of employee satisfaction."
- "Only by helping employees build their skills and capabilities can companies hope to attract and retain talented workers. They join companies and stay there because they believe they'll learn faster and better than they would at other employers."
- "Extreme surfers have used global practice networks to push the limits of their sport. In the 1950s, six-foot waves were considered challenging; today, big-wave surfers routinely and successfully ride sixty-to-seventy-foot waves. Big-wave surfers tend to congregate at specific beaches and breaks to learn their craft, and they connect at competitions and, increasingly, through the Internet. They gain from carefully

watching each other and observing new techniques and
practices under different wave conditions."

- "Cisco . . . has invested heavily in an e-learning platform
  that blows up the notion of centralized training facilities
  and creates a pull platform for employees from more than
  forty thousand business partners, all of whom can access
  analytic tools and information regarding Cisco products on
  an as-needed basis."

So what has this to do with me? I'm just a poor working stiff out on
my duff, looking for a job.

Companies want to hire people with that special pixie dust called
talent.

Talented people:

- recognize the importance of compensation and benefits but
  always rank the opportunity for "professional development"
  as the leading priority in picking their next job;
- join companies and stay there because they believe they'll
  learn faster and better than they would at other employers;
- congregate at skill centers where their skill base is going
  to be demanded and developed the fastest and in the most
  advanced way;
- want the opportunity to "pull" training that nourishes their
  hunger for knowledge rather than waiting for some central
  training office to figure out what program they should be
  spoon-fed next.

If you want to be regarded as talented, your odds are much better if
you maintain—and if you really persuade yourself to believe—that:

- Professional development is your #1 priority.
- You want to join Organization X because it offers the best
  learning opportunities.
- You regard Organization X as a hot spot for learning the
  state of the art in the industry, or you are uniquely skilled to

bring Organization X into contact with those hot spots so it can benefit from them.

- You intend to spend every spare moment and most of your evening hours devouring the best training programs your industry has to offer, and you hope Organization X will help you access them.

Mackay's Moral: The secret of success is really no secret at all: talent plus hard work.

Quickie—
Timing Is Everything

People go around all their lives asking:
     What should I buy?
     What should I sell?

     The real questions they should be asking are:
     When should I buy?
     When should I sell?
     This principle is true when you buy a house.
     It's true when you buy stocks.

     It's also true in managing your career:
     When should I start looking for another job?
     When should I present myself as a candidate when a company
     is conducting a search to fill a vacancy?

Chapter 56

Winning the Circuit:
The *Why* Behind Multiple Interviews

Much can be learned by observing how dolphins feed:

- First, dolphins hunt in packs.
- Dolphin groups, or pods, will herd a school of fish into a dense crowd—known as a bait ball—before attacking. If oceans were boxes, this tactic would be the equivalent of driving someone into a corner. Atlantic bottlenose dolphins actually do drive their fish prey into mud banks.
- Dolphins use clicking sounds known as echolocation. This is the sophisticated animal version of sonar.
- Dolphins may eat plenty of fish, but they don't chew any of them. A dolphin's teeth are structured to catch darting, oily fish that are then gulped down whole.

Modern companies prize teamwork as never before. They want team players because that's how companies work. It's no surprise they interview candidates the way dolphins hunt:

- They do multiple interviews. An interview will be with a person's prospective boss, generally with some probable peers, and sometimes even with a subordinate. In an intense way, the interviewers will bombard a candidate with a barrage of questions. They will often pose leading questions and dangle enticing open-ended statements just to see where a candidate will go.

- A group always has a better chance of pinning someone down than an individual does. For a candidate, a corner is often an inconsistency. Don't, for example, explain a hole in your résumé one way to one interviewer and offer a whole different spin to a second. Let's say you extol team play to the human resources director and boast about being a personal performer to the sales manager. Are they getting Jekyll or Hyde, or both in one, which—as we know—can be far worse?

- Corporate culture is the recognition point of corporations. It's the same shared values that allow the various managers to communicate with each other about their kind of company, people, decision making, teamwork, competitive spirit, approach to innovation, etc. A candidate needs to know everything about a firm's culture before an interview takes place.

- Dolphins swallow fish whole, and it's your job not to be breakfast. In fact, your mission is to persuade your interviewers that you are a smart, spirited dolphin, not a flashy herring, a slippery eel, or a run-of-the-mill cod.

Mackay's Moral: In the job market, you're never the solution to the puzzle if they can't connect the dots.

Quickie—
The Ninety-Day Guarantee

Everyone is offering ninety-day guarantees these days—on everything from goji berry juice to cat litter boxes to contact lenses. If you're desperate for a job, consider what Toni did when she proposed signing on as an accounts payable manager:

- She offered to sign a confidentiality agreement that bound her not to reveal any of the data she learned during her three-month trial period AND a noncompete clause that precluded her working for a direct competitor for twelve months.
- She waived benefit coverage as well as compensation during the trial period and said she would only accept compensation for the ninety-day trial if the company ultimately hired her.
- She said she would represent herself as a consultant if that is what the company wanted and would not comment to anyone inside or outside the firm as to her compensation arrangement.
- She made it clear that she was not restricted to a forty-hour week and that she would happily commit herself to the same work week that other peers in the organization kept.
- If things didn't work out, she agreed in advance to language that made it clear it was her choice to leave, and she had only good things to say about the company.
- She asked for clear standards on which her work could be measured with a commitment to frank, periodic feedback.

Toni not only got the job and the back pay, her attitude won a promotion in a year.

Chapter 57

Landing the Ideal Job

Several years ago, a longtime friend from California called from out of the blue and asked me if I would advise him on getting his dream job, which he was applying for and thought he was a viable candidate. The post was the athletics directorship at a medium-sized university that wanted to take its athletic program to the next level. The bad news was the search committee was interviewing six people for the spot!

Within sixty minutes, I gave him the game plan and I assured him if he followed through on these ideas, he would automatically leapfrog over the competition. Worst-case scenario, it would be a photo finish as to whether he got the job or not. Here's what I urged him to do:

- Write up a three-to-five-year business plan with strategies and tactics describing how he intended to implement the plan.
- Go back and interview the school's last five athletic directors or however many are alive. Ask them, if they had to do it all over again, what would they do differently?
- Lay out a fund-raising program, because most athletic programs are financially under siege.
- Get a list of the search committee members and Google each of them, as well as do your own personal research through your network.
- Travel incognito to the university and walk the campus and talk to students about what they are looking for in their athletic director.

- Discreetly contact the conference commissioner and inhale any feedback you can get.

Of course, my friend got the job, and it was the start of a phenomenal career. Each successive step was built on doing the same sort of preparation that landed him this opening, and doing the preparation better and better each time. The point of the process is this: If you really want a job, there is no such thing as a cold call. (In *Take the Cold Out of Cold Calling*, Sam Richter suggests how to develop this idea in the chapter titled "Bytes.") If you do your homework, you should be able to anticipate every tough interview question thrown at you. If you want to convince people you are the perfect fit for a job, you have to persuade them you know what it takes to do the specific job that needs to be done.

Mackay's Moral: You'll never pass the test without doing the homework.

Chapter 58

Your Designer Job

If you're out of work, and the landlord and bill collectors are the only incoming calls you're getting, who's thinking about how to find the perfect job? Are you nuts? Just give me that old-time paycheck and I'm good to go.

Likely as not, you won't be.

Think about it. If you settle on a job just to settle your accounts, you're likely to lose it. You'll lose the next one. And the next one. And the one after that.

An adage true to my heart: Find a job you love, and you'll never have to work another day in your life.

Joe McCannon is a VP of the Institute for Healthcare Improvement in Cambridge, Massachusetts. He wrote a piece that appeared in the *Hartford Courant* and later was reprinted in the *Minneapolis Star Tribune* on eleven lessons for people about to embark on their new job.

His first piece of advice is to go after "interesting problems, not prestigious positions." The second: "Seek responsibility, not income." The first will keep you engaged in your work, and the second will help you shoulder tasks better.

Down the list, but important to keep in mind, McCannon warns of the "competence . . . trap . . . People who are competent and have a strong sense of responsibility will get used the most." If you don't remind your boss that you're on the lookout for opportunity, you're not likely to get it.

Some people make wish lists when they look for the perfect mate.

Why not do the same as you try to find your next job? This sort of well-constructed list can tell you plenty about yourself and the kind of position in which you are likeliest to succeed. But make sure you are asking the right questions.

The ABC reality show *The Bachelor* has been around for thirteen seasons. Its longevity isn't the most amazing fact about this show. What's remarkable is that at last tally—of the thirteen perfect couples who finished off each season—none have yet made it to the altar, and most have broken up for good. That's probably a lot better than a series of trips to divorce court, but it's also evidence that people often don't ask the right questions in making life's big decisions.

When you design your own "perfect" job, here's my list of the ten most important questions you should be asking yourself:

1. What is my career goal ten years from now, and what are the best kinds of jobs that can get me to that target?
2. What kinds of work do I really enjoy doing? What so absorbs me that I forget the time clock is ticking?
3. What sorts of on-the-job challenges will help me do better what I already do well?
4. What types of skills do I need for a "perfect" job within my reach, and how do I intend to get them?
5. Which sorts of people and organizations earn my trust and confidence?
6. What kinds of people do I work well with? How do I best describe members of the ideal team I want to be part of?
7. What industry and which companies have the best prospects of finding me opportunities to grow when I'm ready to advance?
8. Which companies are most likely to motivate my sense of pride and loyalty, e.g., what organizations will get me out of bed early in the morning or will make me willing to sacrifice my free time?
9. What type of boss do I enjoy working for? What kind of boss gets the best results from me? What kind of boss will

help me grow the most professionally? (These are really three very important but *different* parts of a bigger question: Who is the perfect boss for me?)

10. How important is location (region of the country, large vs. small town, etc.) to my idea of the perfect job, and what sacrifices will I make to be there?

Landing a job you love is a matter of planning and design, not a matter of luck. "Depend on the rabbit's foot if you will," quipped R. E. Shay, "but remember it didn't work for the rabbit!"

Mackay's Moral: When it comes to a job, if you don't love it, you're likely to lose it.

Quickie—
No One Is Immune

In July, I asked readers of my nationally syndicated column if they had any job-search tips that could help other readers. I got a particularly memorable e-mail from a guy named Luke Reisdorf.

Luke had some first-rate tips:

- "Take advantage of classes offered through your unemployment center or local library."
- "Do whatever it takes to keep yourself in a positive frame of mind."
- "Focus your Internet time on networking sites like LinkedIn, Twitter, and Facebook . . . While much can be said about having negative things pop up it can be just as bad to have nothing pop up because it tells a potential employer that that is what you have been up to (nothing)."
- "For a job hunt LinkedIn is perhaps the most important of the sites I mentioned because it is a professional networking site. When you look for a job on LinkedIn and your profile comes with real recommendations from former colleagues and bosses, you have a little more traction."

Luke Reisdorf practiced what he preached. He got a job at Target Headquarters just two months after he was laid off by his former employer. "Even after being in my new job nearly three months, I find myself continuing many of these habits I formed in my job search," Luke wrote me. My hat is off to Luke . . . especially since our firm, MackayMitchell Envelope, was his former employer—a place where he had invested three productive years.

Periodic reductions are the drumbeat of modern corporate life. No one is immune. Not Microsoft, not MackayMitchell Envelope.

"Of course, with the position that has the benefits—medical, dental, et cetera—there is no salary."

Chapter 59

Negotiating Terms in Your
Next Position

When you're getting a job, you're working for yourself. It's time to set higher expectations for yourself than any mean-spirited boss may have in your darkest days.

People always seem to perform better for others than they do for themselves. From time to time, you read about the psychiatrist who has helped so many of his patients rebuild their lives but whose own personal life is a wreck. How about the financial adviser who never picked a stock right for himself but managed to build a tidy pile for his clients?

Not many of us are able to do things for ourselves the same way we do them for others. That translates into whether we're better at our jobs or better at our own affairs. Even people who make their livings negotiating can really mess up in the use of their professional skills in their own personal interests. Not every real estate expert who spends her career negotiating shopping center leases is an expert when it comes to negotiating her own compensation. The insurance company adjuster who knocks heads all day long negotiating settlements with personal injury lawyers still may be a patsy in settling his own salary differences with his employer.

When we accept a new job, most people have to represent their interests, whether they're good at it or not. So we might as well try to learn how to be good at it. Whether or not you've ever negotiated anything else in your life, learn how to negotiate accepting a job offer.

Forget the flowery speeches and concentrate on knowing the other side's strength and weaknesses. In other words, do your homework!

- **Get superior information**. That's why car dealers win in negotiations. They know exactly how much they paid for the car they're trying to sell, and also how much your trade-in is worth. Few ordinary car buyers take the time to learn those two critical numbers. And even when they think they know, the dealer throws in variables like options and financing charges that help disguise the dealership's true profit margin. The result is that only the most sophisticated customers know how to cut a deal without cutting their own throats. The true pro salesperson has customers believing they have stolen the car.

- **Don't make decisions for other people**. When you let them decide, you make them decide. Be clear, friendly, and polite, but don't jump over to the other side of the table if you sense the party with whom you're negotiating is uncomfortable.

- **Stay calm**. If you're tight in the batter's box, you can't hit. Better than average hitters always keep a quiet bat until it's time to swing. Pounding the table only works in the movies.

- **Anticipate questions**. Know the answer to every question you might be asked before you sit down at the table and you won't have to appear as if you are negotiating.

- **Be a spin doctor**. Finesse questions. For example, if you are asked, "What do you need for a salary?" Reply with, "Do you have a salary range established for the position?"

- **Remember silence is golden**. Do as little negotiating as possible. Make your potential employer make the first offer—it could be a pleasant surprise. On the other hand, if you make the first offer and suggest a number lower than the employer was about to offer you, you're giving him a pleasant surprise.

- **Keep evaluating the employer**. What do you know about his or her needs? How long has he or she been looking? Is this proving to be a tough position to fill? Does this firm have the reputation for being a high payer or a low payer? Is it noted for high or low turnover? Does it tend to provide a fast track or a slow track for its employees? A job search can go on for months, and, as we have all seen, market conditions can gyrate overnight.

- **Keep evaluating yourself**. What bargaining advantage do you hold? Top grades? Great potential? Superior past performance? First-rate credentials and experience? Proven skills? Proven loyalty? Will it matter to the company if it doesn't hire you and hires someone else instead? Is your potential to perform of such value to the company that it wouldn't want you to go to the competitor? Can you prove it?

In any job search, the tide can shift constantly and it's easy to lose track of a negotiation. Your counterpart can skillfully maneuver you into a position where you constantly lose ground and never even notice. Document records of each individual encounter and compare positions constantly to detect if you are gaining or losing ground.

Mackay's Moral: The smartest thing you often can do in a negotiation is keep your mouth shut and your eyes wide open.

Chapter 60

Before You Take the Job
They *Offer*, Take the Job You *Want*

The clouds part. The sun shines. You've been offered the job. The brief, beautiful moment in which you can cut the best deal possible for yourself has arrived.

What now?

First of all, return to earth. Don't let the euphoria of the moment cloud your judgment. If a recruiter is involved, remember, recruiters work for the company, not for you. Resist the impulse to prostrate yourself at his or her feet. Recruiters know how to exploit that reaction, and it won't work in your favor. Be happy, not ecstatic. Next, let's get real. Unless you can run a 3.4 forty and throw a football sixty-five yards, you're at a disadvantage.

Most of the time recruiters don't come knocking on your door. You knock on theirs. They know you're panting for the job.

From your point of view, the key is to look at *all* the elements of the package *compared* to your needs.

Now hold that thought: "All" and "compared to your needs" are genuine biggies.

The "all" idea is to eliminate any surprises and disappointments once the marriage is underway. You need to know as much as possible before you sign on. Once you accept the job, there isn't anything left to talk about. You can't negotiate anything after you've agreed to it.

You're in the army now.

"Oh, didn't you know our executives are always expected to turn in time sheets every day?" and "We never, ever allow our people to rent anything but an economy car on the road" and "It's not company policy to allow severance pay unless we agreed to a severance package with you *before* you were hired. Do you have anything in writing?"

These are not the words you want to hear after you've agreed to take the job.

You must have had a few clues that you might be hired before the golden moment occurred. That was the time to do some planning, to map out your ideal package, and to anticipate concessions you'd be willing to make to accept the company's offer.

Don't be too hard-nosed. Be polite, smiling, and, at this point, just gather information. Usually, for management jobs, it takes several discussions to nail down the details and generate a written offer letter.

Now here's the list. The key points that should be covered include:

Salary (and how often it will be renegotiated)
Bonuses and bonus guarantees
Vacation, sick leave, and personal time
Routine work week
Records and reports required
Pension and pension vesting rights
Savings plans and stock options
Medical coverage and other benefits
Interim living prior to relocation
Relocation package (possibly including spouse job search)
Compensation and performance review cycle
Title and reporting relationships
Trade association, community, and club memberships
Office and its decoration, computer and phone equipment
Performance expectations (quantitative and qualitative)
Social obligations and expectations
Community involvement requirements and expectations
Training programs and tuition reimbursement
Advancement and promotion opportunities
Day care policy
Expense allowances

Company car or private car expense reimbursement

Travel requirements—including travel class and accommodations

Severance terms (including noncompete stipulations)

Any other special duties the company expects you to perform (Does the last hire always have to play the Easter Bunny at the annual egg roll?)

Make careful notes during these discussions, and be aware of any slippage as the preliminary talks proceed. It's not uncommon for companies to try to short-sheet candidates they think are really interested in the job or to promise one thing orally and another in writing. Confirm conversations in writing as soon as possible.

Don't accept the offer until you've covered *all*—there's that word again—the topics on your list. That's the best single way to maximize your package.

Don't forget, the secret of negotiating is to negotiate as little as possible. You try to get as much information as you can from the other side while providing minimal information from your side.

Keep that smile working, and if the company starts to backslide, consult your notes and remind it, ever so gently, of what you *thought* you heard before and what you carefully wrote down.

Once you've got the offer, the whole offer, on the table, ready to commit to writing, you're now in a position to discuss the "compared to your needs" part of the equation. This is when you can do some negotiating in the traditional sense. Every company has its own quirky little policies. And so do you.

Your last company, for example, may have provided you with a company car. This one doesn't, even though it has a substantially better pension plan. Is a compromise in order, fifty-fifty on the car?

Another area ripe for compromise is the title you'll be carrying in your new position. Conventional wisdom is: Give in on salary, give in on office size, give in on prime locker space at the executive squash courts, but never, ever give in on title.

That's badly dated advice, and it provides you with an opportunity.

There are more vice presidents around than there are paper clips.

If you're willing to compromise on title, and you should be, you may be the answer to a personnel director's prayers. With all the downsizing and cutbacks, companies are having enormous compression problems with titles.

Consider downsizing your title as a trading card. It's your ace in the hole. Don't throw it away. Hoard it carefully and play it when you need it. It could go a long way toward helping you cut a better deal for yourself.

No matter what the outcome of the horse-trading part of the deal, by using this approach and covering every possible area of employer-employee relations you can think of in your pre-sign-up discussions, you're way ahead of the game, and you're way ahead of 99 percent of all hires.

Mackay's Moral: When you bargain, a demanding style rarely yields a commanding result.

STAY AFLOAT

*"Everybody's getting together after work
to do some more work—you in?"*

Chapter 61

The Multi-Task Master

Mary Weber Nord grew up in Minnesota and got her BA at the College of St. Benedict and her MBA at the University of St. Thomas. After communications management and investor relations positions with Jostens and Hill & Knowlton, she was recruited by the ad agency Fallon Worldwide in Minneapolis in 1984, staying with them until 1992. She then left for eight years to raise three young sons and was lured back in 2000 for another eight-year stint with Fallon as director of talent resources. Mary morphed from being a PR person to a human resources director and ran this segment of the business for Fallon Worldwide for eight years.

Fallon sold to Publicis in the year 2000. This French-based communications and ad mega-agency is one of the four giant global communications firms and also owns Leo Burnett and Saatchi & Saatchi. For the first few years in the Publicis family, Fallon Worldwide operated with considerable independence, much as it always had. Then cost pressures became more intense, and Publicis encouraged more shared services. Pat Fallon became less involved in daily operations.

In 2008, Fallon conducted a round of layoffs, and Mary Weber Nord concluded it might be time for her to strike out in a new direction. She could see a gradual pattern of reengineering that suggested her position might not have the same level of significance it had when she rejoined the company. The expansive growth energy that once characterized the business seemed to be waning, and the spirit of fun was absent. So often, today's human resources officer is seen as the "angel of death"—supervising an endless series of staffing contractions.

Mary voluntarily left Fallon and founded Weber-Nord Consulting in St. Paul. After she was well along with her own plans, the recession hit in 2008. Rather than a recipe for disaster, her new venture proved to be a success. What allowed her to do well? The versatility of her skill mix, and her willingness to do a variety of different things:

- She offers recruiting and human resources consulting.
- She spends part of her time doing fund-raising for her old college alma mater.
- And she's conducting self-defense classes for women.

Mary has taken the multitasking she mastered so well as an agency executive and applied it to managing a diversified series of mini-careers for herself.

Opportunism of this sort only succeeds if you have a diverse mix of skills, and, Mary says, "if you are an accomplished networker who can cobble together the contacts you will need to find opportunities for putting your various skills to work." Finding the different "channels of opportunity isn't always immediately obvious." You have to be willing to paint a fresh self-portrait of yourself, often with a very different paintbrush.

Mary sees her own destiny already taking shape in the lives of her sons. "The oldest is in a medical residency, but the other two are in their early to midtwenties. They're doing multiple jobs, and they don't think anything of earning their living through a mix of specialties rather than just a single career. My new mixed career probably suits my life going forward even better. Originally, I regretted not having more specialized technical skills. Then I realized that those skills I did have probably gave me an advantage. Having spent so much time in communications and client services better equipped me than most for these new job realities."

Baby boomers are up against unique challenges in today's job world. A loyal reader, Shawn Hurley, clued me into an absolute must read for baby boomers. It's a study from the The MetLife Mature Market Institute® prepared in conjunction with David DeLong & Associates. The title: *Buddy, Can You Spare a Job? The MetLife Study of the New Realities of the Job Market for Aging Baby Boomers.* Find it at: http://www.metlife .com/assets/cao/mmi/publications/studies/mmi-buddy-can-you-spare-job.pdf

Get a load of this bombshell: "the Bureau of Labor Statistics estimates a 47 percent increase in the U.S. labor force ages 55+ between 2006 and 2016. This means there will be millions of aging baby boomers looking to prolong their careers in the years ahead."

Those who succeed will match creativity with pragmatism, ready to compete with totally fresh selling propositions for their talents. If you're in this age group, don't let another moment pass before you tackle the implications revealed in *Buddy, Can You Spare a Job?*

Mackay's Moral: A career mixing high-level odd jobs will be the norm, not the oddity, in tomorrow's work world.

Quickie—
Setting Clear Job Measurement Standards

Prioritize and specify the results expected. Don't be trapped by misleading measures. For example, if your primary responsibility is to reorganize your department in the next three months and not to excel in meeting sales goals, make sure this is clearly spelled out.

Clarify the intangibles. Often, people are thrown into situations where they are totally reliant on the performance of others, especially in new product development. Affirm your commitment to perform provided that your associates do their jobs as well.

Investigate failure. If the last person occupying your job failed to meet performance standards, learn why exactly this happened. Your predecessor, for example, may have been skewered for a shortcoming over which he or she had no control. Don't be the second casualty.

Distinguish aspirational from achievable. Who doesn't want to burst through the sales sound barrier? Be sure to clarify what the realistic goal is—not an inspiring, vague desire.

Chapter 62

Knowing When to Upsize:
Asking for a Raise

Asking for a raise can be more traumatic than the first day at the beach in a bathing suit after a long winter of hot fudge sundaes.

Whether it's shipping clerks or CEOs, the common denominator is the same: unvarnished fear.

There's a right way and a wrong way to ask for a raise. Over the years, I have sat across the desk from armies of raise seekers. The sweat-beaded foreheads in those encounters reveal much. Having been a CEO who has responded to raise requests for decades, let me tell you what works and what doesn't:

1. **Remember business is business.** Don't try to use a personal crisis as a lever to increase your income. It's unfair and it won't work. Trotting out little Wanda's orthodontic predicament is going to generate resentment, not sympathy. I'd estimate that over half the people who have asked me for a raise have tied it to a personal emergency in their family. This is worse than a three-base error.

Stellar performance is the only viable basis for a raise increase. If you have a personal crisis, there are a number of means available to deal with it, both inside and outside the company. We're talking business here. Don't try to switch signals from CNBC to the Family Channel.

2. **Know what you're worth.** You can't negotiate anything unless you know the market. Don't try to march in and shoot the lights out by asking for a raise that's out of line with what your company—and your industry—pays people for performing at a similar level.

Learn what your contemporaries and your competitors are getting.

This knowledge can do more than help you win a raise, it can save your job. Ask to be lifted to an unrealistic salary level, and the boss might suggest you get it somewhere else: "Well, Elmo, I know you wouldn't have asked for what you did just now unless you'd checked around and found out what you're truly worth. Since we can't possibly pay it, I can only wish you well getting it from whomever. We're sure going to miss you around here, old sport."

3.　**Don't go in with an attitude.** Calmly decide before the meeting whether you're prepared to live with the consequences of an ultimatum. If you are, then know you can't put it in reverse and back down if the answer is, "Good-bye and good luck." Smart negotiators know that a threat is *not* a sign of strength, it's a sign of weakness, an attempt to get something for nothing rather than a win-win scenario. Once you give the ultimatum, you're forced to back it up, if the other side doesn't accept it.

4.　**Bring backup.** Document evidence of your worth. Like what? Like this:

a. Letters and e-mails from customers praising your worth.

b. Supervisor's e-mails, scribbles, oral comments (preserved in *your* notes, promptly logged) patting you on the back.

c. Your own logs, dated, done at the time, recording services above and beyond the call of duty, such as filling in on different jobs, installing a customer hotline—in short, anything that made or saved the company money or sharpened company performance.

d. Your own files again, now under the banner of "Teamwork." This time, point out your role in the line of duty, and on team assignments.

e. Your progress in education and in training programs. If you've earned any certificates or diplomas, include dates and records.

f. Be prepared to click through your calendar and time planner over the prior year. Highlight what you actually *did*, not what you were scheduled to do.

g. Document your trade association work, your industry work, and also your civic activities, but only those affiliations where the company has encouraged your participation.

This is the short list. I bet you can add to it.

5.   Peg your worth to the future. Show your boss what your goals are for the coming months and how you are going to accomplish them. Specific. Measurable. Documented.

6.   Exploit business timing. Timing is everything. Don't ask for a raise when you just blew the Microsoft account or your firm is recovering from two crash-and-burn quarters. Your future is no more immune from the economic cycle than your company is. Wait until you've just moved a mountain or two or until the sun is shining again. Then go for it.

7.   Read the boss's mood. Know what's going on inside the chief's head. If he or she is stressed out, hold your fire. If the company is doing gangbusters but your department is tanking, cease and desist. Remember your youth. You didn't ask Pop for the car keys if he had had a bad day at the office.

8.   Plan your options if you get turned down. How will you handle a turndown or a counteroffer? Be prepared to be gracious. Ask: What would it take to get that raise next time? How could I make it easy for you to say yes? Should I set a date six months from now to revisit my candidacy? Are your financial goals achievable in the time frame you have defined? Is your salary expectation unreasonable given the job you need done?

That's it. It wasn't so tough, was it? These are just commonsense rules, as easy as one, two . . . eight. Follow them and you will dramatically increase your odds of fattening your salary.

Mackay's Moral: Knowing how to ask for a raise is a skill you can take to the bank.

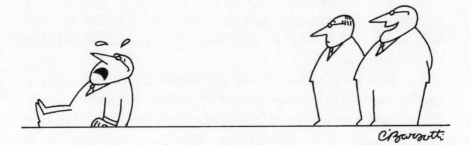

"*Oh, sure, that could be us tomorrow, but it's him today.*"

Quickie—
Peers and Partners

Learn who your silent evaluators are.

Find out quickly which internal candidates were passed over in choosing you for the job you have just gotten. These are not necessarily rivals ready to help you fail. Remember, they know the ropes and have far more internal knowledge of the organization than you do. If they have true potential, could these people be your best backup? Could grooming them to fill your job improve your own chances for further advancement?

Where are lateral relationships in your company the worst? Perhaps you're in manufacturing and your team has a notorious reputation in the distribution department—always finishing production deadlines at the last moment. Maybe you're in advertising and the creative people have a lousy record of keeping accounting records for the control people. You can make great peer group gains by correcting long-standing organizational resentments.

Members of task forces and ad hoc committees are often informal assessment teams of a new player's effectiveness. If a committee's work looks like a thankless waste of time, either help shoulder the drudgery or help change the team's mission.

Stay in touch with recruiters and the personnel department. They will track your placement to make sure it was successful. These people can also help facilitate if a roadblock suddenly emerges, like an uncooperative coworker or if a housing deal goes bust and suddenly sidetracks your time.

Your former company may be eager to torpedo your new job, especially if you left on hostile terms. Monitor the gossip mill.

Chapter 63

This Time Around:
Swearing Off Career Obsolescence

Saloon demolisher Carrie Nation campaigned with irrepressible fervor against drink until her death in 1911. In fact, she claimed to have "smashed five saloons with rocks" ere she ever "took a hatchet" to dens of booze. Her verdict on life: "You have put me in here a cub, but I will come out roaring like a lion, and I will make all hell howl!"

Whether you round out the evening with a Stoli martini—shaken not stirred—is your business, not mine. But it doesn't hurt to put some Carrie-style fervor to work for you in swearing off being a patsy for career obsolescence:

- I will never let a week lapse without having lengthened and strengthened my personal network.
- I will never forget that education is a lifelong pursuit, and I will devote at least as much of my free time to continuing education as I do to personal entertainment.
- Rather than using good times as opportunities to coast, I will always regard them as moments to prepare myself and my career for the inevitable downturn that will follow.
- Rather than using bad times as excuses to languish in self-pity, I will use every spare moment to strengthen my skills and keep myself on top of the rapidly evolving technologies and skill sets of my industry or profession. This will maximize my upside when the economy inevitably surges.

Carrie Nation

- I will remain vigilantly aware of mainstream news, the economic environment, the state of my industry, and the performance of my firm so that I am not surprised by big-picture trends that could affect or even demolish my job.

- I will always discipline myself to "read" the realities of my present workplace and to adjust my job description, working hours, time management plan, and overall game strategy regularly to new business priorities.

- At least twice each year, I will identify people who are in positions I could realistically expect to occupy within three to five years. I will examine their academic and experience credentials, determining how theirs differ from mine, and map out a realistic plan as to how I intend to close that gap.

- In the belief that killing time isn't murder, it's suicide, I will recognize that the Internet and modern information technologies are not eye-candy time wasters. They are, by far, the most powerful information sources ever known, and I will exploit them.

- Since modern life is comprised of multiple career routes and job options, I will regularly have in mind an alternate way to make a living, should my present position vanish for some unforeseen reason . . . and I will have a path in mind of the network of people who can make those options happen.

Mackay's Moral: I will never again tolerate the excuse that I am a victim of circumstances . . . and I pledge to regroup from any serious setback with a passion that will make all hell break loose!

AFTERTHOUGHTS

Kurt Einstein's and Harvey Mackay's
20 Most Revealing Interview Questions

There are always more job candidates than there are jobs, so it's a lot easier to eliminate unsuitable candidates than to attempt to find the one perfect applicant. An interview is a kind of ritual duel, where the interviewer is continually thrusting and probing for information, hoping to draw blood, while the candidate is parrying, trying to stay alive. Every question is a potential trap, where saying either too much or too little can be fatal.

The late Dr. Kurt Einstein was a guru in assessing human talent and coached thousands of executives and candidates in the art of successful interviewing. What Peter Drucker was to management, Kurt Einstein was to talent evaluation. Kurt was not only a consummate professional, he was also one of my best friends. We met through the Young Presidents' Organization (YPO), and both of us traveled the world as resources at YPO universities. I had the privilege of studying at his feet. His comments in the following exercise apply to the interviewer. Mine are advice for the interviewee.

1.   What have you been criticized for during the last four years?
Kurt Einstein: It's interesting to know what the candidate would admit to.

Harvey Mackay: This question is a real test of your negotiating skills—that is, negotiating as in, "He negotiated the rapids without tipping over in his canoe and drowning." You must provide something that isn't so serious as to be disqualifying yet not so trivial as to appear that you're either concealing your flaws or taking the question too lightly. I'd give high marks to a candidate who came up with something like, "I offered some ideas that I felt were constructive, but I was told not to rock the boat" or "I usually finished my assignments more quickly than my peers and some of them resented it" or "I'd take courses at night when everyone else was in the bowling league and I was told I was an oddball." Don't try these answers, though, unless you can back it up, because the inevitable follow-up request is, "OK, wise guy, prove it." I have to admit that other experts are quite critical of the "Little Ms./Mr. Perfect" answer, like "I'm a workaholic," or "I'm a stickler for detail." The answers I give here don't go quite that far, but they are borderline. The other experts would advise shifting the emphasis off yourself with something like, "I'm learning to be more tolerant of the mistakes of others." If you ask me, that's a distinction without a difference. I still think we've got the right approach.

2. Did you agree or disagree with the criticisms and why?

KE: If he agreed with some, you've identified an area of weakness; if he disagreed with all—an inflexible candidate, hard to manage.

HM: Agreeing with some of the criticisms seems to me to be a lot better answer than agreeing with none of them or all of them. Only a megalomaniac thinks he or she is always right and only a schnook thinks he or she is always wrong.

3. Where would you like to be in three to five years?

KE: Observe whether the candidate plans ahead and sets goals.

HM: Bag this answer: "I'd like your job." It's been overworked more than "Officer, I didn't know I was speeding."

3a. And how do you expect to get there?

KE: This will indicate whether the previous answer was truthful or programmed. Ask the candidate to explain in detail.

HM: Get beyond the obvious—e.g., "hard work" or "I plan to take lots of courses." Be clear and specific as to how to meet the requirements and responsibilities and obtain the skills to execute your career plan. You should describe how you set goals, stay focused, and adjust your plan to meet changing conditions.

4. What would you like to change in this job to make it ideal?

KE: Why would he want to change it?

HM: "I don't think it should be changed. I do think it has to be mastered, and that's an exciting and challenging opportunity. Obviously, at some point in my career, I'd hope to be able to handle even more responsibility."

4a. *How would you describe the most and least ideal boss you could choose?*

KE: Indicates personality preferences. Indicates "would he or she fit with future boss?"

HM: Cute, isn't it? Particularly since you probably don't have a clue at this time what your potential boss is like. You should finesse this one a bit: "I've worked with hard-driving, demanding bosses, and I've worked with bosses who've had such a light touch on the throttle, I've barely had any real supervision or direction. I can adapt to any style." And then, move in for the kill: "But if you really pinned me down, I'd say it would be someone who gave me enough direction so I had a specific idea of what was expected of me and had enough restraint to let me do my thing without hovering over me every step of the way."

5. *What activities in your position do you enjoy most?*

KE: Indirect way of ascertaining areas of weakness.

HM: If you have strong feelings about what you like best, you're also revealing the opposite—what you like least. What are good things to like least? Well, for one, "bad morale." So, you might say, "Being part of a winning team." Who wants to be part of a losing one?

6. *How would you describe yourself with three adjectives?*

KE: Delve for three negative adjectives.

HM: Here's another loaded gun. Obviously, no negative adjectives need apply, but even positive ones can have negative implications if they're grouped in a way that suggests a weakness. For instance, "intelligent, efficient, reliable." All great attributes, but when grouped together suggest an absence of human qualities. Is this person arrogant and aloof? Does he or she get along with people? The grouping "friendly, cooperative, a team player" suggests fine personal qualities but a possibly weak performer. Best to combine a few virtues to suggest strengths in both ability and personality, such as "goal-oriented, likeable, successful."

6a. *How would your subordinates describe you with three adjectives?*

KE: What are the differences? Is the candidate sensitive to how other people see him or her?

HM: In my opinion, the correct response is to give the same answer you gave for number 6, and then smile sweetly and wait for the next question.

7. Do you think you praise enough?

KE: Secure people have fewer problems giving praise than insecure people. Psychological attitude toward praise indicates interest and ability to motivate. Development of self-esteem.

HM: "I love to get it, so I love to give it."

8. What would you do if you detected a peer falsifying expense records?

KE: Indicates passive or active approach. Common answers: a. It's not my business, b. Report it, c. Give warning. Gives indication as to morality, honesty, and ethics.

HM: In my opinion, the first answer is so bad I'd be tempted to stop the interview right there, if I were the interviewer, and send the candidate home. If you can't even be trusted to protect the company's interests against dishonesty, why should the company hire you? This isn't swiping cookies out of your third grade classmate's lunch pail. This is the real world. So get real. The third answer is acceptable, barely. It finesses the conflict between being a squealer and letting someone rip off your employer. Understandable, but still weak. Two is best. There's a fourth approach, another finesse, which has the virtue of being a bit more proactive than the third answer: Confront culprits point-blank and try to persuade them to change the erroneous report without issuing a specific threat as to what your conduct will be if they don't.

9. What would you do if the company you just joined gave you three thousand dollars to spend during the first year in any way you felt appropriate?

KE: May reveal areas of weakness if job related, or poor attitude if not job related. Important question is WHY?

HM: The obvious answer is the right one: a job-related use, such as taking courses. But you must be prepared for the inevitable follow-up question "Why?" because it is intended to probe for evidence of weakness, such as your lack of adequate experience or training for the position you're seeking. Be sure if you answer "education," the course work you describe is more advanced than that required for the immediate job.

10. If you had a choice, would you rather draw up plans or implement them?

KE: Draw up: Has tendency to think, innovate, conceptualize, theorize, risk taker. Implement: Has tendency to be a doer, follower (can be positive or negative).

HM: In a booming economy, don't choose "implement" unless the major piece of equipment used in the job you are applying for is a broom. In a down economy, companies want action-oriented players who get results fast. Being an implementer in tough times can be seen as a positive.

11. State three situations in which you did not succeed. Why?

KE: Does he or she admit to any? Blame others? Is the candidate self-assured? Has he or she learned from it, and if so, what?

HM: Kurt's notes are the elements of a winning answer. First, admit to having failed at some things. One example is too few: It suggests rigidity, a willingness to make only the barest, most grudging admission of the possibility of error. Three examples are too many. That response suggests that had the questioner asked for more than three, hey, no problem, you would have been able to come up with whatever number of additional failures were needed. Pick two—e.g., an attempt to get an A+ that netted only an A. Or a second-place finish in whatever. Hardly "real" failures, but admitting to having caused several total disasters is not in your best interests. Next, obviously, you don't "blame others" for your own failures. And, of course, you are "self-assured." Finally, what "you've learned" is to try harder next time, be better prepared, not to let defeat get you down or become a habit, and that succeeding is a lot better than failing.

12. When you fire somebody, what would be your key objective? Why?

KE: Look for: "It was deserved." "It's beyond my control." "Protect myself legally." "Keep company image clean." "Get inside scoop/grapevine." Or: Considers employee's feelings, shows sympathy.

HM: "I felt I was acting in the best interests of both the company and the employee in question." Follow-up question: "Why?" Follow-up answer: "From the company's point of view, the employee's performance did not meet our standards and expectations. Despite repeated attempts to help the employee improve, performance remained inadequate."

13. What personal need do you expect to satisfy by accepting this position?

KE: This gives candidates the chance to identify their most important career needs.

HM: Your needs better track the company's needs pretty closely, or what you're still going to be needing is a job. I would lean toward answers that stress the satisfaction of setting goals, achieving them, and setting new goals. Companies see employees the way track-and-field fans see high jumpers. Every time the athlete clears the bar, they want to set it a little higher for the next jump.

14. *What would you like to change in this job to make it ideal?*

KE: How does the candidate respond when an authority figure makes an error?

HM: Here's the all-time trick question: Question 4 is repeated here as question 14. Did you notice? If so, now what? Is this some kind of weird psychological test? A memory game? Do you pretend it didn't happen? Is the interviewer trying to see if you change your answer? Do you correct him or her? Are you made noticeably nervous by the interviewer's "error"? Kurt doesn't give us a clue as to what the "right" response is, but my guess is that the only really wrong one is to overreact and make a big deal out of it. I'd answer in totally deadpan fashion, "I think this may have come up earlier, and as I recall, I said I felt no need to change the job itself; the need was to master the job as it is and then, if the opportunity arose, to assume even greater responsibilities at some later point."

15. *We all fib occasionally. Would you say something that is not entirely true? Give me three examples when you did.*

KE: Discuss: Significant, insignificant, borderline lies.

HM: A tougher version of question 1. Again, this is to test your ability to walk the line between the answer that is too revealing and the answer that is too concealing. But there's really a lot more happening here than meets the eye. Like question 14, this one is designed to measure how forthright and honest you are in your reactions to an authority figure. This time, the authority figure has not just made an inadvertent "error." He or she has issued a *pronunciamento, a* moral judgment set forth as a statement of fact. The interviewer is saying that everyone lies, and everyone includes you, so the premise on which the question is based is: you lie. All beautifully contained and concealed in this perfectly innocent-sounding, perfectly conventional, perfectly legal, plain vanilla interview question. What's happening here is you're being tested not only on whether you fib but whether you will allow a perfect stranger to say that you do, when the person saying it can have a considerable impact on your future. Am I reading too much into this? Perhaps. Most of us do, in fact, fib. But remember, this test isn't designed to provide employment for candidates who most nearly correspond to the norm. It's designed to weed out average applicants and locate exceptional ones. I don't see anything the matter with challenging the we-all-lie premise. I'd answer as follows: "Oh, I don't think everyone lies, or, as you say, fibs. In my life, I've known people I believe never to have lied. So I have to tell you, I don't think your premise is correct. I cannot say I have met that standard myself and have never lied. I know I have. I will say, though, that when I have lied, I've tried to confine it to social situations. I'm afraid not every baby I've seen is movie star material, and not every meal where I've been a guest has been worth four stars in the Michelin Guide."

16.   What benefits can be expected from threatening an employee to do better?

KE: If answer is other than "none," probe further for candidate management and motivation style.

HM: Threatening employees is usually not an attempt to improve performance. It's a calculated prelude to discharge. The threat is used in hopes of thwarting subsequent legal action—"We warned him or her, so the firing shouldn't have come as a surprise." No one is fooled. The hope is that the employee will get the message and move on before the discharge takes place. And *that* is the only benefit of threatening.

16a.   When would you threaten an employee in order to improve his or her performance?

KE: Ask for examples.

HM: Threats are as common in business as coffee breaks. Employers threaten employees. Unions threaten management. Management threatens unions. A customer threatens a supplier with replacement if punctuality doesn't improve. By threatening, the customer is looking for an easy way out. Thus, a threat is very often a sign of weakness rather than of strength. The same is true for an employer dealing with an employee. Threats only make real sense when they are part of a disciplinary process that might end in firing the employee.

17.   If you encountered serious difficulties on the job for which you are now interviewing, what would they be?

KE: Reveals candidate's area of weakness or fear.

HM: By now you should be able to ace this kind of probe. What you're concerned about, of course, is not failure but success. You anticipate no difficulties but would hope to work in an environment that values teamwork, rewards initiative, provides opportunities for advancement, achieves its goals, and is a congenial place to work.

18.   What are three things you are afraid to find in this job?
KE: Explores candidate's fears (realistic or not).
HM: Another attempt to get you to spout negatives and reveal yourself as a bundle of psychoses. Since you fear nothing, you give the time-honored positive response. Your only concerns are that you have the opportunity to excel, and since your research has led you to believe this is the kind of place you can do it in, well, it's not a concern at all.

19.   We all have negative areas we would like to improve. Do you agree? If you do, could you give me three areas in which you would like to improve?
KE: Weakness; understanding of oneself.
HM: Another "we-all" question, but this time worded in such a way that you're given the option of agreeing or not. So, now you can agree. Again, I'd stick with providing two instead of the requested three, on the theory that giving only one shows arrogance and inflexibility and three is a classic display of wimpiness in going along with whatever the authority figure demands. And again, I'd try to turn the question around so you can give yourself the opportunity to play to your strengths and not to your weaknesses. Thus, you want to continue to grow professionally. While you are certain you have the tools necessary to perform the job in question, no one can have too much education or preparation, and you're going to continue to take self-improvement courses, both those that provide professional training and those that are designed to help upgrade personal and interpersonal skills. Secondly, you never seem to have enough time to perform service work on behalf of others, and there are various volunteer organizations you're interested in, such as Habitat for Humanity, Rotary, and so on.

20.   How do you motivate people?
KE: a. Threat, b. Fear, c. Example.
HM: I've already indicated why I believe threats are overrated and misunderstood. Fear works. For example, Bob Knight, the former Indiana University and

Texas Tech basketball coach, is a master at goading players into performing. But what motivates a nineteen-year-old college sophomore to excel in athletics over a brief, intense time span as part of a team, all of whose members have been equally abused by "Coach," won't work in just any setting. Where the personnel are mature, experienced, and professional they will not regard mistreatment and claims of absolute authority as a source of inspiration.

One of the most powerful motivators is "peer pressure." That's what the Armed Forces use to motivate soldiers. What makes an eighteen-year-old kid risk his life in combat? It sure isn't because he thinks his second lieutenant is such a prince. It's because his buddies, the guys he's bivouacked with since boot camp, will think he's a coward if he doesn't go with the flow. But peer pressure, despite its powerful impact as a motivator, is, like the other motivators, imposed from without, which means the values expressed are someone else's. It tends to work best on young people, because their personal set of values is not yet fully formed, and they are more easily influenced by others.

I think the best motivator, the one that is most likely to stick with you, even for a lifetime, is the one that comes from within, the voice inside you that tells you to show 'em your stuff. If you're looking for a one-word description of a truly motivated person, I'd say "self-starter." Sure, the spark that lit that fire had to come from somewhere. It can be the product of your home environment, your religious upbringing, your drive to achieve success. But wherever that spark comes from, once it becomes part of you, what you believe, then external forces are merely temporary, coming and going with the people who are imposing them.

To stay motivated, you sometimes have to play a trick on yourself. I call it the peas/pie routine. (That is, you have to eat your peas if you want a piece of pie.)

EXTRA: When do you think you have arrived? (Definition of success)

KE: a. When I can collect Social Security, b. When I am president of the company, c. When I have your job, d. I will never arrive—neurotic need, constantly chafing at the bit. Explain "compulsive achievers." Difference between "wanting" and "having" to succeed.

HM: My definition of "having arrived" is when you learn how to realize your passion in life in a meaningful way, and are rich enough to value time and respect how you use it in realizing your goals.

The Mackay Lucky 13
A List of Life-Changing Books

Perhaps I'm shooting myself in the foot here, but since the purpose of this book is to help you get a job, I'm going to provide you with my list of some of the *other* best job-hunting books out there. I consulted head-hunters, human resources managers, recruiters, job hunters, and book-stores. I reviewed dozens of their suggestions, found a few others on my own, and compiled this list, "The Mackay Lucky 13."

Following, in no particular order, are brief descriptions of these books, all currently in print, readily available at bookstores or the library, and written by people who want to help you, too.

Good luck!

What Color Is Your Parachute? **by Richard N. Bolles, Ten Speed Press**

This granddaddy of job-search books has been revised and updated annually since 1970 to give job hunters the most current information. There is good reason this book has sold more than ten million copies since it was first published: It is a practical manual divided into two main parts, "Finding a Job" and "Finding a Life."

Part I, "Finding a Job," takes the reader from the hard times to the things they never taught you in school about job hunting. It offers sixteen different ways to find a job, including the five best and five worst ways; Web sites to direct you through the ins and outs of hunting on the Internet; plenty of advice on résumés, interviews, and salary negotiations; and special tips for changing careers, starting your own business, and what's in store for workers over fifty.

Part II, "Finding a Life," shifts the focus to the moment you decide that "this time you're not going to do just a traditional job-hunt; you're going to do a life-changing job-hunt or career-change: one that begins with *you* and what it is that *you* want out of life." The workbook format assists the reader in thinking through goals and reasons. The bulk of this section focuses on the seven steps to finding a life that has meaning and purpose. It's not a book you can read in an afternoon, but it is a great start to figuring out what you really want to do and be "when you grow up." You'll never regret buying this book—it's a keeper.

You, Inc. by Harry Beckwith and Christine Clifford Beckwith, Business Plus

The subtitle of this book is *The Art of Selling Yourself*. As I have pointed out repeatedly in my book, this is the biggest sales job you'll ever have. When *You, Inc.* was published a few years ago, I was asked to provide an endorsement, which I eagerly gave: "The one book on marketing I'd have if I could have just one."

While this book is not specifically aimed at the job hunter, the hundreds of short lessons would prepare any job seeker to present the best possible image. The inspiring stories, true-life examples, and solid advice flow freely throughout the commonsense lessons in a very readable format. Some examples: "Living Is Selling." "Life is a sale. And the path to success at both living and selling is the same." "Be grateful for your strengths, but work on your weaknesses." The shortest lesson in the book is entitled "Tricks and Shortcuts." The complete text is this: "There are none." The authors discuss communication skills at length, summing up the "real first rule" of communication: "Communicate so that you cannot be misunderstood."

One of my favorite gems concerns the heart of every transaction: "Inexperienced sales people start their pitches with the price and the product, then talk about the company. Only at the end, and perhaps not even then, do they finally sell themselves. Experienced salespeople proceed in the opposite direction. They sell themselves and their organization, then discuss the product. At the end—at the very end—they say, 'Now, let's talk about how little this costs, considering everything you will get.'" What interviewer wouldn't be impressed?

If You Don't Know Where You're Going, You'll Probably End Up Somewhere Else by David P. Campbell, Sorin Books

Your first clue that this book will be helpful is that it's written by the coauthor of the Strong-Campbell Interest Inventory, an assessment tool used by many schools to guide students toward career choices based on their personal interests.

While the advice seems at first to be geared toward those who are looking for their first "real" jobs, it has plenty of useful information for anyone interested in reevaluating his or her career choices. Campbell starts with the premise that what we all want are choices, and focuses on how to create opportunities for yourself. He writes, "You will realize that the greatest tragedy in life is to have no options, to have no choices. Consequently, when you are planning your future, you should plan it in a way that will give you a range of choices."

Planning is "a matter of probabilities," he says, which means that your plans will work sometimes, and not work other times. "Nothing in life is a sure thing," he counsels, "and any plans you make for the future will have to deal with uncertainty." Clearly, this approach makes sense for job hunters at any stage.

Campbell takes planning a step further by showing his readers how to best assess their assets, which include talents and skills, intellectual intelligence, emotional intelligence, education, friends, family, experiences, appearance, and health. It's the longest chapter in this short book, but what a self-examination it is. In his words, "If you have it, use it." Trust me, if you have this book, you'll use it.

60 Seconds & You're Hired! by Robin Ryan, Penguin Books

Career coach Robin Ryan says, "You will not land the job unless you excel in the interview." Her latest edition of this book contains 125 answers that have been used successfully in real interviews, and spends the bulk of the book explaining how to adapt them to your particular situation. Here's the news: You need to answer in sixty seconds or less.

Why just sixty seconds? Ryan says "verbose, lengthy answers bore the interviewer into not hiring [the candidate]. Nervousness and lack of preparation often result in long, rambling, erroneous, or never-ending answers." When you notice that interviewers don't seem to be listening to you, it's probably a sign that your answers aren't impressing them. So never use more than sixty seconds on any answer, she says.

Starting with the simple "tell me about yourself" opener, Ryan explains how to prepare the "60 Second Calling Card," which summarizes your skills, abilities, and previous experiences in an organized, thoughtful fashion that will immediately make the interviewer want to listen. Her next strategy is called the "5 Point Agenda," in which the job hunter selects the five most marketable points and repeatedly illustrates them throughout the interview process. Both these strategies can be tailored to the specific interview or job, and help job seekers clarify the reasons they would be the best fit for the position.

Chapters on interview etiquette, salary negotiations, pitfalls, and questions job hunters should ask also offer valuable advice for the big interview. If it's been a while since you've had an interview, spend some time studying the 125 answers—your interviewer will be glad you did.

The Right Job, Right Now by Susan D. Strayer, S.P.H.R., St. Martin's Griffin

"There is no such thing as the perfect career," Strayer writes. "But there is a career that's perfect for you." The author leads job hunters toward that perfect job through the use of the Kaleidoscope Career Model, her trademarked system which she describes as an "uncomplicated way to take an inventory of all you can give to a career or job and determine everything you want in return."

Through workbook-style charts and graphs, the model goes through five steps: defining values and setting boundaries, defining skills, determining behaviors, defining environmental and cultural factors, and examining benefits and monetary rewards.

Once the self-examination is complete, part two of the plan is taking career action, because the author warns, "Most career problems can usually be attributed to continuing to do the wrong thing, or spending way too much time making excuses."

Strayer doesn't stop with getting the job; she next concentrates on helping you manage your career. "Many professionals make the mistake of thinking that career management ends when a new job begins . . . whether you're in your position for a few months or a few years, from salary to performance, you need to keep tabs on how you're doing, what you're making, and how you'll get ahead." Keep your kaleidoscope handy, she says, because you can use it again and again.

Finding Your Perfect Work by Paul and Sarah Edwards, Jeremy P. Tarcher/Putnam

Paul and Sarah Edwards have authored a long list of books on self-employment, including the Working from Home series. In *Finding Your Perfect Work*, they tackle the problems presented by the changing job market. They explain how "what's happening in our society today is making it economically possible for the first time in history to truly find your perfect work outside the confines of a job so you can build your work around your life instead of the other way around."

Their master guide for job hunters is divided into three parts. Part 1, "The Destination," helps readers envision the life they want to create. Part 2, "The Path," explores the many avenues that lead to the desired outcome and how to choose the most appealing path. Part 3, "The Means," explains how to evaluate the many opportunities to earn a living along the chosen path.

Real-life examples of their process illustrate how the master guide works. One profile describes a woman with a gift for managing money, a passion for performing, a mission to free people from financial distress, assets including a background in acting and experience in bookkeeping. Her means to her dream: a bookkeeping service offering financial awareness seminars.

In addition to charts, worksheets and questionnaires, the book features detailed appendixes including an alphabetical listing of self-employment careers and professional and occupational licensing.

Anyone considering self-employment will get plenty of inspiration from this book. The authors remind us that "the greatest dreams are often born in periods of the greatest distress. Change presents us with new choices and causes us to seek new options that fire up our dreams."

Can I Wear My Nose Ring to the Interview? by Ellen Gordon Reeves, Workman Publishing

And the answer to the title question is, "Yes. If you wear a nose ring every day and you're not going to give it up, then you need to show your true colors." Aimed at first-time job seekers, this book answers questions that newbies may not even think to ask.

Reeves says that the first step in setting yourself up for success is to stop looking for a job. Instead, she says, start looking for a person. "The right person will lead you to the right job." She starts with the absolute basics: "Being professional means being well-dressed and well-groomed; being punctual, proactive, and efficient; presenting your experience and abilities articulately and with confidence; and making sure the documents that support your candidacy are impeccable." Additionally, she stresses the importance of the job seeker's online presence. Google yourself, she says, and see what's out there that will derail your search.

Topics from "What If They Hate Me?" to "Should I Use My Nickname?" to whether to send a digital or hard copy résumé get thorough, useful answers. In fact, the text is peppered with real questions posed to the author over her years as a consultant, and the advice spans the job hunt from résumés, applications, cover letters, references, the interview, clothing, tricky questions, follow-up, weighing the offer, being a good employee, and how to move on when the time comes.

It's a back-to-basics, fun read that lays the foundation for lifelong skills.

In Search of the Perfect Job by Clyde C. Lowstuter (with Cammen B. Lowstuter), McGraw-Hill

You will realize that this book appeals to a very specific audience as soon as you read the subtitle, *8 Steps to the $250,000+ Executive Job That's Right for You.* I've included it in my list because those are the jobs that are often most difficult to find; there are fewer of them and even fewer qualified candidates.

Lowstuter begins with his own experience of being fired from a job that he thought was secure, given his excellent performance reviews. He hadn't realized how distant he and his boss had become, and blames his departure on a lack of chemistry with the boss. And he warns others that while the experience is not unique, it can have a positive outcome: "Traumatic situations will always be with you. Tough, unsettling times represent opportunities for profound learning and personal growth."

His eight steps start with the "Inner View," which covers how to take charge of your career. "Strategies and Options" focuses on strengths, career options, and entrepreneurship. "Credential Building" reviews résumés, marketing letters, and references. "The Search Process" shows job hunters how to find where the jobs are, networking, search firms, and Internet searches. "Selling Yourself" takes a hard look at interviewing and handling tough questions. "Managing the Campaign" examines successful career search strategies and formulas. "Negotiations" gets down to the nitty-gritty on what to expect in a reasonable offer. Finally, "The Next Step" tackles the topic of executive onboarding and a survival plan in your new position.

Lowstuter's exercises, tools, examples, worksheets, and personal experiences comprise a comprehensive guide and a fresh perspective.

Highly Effective Networking by Orville Pierson, Career Press

"There's no doubt that networking can help you conduct a better job search and find a better job—if you can find comfortable and effective ways to network," the author begins. Obviously, I couldn't agree more. Job search networking comes in four stages: decide to work more effectively, prepare for job hunting, talk to personal and professional contacts, and land a new job.

Job hunting is a big project, requiring you to understand your goals, do some preparation, and have a structured approach. With the ultimate goal of getting a new job, Peterson lays out four networking goals: Get the word out about your search and yourself; gather the information you need; meet insiders at places you'd like to work; and get in touch with decision makers.

Several points in particular caught this networking junkie's attention. First, no Web site can do your networking for you. Pierson discusses using social and professional networking sites as a research tool, but not as a first direct contact. He explains the steps that will save you time and still allow you access to the greatest number of contacts. And he debunks a number of networking myths, such as that you have to know a lot of people to build a successful network. His book walks the job hunter through the process of moving from networking to interviews to job offers.

The strength of this book, though, is that it shows you how to use your network. Pierson's best advice: "Talk to as many people as possible about your job search. If you're smart about who you talk to and what you say, your search will go faster and better."

Do What You Are by Paul D. Tieger and Barbara Barron-Tieger, Sphere

The subtitle of this book is *"Discover the Perfect Career for You Through the Secrets of Personality Type."* The authors say their book is different in that it "does not offer generic, one-size-fits-all advice . . . the Personality Type (system) enables us to truly individualize the career discovery process—to give you invaluable insights about yourself, and to enable you to find a career that makes the best use of your natural talents."

The authors say the secret of career satisfaction lies in doing what you enjoy most, and provide a list of questions to help readers determine whether they are in the right job. It is important to "spend some time figuring out what makes you tick."

Much of their discussion is based on the Myers-Briggs Type Indicator (MBTI) and the sixteen different personality types and four personality preference scales that are described in the writings of Isabel Briggs Myers. The authors remind job hunters, "[Personality] Type does not determine intelligence or predict success . . . it does help us discover what best motivates and energizes each of us to seek these elements in the work we choose to do."

Chapters on "The Four Different Temperaments," "Identifying Your Innate Strengths," and "Developing Your Abilities over Time" give the job hunters an overview of how the research applies to them. The bulk of the book, devoted to case studies of the sixteen personality types, provides detailed profiles of career-satisfied people and analysis to show readers how their jobs let them use their natural strengths. The authors then offer advice for "Putting It All Together," with ten steps to creating a personal career plan.

With solid advice, clear examples, and a proven track record, this book is high on my recommended list.

Crash Course in Finding the Work You Love by Samuel Greengard, Sterling

"Not until middle age do many of us gain the perspective and wisdom needed to recognize, amid all that noise, the signals to which we are truly attuned," the author says. "The professional path we 'selected' (or were shunted into) at age 25, we realize, now differs radically from the one we would choose from scratch at age 50. At this stage of life, however, with the clock inexorably ticking, achieving life goals and leaving a legacy assume a new sense of urgency. Fortunately, it's also at this point that we're finally able to dream like children—while putting a lifetime of knowledge and experience to work."

That's good news in this job market, especially with older workers facing layoffs, involuntary retirement, and a tough job market at a time when many will need to work longer than they originally planned. Greengard defines re-careering as "a deliberate transition to a new position with entirely different responsibilities," and says it only knows the bounds we impose on ourselves.

His career-change checklist presents guidelines to keep a career moving forward, and he offers strategies for finding happiness and comfort beyond your comfort zone. He devotes chapters to a practical discussion of career and personality tests, career-counseling options, online resources, and career options ideal for baby boomers and older workers.

Other considerations that Greengard covers are money matters, volunteerism, alternative work options, social networking sites, polishing your résumé, and interviewing. He encourages older job seekers: "Especially for those in midlife and beyond, changing careers can transform an existence . . . it may deliver us to a place where reality finally dovetails with imagination."

Knock 'em Dead by Martin Yate, C.P.C., Adams Media

Since it was first published in 1985, *Knock 'em Dead* has sold over five million copies, which should reassure any job hunter that there's some good advice within. Yate divides the book into five sections, starting with "The Well-Stocked Briefcase," an examination of ways to package your professional skills and job search techniques. As Yate says, "There is no magic bullet when it comes to successful job search techniques, no single best approach . . . The best technique—and there are a dozen different choices when it comes to job searching—is the one that unearths that perfect opportunity."

Part II, "Getting the Word Out," spans contacts, dress, body language, and interview preparation, which leads to Part III, "Great Answers to Tough Interview Questions," a study of what the questions mean and how to handle strange settings and even table etiquette. Also included are dos and don'ts for leaving a favorable impression. Part IV discusses finishing touches, such as interview follow-up, negotiations, multiple offers, and psychological tests. Part V looks at specific crises, like job hunting while still employed, clouds on the horizon, and financial considerations.

While appendixes are a nice touch, this book has a novel approach. The first appendix is six pages long, listing questions that job hunters have and references to the page on which they are answered. It's a great tool. The second appendix concentrates on age discrimination in a youth-oriented culture. There's valuable info here, too.

"A company rarely hires the first competent person it sees," Yate writes. "You must develop a strategy to keep your name and skills constantly in the forefront of the interviewer's mind."

Getting the Job You Really Want by Michael Farr, JIST Works

"While career planning and job seeking can be complicated topics, only two things are truly important in planning a career and in looking for a job: 1. If you are going to work, you might as well do something you enjoy, are good at, and want to do. 2. If you want to find or change your job, you might as well do it in less time," according to the author.

He begins the book with a series of exercises designed to get the job hunter to think about the kind of life he or she really wants. From there, he looks at skills and says, "Because we take our many skills for granted, most people are not good at explaining the skills they have." One study of employers found that three out of four people who interviewed for a job did not present the skills they had to do the job.

The chapter on identifying job objectives lists more than one thousand job titles to help job seekers find interests that they may not have considered. The next likely step is to look beyond what you are qualified for and consider what other fields you may have an interest in and look for other possibilities.

The chapters on applications, résumés, e-mail, and cover letters are very helpful, but Farr takes it a step further with JIST cards, business card–sized mini-résumés. The cards contain what an employer needs and wants to know, with no extra information that might be used to screen you out. Plenty of examples and a worksheet to help the job hunter design one are especially helpful.

Trust yourself, Farr says. "No one can know you better than you. So make the best decisions you can, and keep moving ahead in a positive way."

University of Southern California (USC)—MBA Commencement Speech, May 15, 2009

In May 2009, I was asked to deliver the commencement address to the graduates of the University of Southern California's MBA programs. In addition to the deservedly proud degree recipients, the audience of five thousand included friends and family of the grads.

My talk focused on seven essential aspects of a career well spent: education, networking, adversity, change, communication, ethics, and success. Many appreciative listeners told me afterward that the talk's wisdom was unimpeachable. Others just had a good time taking in the stories and some astounding facts.

You will find some of the comments in the body of the book, but my editors encouraged me to include the entire talk anyway, because they felt it was a good example of public speaking. As such, they maintain, studying this kind of communication can benefit a job candidate. A big part of getting your foot in the door is the ability to hold someone's attention.

Thank you, Dean Ellis, for that kind introduction.

Graduates, parents, and families, members of the administration and faculty . . . Thank you for inviting me to share this wonderful occasion with you.

I remember another very special graduation here, when my son David graduated from the USC Film School. David is now a film director in L.A., and our family borrowed an expression from his industry: "It's in the can," which means it's done and no one can take it away from you.

We use this expression in our family after we have just had a terrific holiday or a wonderful vacation. So, congratulations to all of you.

Tonight, it's in the can. And no one can take this evening away from you.

Let me start by asking all of you in the audience this question:

How many people talk to themselves?

Please raise your hands.

I count approximately 50 percent.

To the other 50 percent who didn't raise your hands, I can just hear you now, saying to yourself, "Who me? I don't talk to myself!"

Well, I think all of you will be talking to yourself about the day's events on your way home this evening. This is an unforgettable moment among many fine hours you will have in your career and life.

I promise to be brief.

I've always heard that being brief is the soul of being witty. But there is another way to describe being brief.

Example: A third-grader had to do a book report, and he chose Socrates.

His report consisted of three short sentences:

Number 1. Socrates was a philosopher.

Number 2. He talked a lot.

Number 3. They killed him.

I will keep that in mind as I share some thoughts on seven important topics:

- Education,
- Networking,
- Adversity,
- Change,
- Communication,
- Ethics, and, finally,
- Success.

Let's start with *EDUCATION*.

As you leave the halls of this great institution, keep one idea firmly in mind: Learning is a lifetime occupation. It ain't over till it's over.

I'm sorry . . . It isn't over until it's over. Where is my education?

I am delighted to share the stage tonight with my longtime friend Warren Bennis, who has provided me with continuing education. Warren said, "Taking charge of your own learning is a part of taking charge of your life."

Consider the story of the mother in the kitchen who hollers up to her son, "You get down here this very minute because you are late for school."

The son hollers back,

"I don't want to go to school, and I'm not going to school.

- The kids don't like me.
- The teachers don't like me.
- And everyone is talking behind my back."

The mother rushes upstairs and pushes the bedroom door open, points to her son, and says, "You get out of bed this very minute because you are going to school for two reasons:

1. You are forty-one years old.
2. And you're the principal of the school."

My father was head of the Associated Press in the Twin Cities of Minneapolis and St. Paul for thirty-five years. He was fond of aphorisms and was constantly posting them on our refrigerator.

I grew up on a diet of aphorisms. Here are several of my dad's favorite wisdom statements about education:

- There are really no mistakes in life—there are only lessons.
- "Learn from the mistakes of others. You can't live long enough to make them all yourself." That's from former First Lady Eleanor Roosevelt.
- Experience is a good teacher, but a hard one. She gives the test first and the lesson afterward.
- Information does not become power until it is used.

- And lastly: If you think education is expensive, try ignorance.

As you continue your education outside the classroom, your first assignment from Professor Mackay is to learn how to *NETWORK* effectively.

If I had to name the single characteristic shared by all the truly successful people I've met over a lifetime, I'd say it is the ability to create and nurture a network of contacts.

A couple of years ago in my syndicated column, I wrote about the best alumni networks in the country.

I said USC tops my list. I went on to write:

"I don't know if they take a blood oath to help, hire, mentor, and generally take care of each other, but they act as if they do.

"From the day you graduate, the USC network is there for you. And, in turn, you, as a graduate, are expected to be there for other USC alumni."

These are the people you can depend on for:

- Advice,
- Introductions,
- Information, and
- Support.

But your network only works if you listen to the people in it.

Did you know that 70 percent of all jobs are found through networking?

(And you thought it was Monster.com!)

It's nice to go to events like this and hear speakers. However, never forget that the person in front of you, behind you, to your right, and to your left can be more important than any speaker. In fact, I strongly suggest you take a moment to make those introductions before you leave here tonight.

Your network will be there for you, and you will be wise to pay attention to them.

My belief has always been . . . You can take:

- My money from me,
- My home from me, and
- My factories . . . whatever . . .

But leave me:

- My good name,
- My reputation, and
- My network.

And I'll be back to where I was in two years, because one thing a great network helps you overcome is *ADVERSITY*.

I've never yet met a successful person who hasn't had to overcome either a little or a lot of adversity in his or her life.

Why do some of us have what it takes to pick ourselves up off the canvas when others are ready to throw in the towel?

I don't know the answer, but if I did, I'd bottle it.

I do know this: It isn't all that rare.

The human species comes equipped with built-in mental toughness.

Some of us just don't know it's there.

Take it from an old peddler: The hardest sale you'll ever make is to yourself. But once you're convinced you can do it, you can.

Adversity is the grindstone of life. Intended to polish you up, adversity also has the ability to grind you down. The impact and ultimate result depend on what you do with the difficulties that come your way.

American business hasn't had such a huge dose of adversity since the Great Depression. When I was growing up as a kid, the GDP was in the hundreds of millions, then it went to billions. And today we have a 13.8-trillion-dollar economy.

The media is constantly confusing billions for trillions and vice versa.

We have been so desensitized with these numbers, it's hard to comprehend them.

So let's put it in its proper perspective.

A quick little drill: All of us are going to count from one to a trillion right now and we are not going to sleep. I want each of you to make a prediction to yourself, how long this will take? You have your answer . . .

It takes 31,658 *years* to count to a trillion.

I don't know about you, but I don't have that kind of time.

Recently, *Fortune* magazine did a telling rundown on the "Lessons of Adversity."

"What has corporate America learned from the economic crisis?" the magazine asked.

"The Fortune 500 is having its worst slump ever, but the survivors have been taught a few things about thinking long term and sticking to principles. Let's think of 2008 as one hell of a school year. What have we learned?"

We learned that "Gorging on easy profits can be fatal." AIG lost an unbelievable $99.3 billion and Fannie Mae burned through $58.7 billion.

But look at the companies that are weathering the storm. Some of the showcased firms are no surprises. They include:

- Apple,
- IBM, and
- Johnson & Johnson.

As *Fortune* points out, "Highly disciplined companies can thrive in all seasons." The same can be said about people.

And hiring is coming back. Some "Fortune 100 employers have at least 150 openings as of mid-April." They include:

- Walmart,
- Hewlett-Packard, and
- State Farm Insurance.

Adversity teaches us the importance of facing and embracing *CHANGE*.

Here's a little lesson in change:

When I graduated from the University of Minnesota in 1954:

- A gallon of milk cost ninety-two cents.
- The average for the Dow Jones was 338.
- And I drove a fire-engine red Pontiac Star Chief with a sticker price of $2,500.

In 1981–1982, many of you were born. That's about twenty-seven years later:

- Milk had risen to $2.23 a gallon.
- The Dow was at about 900.
- And a Pontiac Firebird went for around $8,000.

Today in 2009, that's another twenty-seven years further on the timeline:

- A gallon of milk is $2.69.
- The Dow has bounced back above 9,000.
- And the Pontiac? That model won't even be around by next year.

Clearly, times change. And so must you, if you are to survive and thrive.

Consider the three Generals:

- General Electric,
- General Motors, and
- General Mills.

In 1981, General Electric was celebrated as one of the world's truly great companies.

Recently, some General Electric lightbulbs were selling for more than the price of General Electric stock. (It's curtains for Pontiac and much more at General Motors, as GM teeters on the brink of bankruptcy.)

But General Mills has been holding its own. Wheaties remains the breakfast of champions, as it was when I was a kid snipping off box tops and idolizing Yankee slugger Lou Gehrig, the first sports poster boy on a Wheaties box.

Recently I saw a video on YouTube that Sony played at an executive conference this year. It points out how dramatically the world has changed and is changing:

- Soon China will become the #1 English-speaking country in the world.
- I also heard this statistic when I was at the Olympic Games in China last summer: Three hundred million people play basketball in China. Their basketball court must be enormous! Seriously, those three hundred million people playing basketball in China is equal to the total number of people in the United States.
- The 25 percent of India's population with the highest IQs is greater than the total population of the United States. Translation: India has more honors kids than America has kids.
- We are living in times of exponential change. There are thirty-one billion searches on Google every month. In 2006, this number was less than a billion.

For students starting a four-year technical degree, half of what they learn in their first year of study will be outdated by their third year of study.

Change certainly includes changes in jobs. And this is even truer in careers.

We now know that today's grads will have many job changes in his or her career. And in the near future, three to five career changes.

And the Labor Department has updated that job-change projection: Today's student can expect to have "10 to 14 jobs by the age of 38."

Yes, you heard that right—ten to fourteen jobs.

The Sony study I mentioned earlier elaborates more remarkable statistics on jobs:

The top ten jobs in demand in 2009, experts contend did not exist in 2004.

The U.S. Department of Labor estimates that:

- One in four workers has been with their current employer for less than one year.
- One in two has been there less than five years.

Firms are choosier because they can afford to be. If you want to get picked these days, be prepared to satisfy very picky people.

The amount of change is overwhelming—in demographics, technology, standards, and the employment market. But every time I reflect on change, I always think about how certain principles endure.

No person "will make a great leader who wants to do it all himself, or get all the credit for doing it." That wasn't said by Dr. Phil, but by Andrew Carnegie.

One factor that will never change is the importance of good *COM-MUNICATION.*

The key to good communication is knowing your audience. A classic example is the following letter to the parents of a daughter away from home for the first time at college.

She writes:

Dear Mom and Dad:

I am sorry to be so long in writing lately, but all my writing paper was destroyed the night the demonstrators burned down the dormitory.

I am out of the hospital now and the doctor says my eyesight should be back to normal sooner or later.

That wonderful boy, Bill, who saved me from the fire, kindly offered to share his little apartment with me until the dorm is rebuilt. He comes from a good family, Mom and Dad, so you won't be too surprised to learn when I tell you we are going to get married. In fact, Mom and Dad, you always wanted to have grandchildren so you should really be happy to know that you will be grandparents next month.

Please disregard the above practice in English Composition. There was no fire, I haven't been in the hospital, I am not pregnant, and I don't even have a boyfriend.

But . . . I did get a "D" in chemistry and an "F" in French. And I wanted to be sure you received this news in the proper perspective.

Love,
Mary

Mary got an A for Audience Anticipation.

Getting your message across is critical, whether you're selling, managing, developing products and services, or chatting with your neighbor in the next cubicle.

And remember, good communication is a two-way street. We have two eyes and two ears but only one mouth, which shows us we should watch and listen twice as much as we speak.

You've been writing papers and making presentations to your classes with plenty of feedback, even grades, up to now.

But what will happen once the audience has real money to spend and your company's future depends on your communication skills?

Your communication has to be clear, meaningful, and, above all, truthful. You must present your company or product in a way for which you would never need to apologize.

After all, the image you communicate is what shapes your reputation. And there had better be plenty of substance to back up that image.

There should be no question about your *ETHICAL STANDARDS*.

If you have integrity, nothing else matters.

If you don't have integrity, nothing else matters.

You may have noticed that recently business publications have been reporting on some serious problems with integrity and ethics, on people and companies not practicing truthful communication.

Unfortunately, the business community—of which I am a part—does not get stellar grades for ethics the past few years.

And a large part of the current economic crisis can be attributed to greed and ethical lapses.

The arrow has clearly been pointed in the wrong direction.

Most of you are headed for business careers. Ethics and integrity must be the cornerstone of your existence. They are not electives.

Let me tell you a true story about Professor Bonk, introductory chemistry professor at Duke University. He's taught chemistry so long his course is known affectionately as "Bonkistry."

One year, three guys were taking chemistry and doing well. They were each getting a solid "A" going into the final exam.

They were so confident, that the weekend before finals they decided to go up to the University of Virginia to party with some friends. Due to bad hangovers, they overslept all day Sunday and didn't make it back to Duke until early Monday morning.

They explained to Professor Bonk that they had driven up to the University of Virginia for the weekend and had planned to come back in time to study.

However, they had a flat tire on the way back and didn't have a spare, so they didn't get back to campus until late Sunday night. Professor Bonk thought this over and then agreed that they could make up the final on the following day.

The three guys were elated and relieved.

They studied that night and went in the next day.

Professor Bonk placed them in separate rooms, handed each of them a test booklet, looked at his watch, and told them to begin.

They opened up the test booklet and saw the first question about oxygen was worth five points.

"Cool," each of them thought. "This is going to be a slam dunk."

Then they turned the page and saw the second question worth ninety-five points: Which tire?

Honesty is the best policy, and sometimes it has a high premium.

If you want to get it right on ethics in business, I have one simple tip: Always act like your mother is watching. Because your mother wants you to succeed.

All the points so far lead to what I'm hoping for all of you: continued and well-deserved *SUCCESS*.

As to success: *LISTEN* to that voice in your head that says you really can do it!

Believe in yourself—even when no one else does. Surround yourself with top-quality people and truly listen to their input.

Life is not a parabolic curve.

It doesn't go straight up.

There are a lot of lumps and bumps.

A lot of throttling up, and throttling down.

Don't wait until it's too late to change. Start to take the true measure of your success now. What do you possess that you can offer to other people, to your community, to the world?

To simply ask the question, "How can I make a difference?" is to answer it, because the answer is to never let yourself stop asking the question.

Some people succeed because they are destined to, but most people succeed because they are determined to.

The final key to success may sound funny to you—and that is, eat the heart of the watermelon.

When I was a kid, my father knew a guy named Bernie who had started out his career with a vegetable stand, worked hard all his life, and eventually became wealthy as a fruit and vegetable wholesaler.

Every summer, when the first good watermelons came in, Dad would take me down to Bernie's warehouse and we'd have a feast. Bernie would choose a couple of watermelons just in from the fields, crack them open, and hand each of us a big piece.

Then, with Bernie taking the lead, we'd eat only the heart of the watermelon—the reddest, juiciest, most perfect part—and throw the rest away.

It's like cutting the crust off your sandwich. All that's left is the best part.

My father never made a lot of money. We were raised to clean our plates and not waste food. Bernie was my father's idea of a rich man.

And I always thought it was because he'd been such a success in business.

It was years before I realized my father admired Bernie's "richness" because he knew how to stop work in the middle of a summer day, sit down with his friends, and spend time eating the heart of the watermelon.

Being rich isn't about money.

Being rich is a state of mind.

Some of us, no matter how much money we have, will never be free enough to take the time to stop and eat the heart of the watermelon. And some of us will be rich without ever being more than a paycheck ahead of the game.

Sometimes it seems like if we want to triple our success ratio, we have to triple our failure rate.

From my standpoint, that's what it's all about:

- Never stop learning.
- Believe in yourself, even when no one else does.
- Eat the heart of the watermelon.
- Find a way to make a difference, and
- Odds are good you'll change the times you live in and the world around you.

Because today may be "in the can," but your future is a work in progress.

You've been a marvelous audience. It's been an honor to be here.

Thank you very, very much . . . And good luck!

Appendix: An Open Book

I encourage readers to get in touch with me. Here's how you can:

My Web site is: www.harveymackay.com.

Please send e-mails to: info@harveymackay.com.

If you want to write to me or call my office (please, no requests for personal advice), the address and phone number are:

Harvey Mackay

MackayMitchell Envelope Company

2100 Elm Street S.E.

Minneapolis, MN 55414

1-800-905-8939

The Harvey Mackay online store on the Internet can be visited at: http://store.harveymackay.com.

I'm committed to continuous learning for everyone, including myself, and want to share what I learn on a timely basis.

My nationally syndicated column for United Feature Syndicate appears weekly in fifty-two newspapers. At my Web site, you can read my current weekly column. That's also the place to sign up for my weekly e-mail alert and never miss a column. You can also get each new column delivered right to your desktop by subscribing via RSS.

Periodic blogs are posted on the Web site.

My official Facebook page is:

http://www.facebook.com/harveymackay

Or just Google: Harvey Mackay Facebook and click on the site.

You will find recent Job Search stories discussed on my Facebook Discussion Board.

For the latest tweet, visit http://twitter.com/HarveyMackay.

Index

ABC, 253
ABC News, 55
ActiFi, 189
"Actors Moonlighting on Horror
   Flicks" (Kleinschrodt), 66
Adams, John Quincy, 51
Aesop, 60
Affleck, Casey, 66
aging and employability, 63–64
Ali, Muhammad, 6
alumni affiliations, 90, 102, 138, 237
Amelia, 82
American Academy of Facial Plastic
   and Reconstructive Surgery, 55
American Management Association,
   160
American Psychological Association,
   174
American Red Cross, 99
America's Next Top Model, 115
"Angel of Iran," 149
anger, 43–45
Ant and the Grasshopper, The (Aesop),
   60
AOL/Time Warner, 220
aplastic anemia, 92–93
apparel. *See* clothing
appearance and impressions, 18, 45,
   56, 82, 84, 169, 202–4, 209
asking questions at interviews, 215–17
aspirational networking, 132–33
attitude
   aging and, 63–64
   anger, 43–45
   contrarian, 56–57
   discouragement, 46–48
   and entrepreneurship, 93, 97

at firing, 32–33
   overconfidence, 25–26
   personal makeovers, 55
   pitchmanship, 52–54
   pursuing MBA during downturn,
      58–60
   recruiter, advice from, 70–76
   rejection, rebounding from,
      49–51
   self-confidence, and interviewing,
      173–74
Augsburg College, 95

Bachelor, The, 253
"back-to-basics"-style employers,
   pitching to, 53
Bailey, Greg, 5, 70
Bailyn, Charles, 61
Barron-Tieger, Barbara, 298–99
Beckwith, Christine Clifford, 292
Beckwith, Harry, 292
Bells Are Ringing, 205
Benson, 30
Berra, Yogi, 213
Berry, Halle, 66
Beverly Hills, 90210, 82
*Beware the Naked Man Who Offers You
   His Shirt* (Mackay), 219
Big Ten schools, 103, 130
Bintro.com, 142
BlackBerry, 9, 121, 146, 203, 220, 238
Blanchett, Cate, 66
blogs, 118, 142
Bloomberg.com, 85, 242
Bolles, Richard N., 291–92
Boston Celtics, 5
Boylan, Jim, 5

Boys Don't Cry, 82
Brin, Sergey, 61
Buck, David, 116
Buffett, Warren, 204
Burbank, Luther, 132
Burns, Karen, 66
Burton, Richard, 51
BusinessWeek, 130

California Angels, 66
California Institute of Technology
    (Caltech), 10
Cambridge University, 59
Campa, Al, 67
Campbell, David P., 293
candidates, passive vs. active, 70–71
can-do approach, 201
Canfield, Jack, 30–31
*Can I Wear My Nose Ring to the
    Interview?* (Reeves), 296
Carlson, Bob, 94, 96
Carlson School of Management,
    218
career choices, following your heart in
    making, 102–7
career obsolescence, 276–78
career planning resources,
    Department of Labor, 99–100
career positioning, long-term, 56–57
Caruso, David, 80
CBS, 18, 175
cell phone, 144, 146–48, 206, 210,
    212, 221
Cerberus, 11
certification, 101
Chambers, John, 176
Chandler Hill Partners, 68
change, 14–15
Charlie's Café Exceptionale, 104
Chemical Bank, 225
Chicago Bears, 106
Chicago Bulls, 5
Chicago Tribune, 55
Chicken Soup for the Soul (Canfield and
    Hansen), 30–31

Chng-Castor, Alexis, 101
Cisco, 176, 244
Citadel, 153
Citigroup, 241
C-level job search, 117–23
    executive agility, 117–18
    Internet networking, 118–19
    language proficiency, 120
    skillset of executive, 119–22
    specialization and, 122
    technological literacy, 121
    women executives, 122
C-suite, 8, 72, 117, 242
Clinton, Bill, 26
Clinton, Hillary, 26
Clooney, George, 66
clothing
    for interviews, 169, 202–4, 209
    at work, 18
CNBC, 14
CNET News, 87
CNN Money report, 240
Coastal Occupational Medical Group,
    134
cold call, 103, 192, 193, 251
Colgate, 153
College of St. Benedict, 267
College of St. Thomas, 95
Commercial Credit, 225
community service, 90–91
competitors, getting to know,
    135–37
Conference Board Review, 243, 244
Contact Management System (CMS),
    9, 89, 128
contacts, 6, 86
contrarian attitude, 56–57
Coomber, Steve, 59
corporate culture, 88, 96–97, 203,
    248
correspondence cards, 213–14
cosmetic surgery, 55
Craigslist, 85, 110
*Crash Course in Finding the Work You
    Love* (Greengard), 299–300

creativity, 156–58
CSI: Miami, 79

daily planner, 79–81
danger signals of impending job loss, 8–9
Davanni's, 93–98
Decisive Seven concessions to age, 64
Del Negro, Lynn, 3
Del Negro, Vinny, 3–5
Deloitte, 243
De Meyer, Arnoud, 59
Department of Labor, career planning resources of, 99–100
D. E. Shaw & Company, 168
designing ideal job, 252–54
determination, 3–6
Deutschlander, Ed, 218
Dillard, Annie, 81
Dinner: Impossible, 153
Disabled American Veterans, 90
discouragement, 46–48
documentation, supporting raise requests, 272
documenting, terms of offer, 259
Dodgers, Los Angeles, 66
dolphin feeding style, 247–48
Donkers, Rob, 203
Doostang, 237
Do What You Are (Tieger and Barron-Tieger), 298–99
"Downturn Is Right Time to Take an MBA" (Coomber), 59
Drucker, Peter, 24, 133, 281
Drudge Report, 80
Dubin, Burt, 214
Dun & Bradstreet, 196
Dungy, CleoMae, 103–4
Dungy, Tony, 102–7
Dungy, Wilbur, 103, 104

Earhart, Amelia, 82
Earle, Sylvia, 80
Eastwood, Clint, 82
Edmondson, David, 154

education, 18
    free online courses, 61
    pursuing MBA during downturn, 58–60
Edwards, Paul, 295–96
Edwards, Sarah, 295–96
Einstein, Kurt, 281–89
e-mail, 8–9, 121, 170
    to contacts, 86
employer styles, and pitchmanship, 52–53
enlightened firing, 39–40
entrepreneurship, 92–98
    attitude, 93, 97
    corporate culture, 96–97
    expense control, 95–96
    location, 95
    marketing concept, 94–95
Erickson, Lou, 131
etiquette
    for business lunches, 208–14
    cell phone use and, 146–48, 206
executive job searches, 117–23
experience, learning from, 34–35
extra hours at work, 16–17
eye contact, 211

Facebook, 74, 75, 84, 118, 130, 142, 144, 149, 166, 255
failure, analyzing, 49–50
Fallon, Pat, 158, 198, 267
Fallon Worldwide, 158, 267
Farr, Michael, 300–1
Feldman, Mark D., 38
Fey, Tina, 79
"15 Best Places to Waste Time on the Web, The" (*PC World* article), 110
Financial Times, 80, 85
Finding Your Perfect Work (Edwards, Edwards and Tarcher), 295–96
Fink, I. D., 135–36
firing
    attitude and remarks upon, 32–33
    enlightened, 39–40

firing *(cont.)*
  learning from, 34, 120
  negotiating termination, checklist
      for, 36–37
  positive applications, 39–40, 92
  support groups, 38
Flaig, Sally, 99
Flynn, Nancy, 147
Foley, Fran, 153–54
following your heart (in career
      choice), 107
Food Network, 153
foreign language skills, 120
Fortune, 17, 67
Fort Worth Star-Telegram, 154
Framingham State College, 154

gatekeepers, 131
  dealing with, 183
  electronic résumé screening,
      67–68
  interviewers as, 215
Gates, Bill, 61
General Mills, 104, 105
General Motors, 241
Generation Xers and Yers, 208
Getting the Job You Really Want (Farr),
      301
Gigwise, 80
Gillman, Sid, 105
G & K Cleaners, 135–36
Gladwell, Malcolm, 80, 218
gloom and doom personalities,
      avoiding, 17
goal setting, 83–84
Golden State Warriors, 3
Google, 15, 61, 75, 87–88, 127,
      141, 142, 170, 202, 205, 237,
      250, 296
  Chrome, 85
  Timeline Search, 193–94
graduating college student's job
      search, 231–38
  contacts, making, 233–34
  internships, 231–233
  interviewing, 234, 235

managing online identity, 237–38
networking, 235, 236–37, 238
time management, 238
Grant, Cary, 51
Greengard, Samuel, 299–300
grooming. *See* appearance
guarantee, ninety-day, 330

Habitat for Humanity, 99, 288
Hammer, Langdon, 61
handshakes, 209
Hansen, Mark Victor, 30–31
Hartford Business Journal, 99
Hartford Courant, 252
Harvard Business Review, 242
Harvard University, 50, 59, 168
Hawthorne, Nathaniel, 47
Hawthorne, Sophia, 47
Hayes, Christine, 61
headhunters. *See* recruiters
Hercules, Labors of 11
Highly Effective Networking (Pierson),
      297–98
Hill, Sarah Hightower, 68
hiring process, 69
  criteria, 69
  designing ideal job, 252–54
  extending process, 177–79
  game plan for landing ideal job,
      250–51
  human resource executives, role of,
      242
  job search of graduating college
      student, 231–38
  money-back guarantees, offering,
      248
  multiple interviews, purpose of,
      247–48
  negotiating terms of employment,
      257–59, 262–63
  offer details, 260–63
  pay cuts and, 240–41
  pickiness in approach to, 201
  psychologists' perspective on
      (*See* psychologists' perspective
      on staffing decisions)

talent and, 243–45
timing, 246
Hitchcock, Alfred, 51
Hively, Jan, 116
Hoffman, Jan, 138
Holiday Inn, 16
Holmes, Oliver Wendell, Jr., 34
Holtz, Lou, 49
Home Depot, 112
Horowitz, Etan, 144
HR Certification Institute, 101
http://davidleisner.com/
   guitarcomposer/noname.html 172
http://store.harveymackay.com 317
http://twitter.com/Harvey
   Mackay 317
human resources executives, 242

Iacocca, Lee, 242
IBM, 88
ideal job. *See* perfect job
identity on Internet, managing,
   127–29, 130, 237–38
*If You Don't Know Where You're Going,
   You'll Probably End Up Somewhere
   Else* (Campbell), 293
Indianapolis Colts, 106
Indiana University, 288
indispensability, 16–19
industrial psychologists, 159–67
information sources, 21–23, 278
InfoUSA, 196
In Search of the Perfect Job (Lowstuter
   and Lowstuter), 296–97
Institute for Healthcare Improvement,
   252
Intel, 10
International Software Testing
   Qualifications Board, 101
Internet, 74–75
   avoiding wasted time on, 110
   educational resources on, 61
   identity on, presenting, 127–29,
      130, 237–38
   for job searching, 85–86
   research resources, 193–97

résumé writing resources, 109
social networking, 141–43, 144,
   149, 166
support groups, 38
interviews
   appearance, 84, 169, 202–4, 209
   asking questions at, 215–17
   Chambers' question, 176
   fine-tuning résumés following,
      108–9
   Know More! Job Interviews approach,
      191–93
   lunch, 208–14
   Mackay 44 preparation checklist,
      169–71
   mealtime, 208–14
   multiple, purpose of, 247–48
   people building skills, question on,
      179
   performance anxiety, conquering,
      172–75
   post-interview homework,
      219–24
   preparation for, 169–71, 225–27
   questions during, 215–17, 281–89
   rehearsing, 180
   research for, 86–88, 189–97, 203
   revealing questions and answers,
      281–89
   scheduling of, first versus last,
      198–200
   second-round, 225–27
   thank-you notes, 88–89, 171, 185,
      204, 213–14, 220,
   video training for, 112–15
iPhone, 6, 44, 80, 146, 198
Irvine, Robert, 153

Jackson, Andrew, 51
Jefferson, Thomas, 51
job description, fine-tuning of, 24
job loss, signals of pending, 8–9
job market, and change, 14–15
job measurement standards, setting,
   270
job offers, 260–63

jobs
  danger signals of impending loss of, 8–9
  keeping, tips for, 16–19
  Mackay's Law and, 10–11
job search
  appearance, 84
  C-level job search, 117–23
  competitor firms, getting to know, 135–37
  creativity and, 156–58
  daily planner, 79–81
  goal setting, 83–84
  of graduating college student, 231–38
  interviews (*See* interviews)
  as job, 83–91
  networking (*See* networking)
  note taking, 89–90
  psychological evaluations and, 159–61
  reading, 84–86
  recruiters' advice, 70–76
  researching company culture, 86–88, 203
  thank-you notes, 88–89
  volunteer work, 90–91
job specifications, 178
Judge Business School (Cambridge University), 59

Kahn, Robert L., 63–64
Kansas City Chiefs, 105
Kaufman, Ron, 201
Keppie Careers, 144
keeping job, tips for, 16–19
Kiam, Victor, 217
Kirkpatrick, Bill, 162–67
Kleinschrodt, Michael H., 66
Knight, Bob, 288
Knock 'em Dead (Yate), 300
Know More! (training program), 189, 191
Know More! Job Interviews (training program), 191–93

Korn/Ferry International, 117, 119
Kowitt, Beth, 67

Langer, Amy, 149
Langley, Monica, 225
Law of Large Numbers, 18
Lehigh University, 138
Leisner, David, 172–74
library research, 195–96
lifetime job strategy, xix
LinkedIn, 74, 75, 118, 142, 149, 194–95, 237, 255
Lipp, Robert, 225
Lombardi, Vince, 49
Lowstuter, Cammen B., 296–97
Lowstuter, Clyde C., 296–97
lunch interviews, etiquette for, 208–14
  appearance, 209
  asking interviewer questions, 212–13
  eye contact, 211
  follow-ups after, 213–14
  handshakes, 209
  ordering, 210
  paying bill, 213
  punctuality, 208–9
  résumé, discussion of, 211–12
  at table, 209–10

Macalester College, 95
MacArthur Foundation, 63
McCannon, Joe, 252
McCombs, Red, 106
MacGregor Fast Pitch Softball, 206
Mackay, Carol Ann, 3
Mackay, David 199
Mackay, Harvey, 29, 89, 92, 117, 177, 219, 281–89
  MBA Commencement Speech, University of Southern California, 303–15
  Web site and contact information, 317
Mackay, JoJo 158

Mackay 44 Interview Preparation
    Checklist, 169–71
Mackay Lucky 13, 291
MackayMitchell Envelope Company,
    32, 70, 95, 162, 189, 255
Mackay 66 Customer Profile, 89, 219
Mackay's Law, 10–11
Mackay Sweet 16 questionnaire, 219
Mackay 33 for Employees and
    Managers, 219
Mackay 22 Post-Interview Homework,
    219–20, 222–24
Madison, Gail, 146, 147–48, 208–14
Masterpiece Theatre, 135–36
Mazzitelli, Teresa, 70–76
Mazzitelli Group, 70
MBA, 58–60, 133, 208, 232, 237
MBA Commencement Speech,
    University of Southern California
    (Mackay), 303–15
Medtronic, 242
Metropolitan Opera, 66, 162
Michelangelo, 64
Midas Touch, 83
Midternships: Internships @
    Midlife™, 116
Milwaukee Bucks, 3
Million Dollar Baby, 82
Mills, Elinor, 87–88
Minneapolis Star Tribune, 149, 153–54,
    252
Minnesota Rubber, 94
Minnesota Vikings, 105–6, 153–54
Mirrione, Gloria, 202
Miss America (beauty pageant), 55,
    184
MIT, 61
modesty, 19
money-back guarantees, offering,
    248
Monroe, Marilyn, 51
Monster.com, 85, 237
moonlighting, 66
Moore, Gordon E., 10
Moore, Tom, 104–5

Moore's Law, 10–11
"Most Likely to Succeed: How Do
    We Hire When We Can't
    Tell Who's Right for the Job"
    (Gladwell), 218
Mount Sinai Hospital, 63
Mozilla Firefox, 85
multiple interviews, 247–48
multi-task careers, 267–69
Murrow, Edward R., 175

Nation, Carrie, 276, 277
National Basketball Association
    (NBA), 3–5, 47
National Football League (NFL), 49,
    104–7
NBC, 30
negotiation
    of employment terms, 257–59,
        262–63
    of expected results on being hired,
        270
    of raises, 271–73
    of termination, 36–37
networking, 6, 74, 86, 134
    agile networkers, 165–66
    alumni affiliations, 138
    assessing and maintaining network,
        131–33
    and C-level job searches, 118–19
    contact outlook, 127–29
    network pruning and maintenance,
        132–33
    octopus exercise, 139–40
    social, 141–43, 144, 149, 166
newspaper databases, 196
New Yorker, 80, 218
New York Times, 61, 85, 138, 146, 147,
    162, 168, 176, 202, 203
niche hiring, 87
Nichemanship and Pitchmanship, 18,
    52–54
niche marketing, 18, 52, 87
Nielsen (ratings), 30
ninety-day guarantee, 330

Nixon, Richard, 94
Noll, Chuck, 105
Nord, Mary Weber, 267–69
North Carolina State, 3
North Star Resource Group, 218
notchmanship, 18
note taking, 89–90
Nozkowski, Thomas, 173
Nutrition World, 93

Obama, Barack, 168
obsolescence, sweaing off career,
    276–78
octopus exercise, 139–40
offers, 260–63
O'Leary, George, 153
Ohio State University, 158
O'Neal, Lucille, 47
O'Neal, Shaquille, 47
Olympics, 15
One-Stop Career Centers, 99–100
"OpenCourseWare" (MIT course),
    61
OSHA, 97
overconfidence, 25–26
overweight persons, discrimination
    against, 84
Oxnard Chamber of Commerce, 134

Packer, Gregory F., 198
Page, Larry, 61
Paige, Satchell, 64
"pain-points" of organization, 227
Paxson, John, 5
pay cuts, 240–41
Peale, Norman Vincent, 200
peers as career factors, 275
people building skills, 179
perfect job, 250–54
    checklist for, 253–54
    game plan for landing, 250–51
performance anxiety, conquering,
    172–75
performance standards, setting, 270
perseverance, 3–6, 18
personal intelligence system, 21–23

personal makeovers, 55
Phelps, David, 149
Phelps, Michael, 75
Phoenix Suns, 3–4
phoning contacts, 86
physical conditioning, 63–64, 82, 84
PhysOrg.com, 144
pickiness, in approach to hiring, 201
Pierson, Orville, 297–98
Pillsbury, 92
Pipl.com, 195
pitchmanship, 52–54
Pittsburgh Steelers, 104–5
Pontiac, 14, 15
Pontillo, Tony, 96
Porter, Terry, 5
positioning, for career opportunities,
    18
post-interview debriefing, 89
post-interview homework, 219–24
Potter, Harry, 39–40
power clothing, 209
PowerPoint, 57, 157
preparation, 3–6
    for first interviews, 169–71
    for second interviews, 225–27
presence on Internet. See identity on
    Internet, managing
"Price of Pressure, The," 174
Printz, Mary, 205
promotion, analyzing loss of, 25–26
psychological evaluations, 159–61
psychologists' perspective on staffing
    decisions, 162–67
    downscaling, 162–63
    networking, 165–66
    role of psychologist in hiring
        decisions, 163–64
    temporary positions, 163
    traits sought after, 164–65
Publicis, 267
punctuality, 208–9

Quiet Strength (Dungy), 105
Quality Assurance Institute, 101
questions for interviewers, 215–17

RadioShack, 154
"Rah, Rah, Résumé!", 138
raise, asking for a, 271–73
Rather, Dan, 18
reception areas, 205–7
    C-level jobs, 117–23
    contacts with, 127–29
    extended hiring process, 177–79
    job search advice from, 70–76
recruiters, 21, 70–76
Reeves, Ellen Gordon, 296
references, 178
ReferenceUSA, 196
rehearsing interview questions, 180
Reinsdorf, Jerry, 5
Reisdorf, Luke, 255
rejection and setbacks, 46–48
    adjusting résumé after, 108–9
    dealing with, 28–31
    learning from, 34
    reactions to, 184–86
    rebounding from, 49–51
Remick, Tierney, 117–23
Remington Products, 217
research, 54, 86–88, 170, 189–97, 203
    Google Timeline Search, 193–94
    libraries, 195–96
    LinkedIn, 194–95
    newspaper databases, 196
    Pipl.com, 195
résumés
    electronic screening of, 67–68,
        141–43
    of executives, 123
    fine-tuning, after setback, 108–9
    holes in, options for plugging, 154
    limits of, as a credential, 168
    lunch interviews, discussion at,
        211–12
    padding, 153–54
    strategies for, 68
return calls, motivating, 181–82
"Return of the Interview Suit, The,"
    202, 203
Richards, Phil, 218
Richter, Sam, 189–96, 251

Right Job, Right Now, The (Strayer),
    294–95
Right Words at the Right Time, The
    (Thomas), 47
Rockport Institute Web site on résumé
    writing, 109
Rolodex, 89
Rotary, 288
Round two interviews, 227
Rowe, John W., 63–64
Rowling, J. K., 39
Rutgers, 154
Ruth, Babe, 51
Rupp, Adolph, 3
Ryan, Robin, 293–94

St. Olaf College, 116
St. Petersburg Times, 153
St. Vincent de Paul, 90
Saltpeter, Miriam, 144
San Antonio Spurs, 3
Sarver, Robert, 4
Save the Whales, 90
SBR Worldwide, 189
Scarlet Letter, The (Hawthorne), 47
scheduling interviews, being first
    versus last, 198–200
Schelper, Roger, 92–98
"Secrets of the Résumé Gatekeeper,"
    67
Seinfeld, Jerry, 30, 172
Seinfeld, 30
selectivity of top employers, 201,
    218
self-confidence, and interviewing,
    173–74
self-pity, 50
setbacks. *See* rejection and setbacks
Shakey's Pizza, 94
Shay, R. E., 254
SHiFT, 116
"Six Golden Rules for Conquering
    Performance Anxiety" (Leisner),
    172–74
60 Seconds & You're Hired! (Ryan),
    293–94

SKS Consulting Psychologists, 162
social networking, 141–43, 144, 149, 166
softballs, 206
"Somewhere over the Rainbow," 10
Song, Sora, 174
Sony, 15
Sports Illustrated, 102
Stallone, Sylvester, 28
Stanford University, 231–33, 235, 237
Stanford University Advanced Management Program, 59
Star Trek, 57
Stenson, Mick, 94, 96
Stoll, Cal, 102, 103
Strayer, Susan D., 294–95
Successful Aging (Rowe and Kahn), 63–64
Sullivan, Stacy Savides, 87–88
Summers, Lawrence, 168
Super Bowl, 105–6
support groups, 38
Survivor, 11, 115
survivor jobs, 163
Swank, Hilary, 82
Swanson, Brad, 162–67
Swim with the Sharks Without Being Eaten Alive (Mackay), 177, 219
Syracuse University, 138

Take the Cold Out of Cold Calling . . . (Richter), 190
talent, 243–45
"Talent Is Everything" (*Conference Board Review* article), 243–44
Taleo, 67
Tampa Bay Buccaneers, 105–6
Tarcher, Jeremy P., 295–96
Target Corporation, 255
teamwork, 87, 164, 235, 242, 247–48, 272, 288
Tearing Down the Walls (Langley), 225
technological awareness, 121, 146–48
TEDTalks, 61, 80
temper, tips for controlling, 44

termination checklist, 36–37
Texas Tech, 289
thank-you notes, 88–89, 204, 213
30 Rock, 79
Thomas, Marlo, 47
thought process, 178–79
Tieger, Paul D., 298–99
Time, xix, 174
time management, 79–81, 83–91, 238, 278
Times of London, 59
timing, 198–200, 246
TiVo, 79
Torre, Joe, 66
Toyota, 10
Tracy, Dean, 227
Truman, Harry, 49
truthfulness, 179
25 Secrets to Sustainable Success (Richards), 218
twenty-something, job search of. *See* graduating college student's job search
"Turtle Wax"-style employers, pitching to, 52–53
Twitter, 74, 118, 144, 149, 166, 255
TwitterJobSearch, 144

unemployment rate, xix
United Way, 90
University of Alabama, 38
University of Arkansas, 49
University of Chicago, 116
University of Kentucky, 3
University of Michigan, 63, 158
University of Minnesota, 14, 92, 93, 95, 102, 103
University of Notre Dame, 153
University of Pennsylvania, 208
University of St. Thomas, 267
U.S. News & World Report, 66

"value proposition" for potential employers, 227
Van Ekeren, Glenn, 46–47

video training, for interviews, 112–15
Viscusi, Stephen, 17
Vital Aging Network, 116
volunteering, 17, 90–91

Wall Street Journal, 85, 202, 206, 211
Ward, Brittany, 144
warm call, 103, 192–93
Warm Call Resource Center, 193
Warm Call Toolbar, 193
Washington Examiner, 101
Watson, Thomas, 88
Weber-Nord Consulting, 268
*We Got Fired! . . . And It's the Best
    Thing That Ever Happened to Us*
    (Mackay), 29, 92, 117
Weill, Joan, 225
Weill, Sandy, 225
Wharton School (University of
    Pennsylvania) 208
What Color Is Your Parachute? (Bolles),
    291–92
Wikipedia, 85, 198, 212
William Mitchell Law School, 95
Williams, Alex, 146
Williams Arena, 92
Wilson, Eric, 203
Wilson, Kemmons, 16

women, opportunities for, 122, 165
Wood, Lennette, 134
Woodring, Pat, 94, 96
Workforce Investment Act (WIA
    program), 99
work habits, 179
World Series, 49
Worth Super Green Dot Slowpitch
    Softball, 206
www.facebook.com/harveymackay
www.harveymackay.com 89
www.rockportinstitute.com/resumes.
    html 109
www.samrichter.com 190
www.servicelocator.org 100
www.shiftonline.org 116
www.twitip.com/leverage-twitter-for-
    your-jobsearch/ 144
www.warmcallcenter.com 196

Yahoo HotJobs, 146
Yale, 61
Yate, Martin, 300
You, Inc. (Beckwith and Beckwith),
    292
Young Presidents' Organization
    (YPO), 281
YouTube, 15, 80, 110

Get a Job or Get Your Money Back Guarantee

I hope you enjoy my book. I'm so confident of the effectiveness of this advice that I'll make you the following promise: If you conscientiously apply all of the principles herein for six months without landing yourself a job, I will cheerfully refund the purchase price. Simply write a letter to me at the following address detailing your job-hunting efforts and their results, along with your proof of purchase, and I will send your money back.

Harvey Mackay
c/o Piatkus
Little, Brown Book Group
100 Victoria Embankment
London
EC4Y 0DY